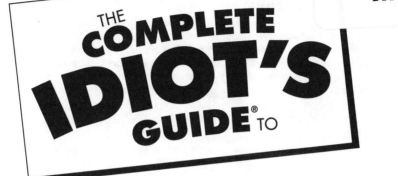

THE COMPLETE IDIOT'S GUIDE® TO

Careers in the U.S. Military

by Bill Harris

ALPHA

A Pearson Education Company

Copyright © 2002 by William Harris

THE COMPLETE IDIOT'S GUIDE TO and Design are registered trademarks of Pearson Education, Inc.

International Standard Book Number: 0-02-864381-X
Library of Congress Catalog Card Number: 2002106345

04   03   02   8   7   6   5   4   3   2

Interpretation of the printing code: The rightmost number of the first series of numbers is the year of the book's printing; the rightmost number of the second series of numbers is the number of the book's printing. For example, a printing code of 02-1 shows that the first printing occurred in 2002.

Printed in the United States of America

Note: This publication contains the opinions and ideas of its author. It is intended to provide helpful and informative material on the subject matter covered. It is sold with the understanding that the author and publisher are not engaged in rendering professional services in the book. If the reader requires personal assistance or advice, a competent professional should be consulted.

The author and publisher specifically disclaim any responsibility for any liability, loss, or risk, personal or otherwise, which is incurred as a consequence, directly or indirectly, of the use and application of any of the contents of this book.

Publisher: *Marie Butler-Knight*
Product Manager: *Phil Kitchel*
Managing Editor: *Jennifer Chisholm*
Acquisitions Editor: *Gary Goldstein*
Development Editor: *Nancy D. Lewis*
Production Editor: *Katherin Bidwell*
Copy Editor: *Amy Borrelli*
Illustrator: *Chris Eliopoulos*
Cover/Book Designer: *Trina Wurst*
Indexer: *Heather McNeil*
Layout/Proofreading: *Angela Calvert, Mary Hunt, Vicki Keller*

For marketing and publicity, please call: 317-581-3722

The publisher offers discounts on this book when ordered in quantity for bulk purchases and special sales.

For sales within the United States, please contact: Corporate and Government Sales, 1-800-382-3419 or corpsales@pearsontechgroup.com

Outside the United States, please contact: International Sales, 317-581-3793 or international@pearsontechgroup.com

Contents at a Glance

Part 1:   **Now Hiring**   1

1   The Best Jobs in the World   3

You aren't going to find these jobs in the classifieds. There are just too many of them. No company in the country, not even General Motors, has as many jobs—or as many different kinds of jobs—open right now.

2   Joining Up   15

Watch that first step! Recruiters aren't going to bop you on the head and load you, unconscious, onto the next bus. They're going to make some incredible offers to make you want to sign up without strong-arm tactics. Can they deliver on them?

3   Oh, No, Not Another Test!   29

Before you can go anywhere in the military, you'll need to take an aptitude test first. It may seem easy—if you have an aptitude for tests. If not, there is a thing or two you can do to make it a walk in the park.

Part 2:   **You're Hired! Now What?**   41

4   The Part You've Been Dreading … Shape Up!   43

It's tougher than joining a health club, but just how tough is Basic Training? Nobody will tell you it's easy. But forget most of what you've heard. It's all about attitude. That's what's going to make the difference. And, after all, it's over in a couple of weeks.

5   The Reserves, National Guard, and ROTC   59

The best reason for joining the service is the fabulous benefits you get. But you don't have to leave home for a few years to collect them. You can have the best of both worlds.

6   Yes, We Are Collegiate   71

Everybody should go to college, right? But not everybody gets the chance. Until now. Not only can you earn college credits on the job, but Uncle Sam is going to give you money to get on with it after your tour is over.

Part 3:   **Special Opportunities**   **81**

   7   Top of the Heap: The Service Academies   83
       This is where the best get better. Think you can cut it? You
       won't know until you try. It's worth a whole lot more to you
       than just a military commission.

   8   An Officer and a Lady: Opportunities for Women   97
       Forget GI Joe. He's just as likely to be a she in today's
       military. And she's doing very nicely, thank you.

   9   An Equal Opportunity Employer   109
       No other career path in America is as wide open for
       minorities as today's military. It's not what you are,
       but who you are that counts.

  10   Perks, Perks, and More Perks   121
       They call them "fringe benefits" in the business world, but
       they are woven right into the fabric of life in the military.
       And no other employer is nearly as generous with them.

Part 4:   **Life in the Military**   **139**

  11   Making Up Your Mind   141
       What do you want to be when you grow up? Don't do a
       thing until you've looked these things over. It's your life.

  12   This Man's Army   149
       A bunch of guys slogging through mud with rifles on their
       shoulders? If that's what you think the Army is all about,
       you've got some surprises coming. More than 200 of them,
       in fact.

  13   Anchors Aweigh with the Navy   167
       You can take a cruise around the world on the QE-2, or you
       can join the Navy and pick up some new skills along the way.
       Not only is it cheaper, but the food's better, too.

  14   The Wild Blue Air Force   189
       Nothing will get you where you want to go faster than a jet
       aircraft—except for active duty in the Air Force. If you're
       looking for a career in technology, there is no better place
       to begin.

  15   The Few, the Proud, the Marines   209
       You can pick out the ex-Marines in any crowd. They're the
       ones taking charge. It's all about pride, the extra-special pride
       of the Marines.

16 Patrolling the Shores with the Coast Guard   227
The Coast Guard has been at the forefront of homeland security since the homeland was just a handful of states along the Eastern seaboard. It gives you a chance to make a difference all the time. In all 50 states.

Part 5:   Special Cases   245

17 A Dream Realized   247
Thinking of going to medical school but don't think you can afford it? How about getting your M.D. degree for free!

18 Fly Me to the Moon   255
You've always wanted to be an astronaut, haven't you? Well, what's stopping you? Here's how to get there.

19 The New Heroes   263
Jobs in law enforcement are more attractive than ever. Here's how to get a head start on making police work a career.

20 Serving as a Civilian   269
You don't have to put on a uniform to serve your country through the military.

21 Cutting-Edge Technology   279
The military isn't just for jocks anymore. If you like playing computer games, you're going to love the military … and they're going to love you.

22 Dive Into the Motor Pool   291
Love cars? Find new vehicles and machines to love, even if you're a woman.

Appendixes

A Military as a Second Language   301

B Team Canada   311

C Surfing Your Way to a Military Career   315

Index   325

Contents

Part 1: Now Hiring   **1**

1 The Best Jobs in the World   **3**

What's Your Dream? 4
   Check Out These Options *5*
   Opportunities for Women *6*
Is It Payday Yet? 6
   What About Raises? *7*
   So What's the Bottom Line? *7*
   How Does That Compare with Civilian Jobs? *7*
   What Can That Mean to You? *8*
   Cash for Joining *8*
What About Benefits? 9
   Food and Housing *9*
   Medical Care *10*
Education Benefits 10
   The Montgomery GI Bill *10*
   Tuition Assistance Program *11*
   Free College Credits *11*
   Servicemember Opportunity Colleges *12*
   What About My College Loans? *12*
The Cutting Edge of Technology 12

2 Joining Up   **15**

Limitations and Restrictions 16
The Ten Commandments of Enlisting 17
How to Deal with Recruiters 18
   Don't Limit Yourself *18*
   Make the Rounds *18*
   Take a Devil's Advocate Along *19*
   Talk with Someone Who's Been There *20*
   No Such Thing as a Stupid Question *20*
   Smart Questions *20*
Call Your Own Shots 21
   No Openings? No Problem *22*
   One Career Leads to Another *23*
The First Step Is Up 23
Free Money 24

How You Qualify 24

"Critical Career" Choices 24

How You Collect 25

The Last Mile 25

The Final Step 26

3 Oh, No, Not Another Test!   **29**

What Is the ASVAB? 30

Can You Prevent Recruiters from Seeing Your Scores? 31

Head Them Off at the Pass 31

When and Why Take the Test 32

Don't Do Well with Tests? 32

Can You Take the Test Again? 32

The Big Day 33

A. General Science 33

B. Arithmetic Reasoning 34

C. Word Knowledge 34

D. Paragraph Comprehension 35

E. Numerical Operations 36

F. Coding Speed 36

G. Auto and Shop Information 37

H. Mathematics Knowledge 38

I. Mechanical Comprehension 38

J. Electronics Information 39

Think You Can Ace the ASVAB? 39

Why Is Your Score Important? 40

Part 2: You're Hired! Now What?   **41**

4 The Part You've Been Dreading ... Shape Up!   **43**

Who Needs It? 44

How Long Does Basic Training Last? 44

Do Women Have an Easier Time? 45

What to Take with You ... and What Not to Take 46

About That Haircut 47

Shaping Up in Advance 48

Making Basic Easy 50

Your First Day 50

Week One 51

Week Two 53

Week Three 53

Week Four 54

Week Five 54

Week Six 54

Week Seven 55

Week Eight 55

Week Nine 55

The Moment of Truth 56

Who Is That Guy? 57

5 The Reserves, National Guard, and ROTC   59

At Your Service 60

Who Are These People? 60

How Will Your Boss Take It? 60

How Guardsman Are Trained 61

Time on Duty 61

What's It Worth? 61

Air National Guard 62

Coast Guard Reserve Force 63

Marine Forces Reserve 63

Naval Reserve 64

What Is ROTC? 65

The Navy and Marines ROTC Program 65

Air Force ROTC Programs 66

Army ROTC Programs 67

You Don't Have to Be a Scholarship Winner 68

6 Yes, We Are Collegiate   71

The New GI Bill 72

You Can Have It Right Now 72

Making College Indispensable 73

Military School Credits 73

Servicemember Opportunity Colleges 73

Career Degrees 73

Testing Credits 75

Concurrent Admissions Programs 75

Learn and Earn Credits While You Serve 75

Community College of the Air Force 76

Opportunities in the Navy 76

Guard and Reserve Opportunities 77

More Than Just College 77

Got Student Loans? 78

The Army's Loan Repayment Program 78

The Fine Print 79

Distance Learning 79

    How Distance Learning Works 79

    High School, Too 80

Part 3:   Special Opportunities **81**

7 Top of the Heap: The Service Academies **83**

The Secret of Business Success 84

How to Get In 85

Money Matters 87

Academic Requirements 87

Personal Requirements 88

The Other End 88

Life at West Point 89

    Time Off 89

    Living Conditions 89

    The Student Hierarchy 90

Military Training 90

Academic Training 91

Basic Training 92

    Air Force Academy—"The Beast" 92

    Making It Past "The Beast" 93

    A Surprise Ending 94

Coast Guard Academy 94

    Summer Training 95

    Academic Training 95

Merchant Marine Academy 96

8 An Officer and a Lady: Opportunities for Women **97**

Better Go in Disguise 98

Making It Official 98

WACs, WAVES, WASPs, and SPARS 99

Down, but Not Out 100

    Changing the Playing Field 100

    Changing the Rules 101

    Changing the Numbers 101

Opening New Jobs 102

What Women *Can't* Do 103

What Women *Are* Doing 104

Training 104

Breaking the Mold 105

The Other Woman—Military Wives 106

9 An Equal Opportunity Employer   109

Getting Better 110
Changing Times 111
    Making It *112*
    A Crack at College *112*
Getting Academic Skills 112
Building a College Fund 113
The ROTC Advantage 113
Building a Career 114
Getting Ahead 115
Opportunities for Hispanics 116
You May Not Need a High School Diploma 116
Language Is No Barrier 116
You Don't Have to Be a Citizen 117
Minority Women 117
The Bottom Line 118

10 Perks, Perks, and More Perks   121

Yours for the Taking 122
A Typical Nonmilitary Scenario 123
Not a Retiree, a Veteran 124
Basic Veterans' Benefits 125
    Disabled Veterans *125*
    Low-Income Veterans *126*
Discharge Status 127
    Altering Your Discharge Status *127*
    Voluntary Separations *127*
Military Retirees 128
Health Care 129
Pensions 130
    Not Your Average Retirement Plan *131*
    A New Retirement Choice *132*
    VA Pensions *132*
Life Insurance 133
Home Loans 134
The Montgomery GI Bill and Top-Up 134
Keep an Eye on Those Discharge Papers 136

Part 4: Life in the Military   139

11 Making Up Your Mind   141

Serve Without Joining Up 142
A Level Playing Field 143

Following a Tradition 143
The Pyramid of Honor 144
Getting the MOS You Want 146
Assume Nothing 147

12 This Man's Army   149

The Draft 150
Not Your Father's Army 151
Different Ways to Be a Soldier 151
Digging Into the Lists 152
Go Beyond the Job Descriptions 153
Choosing the Right Branch 154
  Combat Arms *154*
  Combat Support *155*
  Combat Service Support *156*
Dividing It Up 158
The Pecking Order 159
  Commissioned Officers *159*
  Enlisted *160*
  Warrant Officer *160*
  Special Specialties—Warrant Officers *160*
Up to Your Neck in Sergeants 161
Starting at the Bottom 162
  Your Contract *162*
  Your New Life *163*
  An Organized Life *163*
  Come as You Are *163*
  A Place to Live *164*
Barracks Life 165
  Army Chow *165*
  Where Will You Go? *166*
  Job Security *166*

13 Anchors Aweigh with the Navy   167

New Beginnings 168
  "I have not yet begun to fight!" *168*
  The Navy's Birthday *169*
Navy Strength 169
  The Navy's Fleets *170*
  Ghost Fleets *171*
  The Pacific Fleet *172*

Seagoing Jobs 173
Living Conditions 174
Commuting to the Job 175
A Sailor's Life 175
  Getting Hungry? *176*
  Couch Potatoes *176*
  On-Board Amenities *177*
  Taking a Grand Tour *177*
  Sailing in Good Company *177*
  Air Wings *179*
Ranks and Rates 180
  Commissioned Officers *180*
  Enlisted *181*
  Warrant Officer *181*
Determining the Job You Want 182
  General Enlisted Career Fields *182*
  What's in a Name *183*
Navy-Specific Jargon 184
How Tough Are You? 186

14 The Wild Blue Air Force   189
America Goes to War in the Air 190
An Idea Whose Time Had Come 192
The Air Force Structure 193
  Air Force Units *193*
  Space Operations *194*
Technology Rules 195
Career Paths 195
  How Officers Are Developed *196*
  Career Choices *196*
  The Personnel Department *197*
Special Tactics Groups 198
Pulling Rank 198
  Commissioned Officers *198*
  Enlisted *199*
  Warrant Officers *200*
The Force Behind the Force 200
  Bombers *200*
  Fighters *202*
  Noncombat Aircraft *205*
Getting In on the Action 206

15 The Few, the Proud, the Marines   **209**

Marines on the Move 210
The World Wars 211
    Glory on Top of Glory 212
    Making a Difference 212
Number One 213
    Higher Standards 213
    Why the Marines? 213
A Special Specialty 214
    Toughening Up 214
    Grinding Out Grunts 215
Marine Corps Weapons 215
A Lot to Learn 216
Training Women 216
The Best MOS in the Corps 217
Dress Blues 218
The Marine Emblem 219
Through the Ranks 219
    Commissioned Officers 219
    Enlisted 220
Moving Up 220
    Training Officers 221
    Going Up Fast 222
Instant Response 222
    Gator Ships 222
    Landings Made Easy 223
    Amphibious Transport Docks 223
    Landing Ship, Docks 223
    Amphibious Assault Ships 224
    The Future 224
Life at Sea 225

16 Patrolling the Shores with the Coast Guard   **227**

In the Beginning 230
    The Lighthouse Service 230
    Seagoing Revenuers 231
    Chasing Rumrunners 231
    Gunrunners and Drug Busts 232
Going to War 233
    Full-Time War Footing 233
    Korea and Vietnam 234

Alaska and the Gulf of Mexico 234
The National Strike Force 235
Tools of the Trade 236
    High-Endurance Cutters 236
    Polar Class Icebreakers 236
    Boats 237
    Aircraft 237
    A Trophy Ship 237
Wide-Open Opportunities 239
Coast Guard Ranks 239
    Commissioned Officers 239
    Enlisted 240
    Warrant Officer 240
Picking a Rating 240
    Marine Science 241
    Dive Schools 241
Coast Guard Life 242
The Coast Guard Auxiliary 242
Uniforms 243

Part 5: Special Cases   **245**

17 A Dream Realized   **247**

The Cost of a Medical Degree 247
    How to Get a Free M.D. Degree 248
    How Does a Premed Student Qualify? 249
    What Happens Next? 249
Before You Leave for School 250
What's It Worth? 250
The Fine Print 250
Serving While Learning 251
    Residencies 252
    Active Duty 252
    Where Will You Go? 252
Try It, You'll Like It 253
An Alternative Route 253
    A Few Basic Differences 254

18 Fly Me to the Moon   **255**

The Pioneers 256
The Shuttle Program 257
    How to Qualify 257
    The Screening Process 258

    Making the Cut 259
    Candidate Training 259
    Advanced Training 259
  Other Job Opportunities 260
  The U.S. Space Command 261
  Computers in SPACECOM 262

19 The New Heroes   **263**

  Getting the Perfect Background 264
    Seagoing Stakeouts 264
    Criminal Investigations 265
  Opportunities in the Other Services 266
  Your Postmilitary Career 267

20 Serving as a Civilian   **269**

  What Is Civil Service? 270
  Civil Servants in the Military 270
    Advancement 270
    It Gets Better 271
    Special Educational Programs 272
    The Other Services 272
    Part-Time Jobs 272
    Management Training 273
  Job Opportunities 273
    The Corps of Engineers 274
    Army–Air Force Exchange Service 274
  Why Should You Consider a Civil Service Job? 275
    Why So Many Openings? 276
    How Do You Get These Jobs? 276

21 Cutting-Edge Technology   **279**

  Where It All Started 280
  Building a Dinosaur 281
  Onward and Upward 282
  What It Can Mean to You 283
  Computers on the Battlefield 283
  Electronic Warfare 284
  Picture Yourself in a World of Computers 285
    Research and Development 285
    Virtual Reality 286
    Cyberwarfare 287
  Where Will You Go from Here? 288

22 Dive Into the Motor Pool **291**

Jobs with a Future 292
  A Growing Need 292
  What Kind of Jobs Are They? 293
Get the Best Experience 293
Keeping the Wheels Turning 294
"Mechanic" MOS Training 294
Not for Men Only 295
The Challenge 296
Not Exactly Like Civilian Counterparts 296
The Future Is Here 297
  Driving Into the Future 298
  Reinventing the Wheel 298

Appendixes

A Military as a Second Language **301**

B Team Canada **311**

C Surfing Your Way to a Military Career **315**

Index **325**

Foreword

There has never been a better time to take advantage of the opportunities available in the U.S. military. If you are a young person freshly graduated from high school, or in your late 20s or early 30s needing to escape a job that doesn't seem to be taking you anywhere, the military is an option you should consider.

Even if you are not planning on finishing a full 20-year career in one of the uniformed services, you might want to think of it as a place to build a resumé. The skills and experiences you can acquire will make you more appealing in the civilian marketplace. For instance, the majority of America's airline pilots and many law enforcement, paramedical, and fire and rescue personnel received their training in the military.

The civilian world recognizes that your military training will have provided you with valuable skills using the most up-to-date technology. Military electronics technicians, aircraft mechanics, air-traffic controllers, computer and communications systems analysts are much sought-after employees. But the larger benefit of your time in the military will be the personal maturity and leadership capability that you gain. Military personnel are constantly challenged to take on greater levels of responsibility, increase their skills and education, and develop into competent professionals.

The old barriers to advancement have been removed so that all persons have the same chance. Contrary to the impression left by occasional incidents of negative publicity, the U.S. Army, Navy, Air Force, Marine Corps, and Coast Guard have been the pacesetters since the late 1940s in recognizing the value of a diverse work force where everyone counts. Take a look at today's military leaders—the officers and noncommissioned officers sitting around conference tables setting goals and planning strategies for the twenty-first century—and you will see women as well as men of all colors and backgrounds.

As I reflect on my own career as a military officer, I must say that it has been exciting, rewarding work. I have shared in events that have influenced history, participated in humanitarian missions that have saved lives, and taken an active role in efforts that brought an end to some unspeakable evils. Every year has roused me to offer my very best, and stretched me. In that time, I have seen a parade of young people grow into confident and responsible men and women. Along with all my co-workers, I joined the computer age as the military entered the world of advancing technology. I have worked in places I never thought I would see and done things that I never thought I could do.

However, the best part of being a military member is that I have been a part of a larger family that gave me a lifetime of friends and memories. I recall the men and women I accompanied through the mud of the Amazon rain forest, or those with whom I sat under the canopy of camouflage netting in the 117-degree heat on exercises in the Mojave Desert. I saw the midnight sun reflecting off Alaskan glaciers and watched ships passing at dawn through the Panama Canal. These sights alone were breathtaking enough to guarantee that I would remember them, but to have shared them with the kind of friends I met in the military—well, that was awesome.

This book contains a wealth of information to study as you ponder what the military might offer you. Don't stop there. Talk with people who are serving today, talk with those who have retired from service, talk with employers who have hired them and to as many people as you can find who can shed further light on your decision. Do this before you talk to the recruiters, so you will be prepared to ask the right questions. You will begin to see that the military can open doors to a surprising selection of attractive career options.

—James R. Price
Chaplain, Lieutenant Colonel,
Texas Air National Guard

Introduction

Somebody asked me the other day if I was a Vietnam veteran. I was flattered, but not for reasons you might expect. It was pleasing to know that I still look young enough.

"Afraid not," I replied, "Korea was my war." "Oh," he said, "you don't hear much about those guys anymore, do you?"

Well, no, you don't. It isn't that the woods aren't still full of Korean War vets. It's just that it all seems like ancient history these days—so much has changed since the 1950s.

Nothing, absolutely nothing, has changed quite as much over those years as the military itself. Even Vietnam vets are startled when they find out how much better it has become, and compared to the 1940s and 1950s, military life had already improved by the time they came along, most especially for minorities.

A half century ago, the specter of being drafted into the service brought out all sorts of creative dodges. It never dawned on anyone that they could move to Canada to avoid being drafted. That would come later. But back then, it was more fun to use your brain to try to outwit the Selective Service system. And just about everybody played the game.

When he responded to his "Greetings," a friend of mine put wet blotting paper into his shoes because he thought it would raise his body temperature and make him appear to be a bad health risk. It did, but the medics just held him overnight and he passed his physical the next day.

His story had a happy ending, though; he wound up as an MP in a security detail around the Mercury-Atlas astronauts. He's still talking about it.

He didn't make the Army a career, and now he's retired. He had to work at a job he didn't really care much about for 45 years before he was eligible for a small pension. And not once during those years did he ever get a chance to rub elbows with the likes of John Glenn, Scott Carpenter, or Wally Schirra.

There wasn't much reason for anybody to reenlist back then. In fact, apart from patriotic impulses (which were more often limited to flying the flag), there weren't many incentives for joining up in the first place.

All that has changed.

There hasn't been a time in the history of America when opting for a military career has made more sense. There's a greater variety of jobs available than there ever were, and more ways to turn your service into a first-rate education, and the salary and benefits are as good as they get in most civilian jobs.

There are better benefits at the other end, too, from pensions to home loans. And you can retire after 20 years. There are no bars to joining up or moving up. A military career these days is as rewarding as you want to make it.

It's all because of the draft—or the lack of one.

In my day, you made military service one of the rights of passage into adulthood. Because of Selective Service, you didn't really have a choice, short of shooting yourself in the foot. Then the draft was eliminated. Suddenly, you could skip that step if you wanted to.

But just as suddenly, the whole concept of military service changed. It became an attractive career option. It's not your father's military anymore. Uncle Sam wants the best, and he's changed the system to attract the best.

If you haven't heard how much things have changed, you're going to be amazed at some of the things you'll find in these pages. I was. In fact, if I were 40 years younger, I'd be down at the recruiting office right this minute.

How This Book Is Organized

This book is presented in five sections:

In **Part 1, "Now Hiring,"** you're going to get a taste of just how much the military has changed over the last several years. You'll find out about some of the career choices you have, and how to make sure you get what you want. This is where you'll discover some of the benefits waiting for you, from bonuses to tuition help. It's also where you'll get some tips on dealing with recruiters: what to ask them, what to tell them, and what to watch out for. Finally, it guides you through the first step everybody needs to take, the Armed Services Vocational Aptitude Battery. It's a test you ought to take seriously, and the tips for scoring big will help make it easy.

In **Part 2, "You're Hired! Now What?"** you'll find out what to expect during your first weeks on the job (yes, this is a job!). You've heard all sorts of horror stories about Basic Training. Some of them may even be true. On the other hand, forewarned is forearmed, and this is where you can separate fact from rumor. This part also describes some options you have to an active duty military career, like the Guard, Reserves, or ROTC programs, which will give you a leg up when you join later on. And it's where you'll find the menu of educational opportunities you're going to get, from tuition help later on to free college credits right away, even to relief from those student loans that are worrying you.

Part 3, "Special Opportunities," starts at the top with a rundown of the service academies, including West Point, Annapolis, and the Air Force Academy. Except for the Coast Guard Academy, you'll need an official appointment, usually by a member of Congress, but that's easier than it seems. Most of the other qualifications are tougher, but go for it anyway. The rewards are going to take you beyond your wildest dreams. This part is where women are going to find some pleasant surprises, too. Your mother never dreamed that her daughter would find so many ways to stand out. Parents of minorities, who grew up being put down, are also in for some surprises when they see how their children can succeed in today's military careers. They remember discrimination, but now it has become a thing of the past. And take a look at some of the goodies waiting for you when your military career becomes part of your past.

In **Part 4, "Life in the Military,"** you'll get down to the nitty-gritty with a look inside each of the five branches of military service. How do you decide which one is best for you? It isn't easy. Maybe you picture yourself standing proudly at attention in Marine dress blues, or possibly Air Force blues are more your style. But in the end, you're not signing up for a fashion show. Many people pick a branch because of family traditions. But don't forget that while tradition runs strong through all of the services, none of them is quite the same as it was in your father's day. This is your career decision, and once you know what to expect, you might just find yourself starting a whole new family tradition.

Part 5, "Special Cases," gives you details on a couple of career fields that make joining the military one of the best choices you can make. You'll find out how you can get a medical degree free. Yes, free. If you've always had a longing to get involved in space exploration, the military is your logical first step, and this section will help you plan for it. If machines fascinate you, you may be surprised at how many different kinds of motors and engines the military depends on, and how many opportunities there are to help keep the wheels turning. Even for women. And if you think Uncle Sam is just looking for jocks to fill the ranks, think again.

Information, Inspiration, and Things That Are Fun to Know

The more you look at the military, the more there is to see. You are going to find some material sprinkled throughout the pages that expand on some points or introduce you to some of the people who brought dignity and inspiration to everyone's military career.

> ### In Their Footsteps
>
> Many of the stories under this heading are about people who have earned the Medal of Honor, our country's highest award for valor. It is awarded for actions "above and beyond the call of duty." Although you yourself may never be put in a position to be recommended for the medal, the values it represents are at the heart of the military experience.

Bet You Didn't Know

Full of fun facts and interesting information, these tidbits will put you "in the know."

Warning

Don't get scared. These are just a few things you need to be careful about.

Tip

Sometimes providing historical background, these notes provide you with nuts-and-bolts information you'll find helpful.

Trademarks

All terms mentioned in this book that are known to be or are suspected of being trademarks or service marks have been appropriately capitalized. Alpha Books and Pearson Education, Inc., cannot attest to the accuracy of this information. Use of a term in this book should not be regarded as affecting the validity of any trademark or service mark.

Part 1

Now Hiring

As the Army's slogan once put it, the military offers you a chance to "be all you can be." It is true of all five branches of the service, now more than ever. The American military has more jobs—good jobs—open than any employer you can name. But like any other job hunt, you need to decide what you want to be before you start.

There are things you have to do, like take an aptitude test and meet minimum requirements, and there are some things you should do, like asking the right questions.

The Best Jobs in the World

In This Chapter

- Job hunting made easy
- Opportunities you may never have even dreamed about
- Getting in on the ground floor of new technology
- Big-time benefits you won't find anywhere else
- An eye-opener about how much you can earn

Right now, there are more than a million and a half men and women in uniform working for Uncle Sam. No other branch of the government has that many employees. The country's biggest corporate employer, General Motors, has 367,000 people on its payroll, but the military hires nearly that many people each and every year.

Every day of the week, it hires an average of a thousand new people to replace those who are taking advantage of fabulous retirement benefits. The veterans are taking the skills they developed during their military service to employers who consider them to be perfect candidates for the best jobs they have to offer. For them, it all began with taking advantage of an offer to sign on for the opportunity of the best on-the-job training in the world.

What's Your Dream?

"What do you want to be when you grow up?" How many times was that question thrown at you when you were a kid? Chances are pretty good that at different times you said you wanted to be an astronaut or an airline pilot, a weather forecaster, or even a police officer or firefighter. If you still have those dreams—or have come up with some more in the meantime—the military can help you make them come true. It will also give you some new ideas that will expand on them.

There are so many job opportunities open to you in the military, it would take a book twice this big to list them all. The Navy breaks down its job descriptions under these categories, and each has a long list of subcategories to go with it:

- Industrial engineers
- Intelligence officers
- Electrical and electronics engineers
- Lawyers
- Environmental health and safety officers
- Aerospace engineers
- Life scientists
- Surveying and mapping managers
- Physicists
- Space operations officers
- Air traffic control officers
- Chemists
- Civil engineers
- Computer systems officers
- Marine engineers
- Meteorologists
- Nuclear engineers
- Oceanographers

Every branch of the service has its own unique list, of course. Although, as in the case of the Navy, many are specific to the service's specific mission, you'll find that many of the categories are similar to jobs in the civilian world.

Check Out These Options

Have you always wanted to be an astronaut? Perhaps instead you would rather get involved with *training* astronauts? Among the jobs available to you is testing the equipment astronauts use, from spacesuits to spacecraft, without ever leaving Mother Earth.

Still want to be a TV weather forecaster? Instead of appearing in front of the camera, you can become part of the team that gives the on-air weathermen the information they read, and that can be a whole lot more fun. After all, how many of them ever get to fly into the eye of a hurricane?

Bet You Didn't Know _____

If you expect your military career to evolve into one as an airline pilot, be prepared for some stiff competition. Salary levels in the field can range up to $300,000 a year.

By law, airline pilots can't fly more than 100 hours a month or 1,000 hours a year. The average pilot usually puts in 75 hours of flying and another 75 performing other duties every month. On paper, it seems like a great deal, although the schedules are irregular, and a pilot may be away from home for long periods, and many are constantly fighting jet lag.

The salaries, while relatively high at the start, don't reach the highest levels until after several years on the job. Negatives aside, though, it's an attractive goal. And the most attractive candidates for these jobs are people who have military experience.

Speaking of flying, next time you take a plane trip, ask the pilot where he learned how to handle that thing. If the answer isn't one of the branches of the military, it might be a good idea to book a different flight. It has been a tradition in the airline business almost from the beginning to hire pilots who have earned their wings in the military. Of course, many pilots are graduates of flying schools, but their level of experience at the time they're hired is a good deal less than their co-workers who learned the business in military aircraft.

The fact is, there aren't very many dreams that can't become a reality when they start with a military career. From industrial engineering to environmental sciences, the services offer more than 10,000 specialized courses in some 300 different schools.

Tip _____

According to Defense Manpower Data Center, 88 percent of all military occupations have counterparts in the civilian world. That means that people who have learned a job and accumulated experience working at it in the military can hit the ground running when their active duty careers end and their civilian life starts up again.

Better still, they follow up with hands-on experience through more than 2,000 job classifications. Better than that, you can choose just about any one of them to match your own concept of a dream job.

Opportunities for Women

Although there are some jobs, like a Navy Seal or an Army Green Beret, that are closed to women, there are more positions available to them today than ever before in history. For example, the following list gives the percentage of jobs that are available to women in each of the military branches:

- ◆ 93% Army
- ◆ 96% Navy
- ◆ 99% Air Force
- ◆ 94% Marine Corps
- ◆ 100% Coast Guard

More information on opportunities for women in Chapter 8.

In Their Footsteps

By the time she retired from the Air Force in 2002, Lt. Col. Teri Netter had spent 34 years in uniform. She joined up right after high school and her paycheck of $101 represented a 25-percent increase over what she had been making as a housekeeper.

Back in 1968, women didn't have as many job options as they do today, but she got training in data automation, which she supplemented by going to school on her own with tuition assistance. Within a few years she had earned a degree in computer science and became a commissioned officer. Before she retired, she was chief of command-and-control systems in the Pentagon's Mission Control Directorate.

Is It Payday Yet?

"You'll never get rich," says the old song, "... you're in the Army now." While nobody joins the military to get rich, an impressive array of benefits and bonuses can add up to a great deal that no private employer could ever even think of offering.

How much money you'll make is one of those questions where the answer is, "It all depends ...." That's because military pay is generally divided into different parts. The first, of course, is the base pay. It varies according to your rank and how long you've served.

What About Raises?

As a rule of thumb, you can count on seeing your paycheck grow every two years. But Congress authorizes general increases every now and then as well. In 2000, for instance, military pay went up by 4.8 percent across the board.

The law that resulted in that increase also calls for annual raises over the next several years at a rate of a half percent over growth in the private sector (that is, the general salary levels in civilian jobs as reflected in government statistics that are revised every year).

Above the base pay, you'll be able to collect tax-exempt special allowances for such things as off-base housing and uniforms. And in many specialties, such as submarine duty or piloting an airplane, you'll be entitled to even more in the form of supplementary pay.

So What's the Bottom Line?

The basic pay in the military is the same for every branch of service. Checks are issued twice a month. The amount follows a table issued by the Department of Defense that breaks down the numbers according to ranking scale and length of service. As you can imagine, it's a big table. For a look at it, check out http://militarypay.dtic.mil.

As of the spring of 2002, people with an E-3 rank—Private First Class in the Army, Seaman in the Navy or Coast Guard, Airman First Class in the Air Force, or Lance Corporal in the Marine Corps—are close to the bottom of the pecking order. Their pay is $1,214.70 a month during their first two years of service. If they live in nonmilitary housing, they'll collect about 41 percent more if they're single and 48 percent extra if they have dependents. The actual amount varies according to the housing market where you'll be living.

The base-pay scale goes up every time you get promoted, of course. On average, you can expect to be promoted three times during a four-year enlistment.

The current rate for a commissioned officer, designated "O-8," is $6,838.20 a month for less than two years of service. That's more than $82,000 a year before any of the other benefits are added in.

How Does That Compare with Civilian Jobs?

Back in 1999, Army Times Publishing Company reported that the annual average yearly income in a military household was 9.1 percent higher than for a comparable civilian family.

It was the result of a survey that compared 40 military jobs to their counterparts in the private sector. Military pay was lower in 19 of them, but in 21 of the categories, it was equal to civilian pay and often higher. The comparison included the military's base pay, plus basic allowances and tax savings, but none of the other free benefits that civilian workers don't get (we'll get to those later in the chapter).

At the time the survey of 1.3 million households was made, the average income among the families of military personnel was $56,561, compared to an average for all U.S. households of $51,855.

What Can That Mean to You?

At current pay levels, by the end of Basic Training, an 18-year-old Army PFC earns about $21,000 a year in base pay and allowances that include money for housing and subsistence as well as bonuses in many selected specialties. (You are going to be surprised at how many there are!) Because many of those allowances are tax-free, he or she gets to keep more than $800 in spendable income that would otherwise be lost in a civilian job. By contrast, another member of the same high school graduating class might earn $20,000 a year as a computer specialist after spending some time in a technical school.

That is just for starters. A master sergeant in the Marine Corps with 20 years of service makes more than $50,000 a year. A colonel with the same length of service makes more than twice as much. Among newer people, a recent college graduate can earn $34,000 a year as an ensign in the Navy, about the same as most other entry-level jobs in the civilian world. The big difference is that the ensign will be building benefits toward an eventual graduate degree, which won't be the case with a recent grad who goes into a civilian job.

Cash for Joining

There aren't many civilian jobs that offer a cash bonus just for signing a contract. That's another way the military is different. If you qualify, you can pocket as much as $20,000 in enlistment bonuses when you start a career in the Army. For example …

- ◆ College students are entitled to $4,000 if they have 30 to 59 hours of earned credit, or $8,000 for 60 hours or more. Many college students find it a smart idea to interrupt their college career, collect the bonus, and then finish up later, combining credits they picked up on active duty with more paid-for by the Montgomery GI Bill when their tour of duty is over.
- ◆ Choose airborne training and you'll get a $3,000 cash bonus.
- ◆ Sign up for a two-year enlistment in some specialties and your bonus will be $4,000.
- ◆ Join the Army Reserve with a specialty to offer and you'll be paid an extra $8,000.

Those amounts are just what the Army offers. All of the other services have similar enlistment incentives. For more information, refer to the section "Free Money" in Chapter 2.

What About Benefits?

Starting out in almost any civilian job, you can expect to get a week's vacation after working for a year. You'll get two weeks with pay the following year, and then wait a couple more years before you'll be entitled to more.

The military is different. Everyone, in every branch of the service, gets 30 days of paid vacation every year—they call it "leave," but it's the same thing. They also get the day off on every federal holiday. Most military personnel work five, eight-hour days a week. If they work nights, they get extra pay. If they work weekends, they get equivalent time off.

If you sign up right out of high school, you can retire when you're 33 years old, after 15 years of service, with a lump sum payment of $30,000, plus a pension equal to 40 percent of the average of your highest pay over three years.

Stay in for another five years and the pension will go up by another 10 percent. Think about it: You'll still be under 40 and free to turn your experience into a high-paying civilian job.

You'll also still have some impressive benefits as a veteran, like discount shopping at military supermarkets and department stores. You'll be entitled to low-interest home loans, too.

Food and Housing

It goes without saying that free food is among the most attractive benefits of being in the military. If your vision of what to expect comes from reading the *Beetle Bailey* comic strip where the cook drops cigarette ashes into the stew, you're in for a big surprise.

Bet You Didn't Know _____

Every branch of the service takes special pride in its chow. The Army, Navy, Coast Guard, and Marines compete with one another to see who comes out best in taste tests, which they routinely stage among themselves with all the competitive spirit of a college football rivalry.

Many of the military's cooks take advantage of special training offered at the Culinary Institute of America, the country's most prestigious school for food-service careers. The CIA is well known, not just in America, but around the world for the number of first-rate chefs among its graduates.

Every branch recognizes the connection between good nutrition and good health, too. That doesn't mean you're going to be stuck with a health-food diet, though. The food is as hearty as it is healthy. But if you're a picky eater and prefer to feed yourself, you'll be paid to be able to do it. You will be entitled to what is called a BAS, Basic Allowance for Subsistence. Like the housing allowances, the amount varies according to the cost of living where you are based.

In addition to your dining benefits, during your years in the service, you'll get free housing on base or generous tax-free allowances for a home of your own. And forget about those old barracks movies. For most of your military career, after your schooling is over, you'll have a room with most likely one roommate, and not a couple of dozen noisy people, when you choose to live where you work. Of course, that isn't *always* the case. If you're serving aboard a Navy ship, for instance, there isn't space enough for any privacy.

Medical Care

Like food and housing, free medical care is one of the obvious military benefits. Yes, of course you're entitled to doctor's services, hospitalization, and dental care without any charge at all. But what you might not have known is that, good as they are, you aren't limited just to military facilities. The health-care system extends into private hospitals, too.

You may also not have known that the same level of care is available to your family as well. In some cases, an enrollment fee and yearly deductible may apply. But at a time when private medical insurance plans are pricing themselves out of the average family's budget, this is a benefit worth thousands of dollars, not to mention priceless security.

Tip

It's never smart to drop out of high school, whatever the reason. Officially, you can't enlist without a high school diploma, but the Army offers a "GED Now" option that allows you to enroll in a special General Education Diploma program, which you'll need to finish in a specified length of time. After that, you're free, even encouraged, to go on to higher education.

Education Benefits

One of the first challenges a new high school graduate faces is whether to go to college or to get a job. The military allows you to do both at the same time.

Everyone in the service is trained in a job specialty. Many of the schools offer high-tech training, and many are accredited to offer college credits. But there are more options available to you.

The Montgomery GI Bill

The Montgomery GI Bill program is voluntary, requiring a contribution into one's personal college fund of $100 a month for a year, a total of $1,200. It extends to members of the National Guard and military reserves as well, but at lower rates.

In addition, the Montgomery GI Bill gives $28,000 to anyone who finishes a 36-month enlistment in any of the services. The Army or Navy college fund programs add to it for a total of $50,000 for education, and the Marine Corps or Coast Guard college funds raise the total to $30,000.

To take part, you'll need to score 50 or better on the Armed Services Vocational Aptitude Battery (ASVAB), which will be covered in Chapter 3. You're also going to need a high school diploma or a GED. The benefit isn't available to anyone with prior military service.

To qualify for the added benefits of college funds offered by the Army, Navy, Marine Corps, and Coast Guard, you'll also need to sign up for varying amounts of time up to four years.

Bet You Didn't Know

The Servicemen's Readjustment Act of 1944 offered veterans of World War II $500 a year for college tuition and other education costs. (Yes, it was more than adequate in those days.) It was reinstated in 1984 from a bill drafted by Rep. G.V. Montgomery (D-Mississippi) as a voluntary program. About 95 percent of all military personnel are taking advantage of it. The original law became known as the "GI Bill," and this newer, better version is called the "Montgomery GI Bill."

Tuition Assistance Program

It's in the military's own best interest for you to go on with higher education while you're serving, and it goes beyond the benefits of the Montgomery GI Bill to help you do it without waiting until your tour has ended. When it does, you will still be eligible for Montgomery benefits, but this new program puts you ahead of the game.

During your term of service, a special Tuition Assistance Program pays 75 percent of the cost of tuition or expenses, for courses you take for college credit while you are serving, with a cap of $187.50 per semester-hour credit. There is a maximum of $3,500 per fiscal year for each student.

Free College Credits

The huge variety of schools the military runs may not seem much like colleges. That's especially true if you just look at them as tuition-free institutions. But that isn't how the American Council on Education looks at them. It has certified more than 60 percent of military-training courses for full credit by a majority of America's colleges and universities.

As far as your certification record for a college diploma or certificate is concerned, it is exactly the same as if you had been in a private college or university rather than training for your military specialty.

Servicemember Opportunity Colleges

Known in military-speak as SOC, this is a group of more than 1,400 colleges and universities that have agreed to transfer credits among themselves for military students and their dependents. (Yes, your spouse and your children qualify as well.) These students, who are working on their degrees through the Internet, by mail, or in college classrooms, which are located on many military installations, can keep up their work no matter where the military happens to send them. The student body of this floating institution, by the way, is well over 26,000.

What About My College Loans?

If you decided to go to college first before signing up in the military, it wasn't a mistake. As a college graduate, you can join at a higher rank where the perks are better. But what about those unpaid tuition loans?

The Army, for one, has a great deal for you: For every year you serve, it will repay either $1,500 or a third of your educational debt load (whichever is greater). The Navy has an even better deal, although there are some restrictions. It will pay off your student loans up to a total of $10,000 if you qualify.

The Cutting Edge of Technology

Without development by the military, we wouldn't have radar, helicopters, or jet airplanes. We wouldn't even have microwave ovens. Without people in uniform working behind the scenes, we'd still be staring at the moon and wondering if it's really made of cheese.

Americans are the most inventive people on earth. But an idea is only as good as what you do with it, and you can't always do it alone. It usually takes a team to translate an idea into reality, and more often than not, the teams that do the job are men and women in uniform.

The military is where innovation begins in hundreds of fields, from the development of fuel cells to solid-state lasers and robotics, as well as the development of new vaccines. It is active in less exotic fields, too, like the development of new gizmos for your car, developing better computer software, and innovation in human resources management. And in every discipline, the help-wanted sign is out.

In Their Footsteps

At Edwards Air Force Base in California, a team of airmen and scientists is working on a program to double the capacity of every rocket propulsion system in the country's arsenal. This will not only make weapons systems and satellite launching programs less expensive and more efficient, but will ultimately change the whole concept of space research with miniature payloads. Their research includes the development of micro-thrusters, nozzles about as big as your thumb, that are leading to the possibilities of mini-satellites.

But improving existing hardware is only part of what they're up to out there on the California desert. The team has already developed a superplastic that can hold up in space and will have an infinite number of applications here on earth … when private industry catches up with the concept.

The Least You Need to Know

◆ A military career is the starting point for success in almost any field, and opportunities have changed for the better.

◆ The pay is better than you thought—and you can even make money when you sign up.

◆ The benefits can add up to a significant amount when you consider food, housing, and medical care.

◆ Whether you are working toward a GED or a college degree while in the military, you can receive tuition assistance, get funds for college or help with loan payments, and even receive credits and take classes over the Internet.

◆ The military can be a way to discover new interests; few civilian careers can do as much to build your personal pride.

◆ Whatever you may have believed about a career in the military, it's worth a second look. Everything has changed for the better.

Chapter 2

Joining Up

In This Chapter

- Age limits and other requirements
- When it's a good idea to put off your start date
- Making sure you get the job you want
- Starting out higher up
- What to expect from sign-up bonuses

Not long ago, a scruffy-looking guy who was living on the streets of New York walked into the Armed Forces Recruiting Center in Times Square. He pulled himself up to attention, saluted, and announced, "I want to join the Marines!"

The Marine sergeant never blinked. He pulled out a sheaf of papers and invited the man to have a seat. But the interview had barely begun when he had to tell the man he wouldn't get his wish. It wasn't because of how he looked or how he was dressed. The Marine Corps, after all, has a proud tradition of molding men from the rawest of material. No, this man was simply too old to serve.

Limitations and Restrictions

This section is about the numerous requirements and limitations that you will discover should you decide to join up:

◆ In order to enlist in the military, you must be at least 17 years old and younger than 35. For the Air Force, the cutoff is 25 years old. There are other variations in the upper age limitations, too, such as prior service and whether you are trained in a field that a service regards as critical. But the absolute minimum is 17, and at that age you're going to need the written consent of a parent or guardian.

◆ You'll be expected to have a high school diploma. But in some cases, you might be able to get into a military GED program.

Bet You Didn't Know _____

The GED (General Educational Diploma) program was originally developed for the military during World War II, when many young draftees didn't have high school diplomas at the time they were drafted into the service. In order to help them qualify, special courses were developed so that the basic requirements for a high school diploma could be met. At the end of the course, a test was given and a diploma awarded for passing.

Over the years, the educational community accepted GED diplomas as a substitute for a full high school experience. Thousands of young people have benefited from the program, the majority of whom had been forced to leave school to help support their families.

◆ You can join the American military if you're not a citizen of the United States, but you need to be a legal alien with a green card to confirm it. A student visa will also make you eligible, and many foreign students agree to enlist in the military to take advantage of the educational benefits the American military offers.

◆ There are height restrictions, too. You'll need to be shorter than 6' 8" and taller than 5' 0". Women can slip under the bar if they are 4' 10".

◆ Weight restrictions apply as well, according to age and height. But that is something you have some control over.

◆ Being married is no bar to enlistment, even if you have children. But if you have dependent children and are not married, you'll be out of luck.

◆ The military makes it a point to screen out candidates who seem likely to become disciplinary problems. If you've been arrested and convicted of anything, from shoplifting to DWI to painting your graffiti tag around town, you may be rejected.

But that doesn't necessarily mean that your past is going to doom your future. Individual services look at past offenses on a case-by-case basis and frequently grant exceptions, called "waivers." If you have a problem and one service turns you away, try the others before you give up.

The Ten Commandments of Enlisting

The following is a list of things to keep in mind and consider before enlisting:

1. Take your time. Enlisting is a big step in your life. Don't do it until you're positive you are doing the right thing.

2. Take someone along to the recruiting station. A buddy or a family member will be able to help you sort out all the information. He or she can also ask questions and take notes for you.

3. Talk with people who have been there. Visit a military installation if you can. Get to know a veteran who can tell you what to expect.

4. Think about your opinion of war. When all is said and done, job one in the military is preparing for conflict. If you are uncomfortable with war or the loss of life it sometimes entails, the military may not be right for you.

5. Ask for a copy of the enlistment agreement. There is a lot of fine print to go over, and you need to study all of it. It is your right to take it home before you sign on the dotted line.

6. Remember that there isn't an adjustment period. After you leave for Basic Training, you will be under contract to serve for a specified length of time. It is typically eight years, counting reserve duty. There is no way out of it once you have signed an enlistment agreement.

7. Get all of the promises in writing. In general, most of what a recruiter promises you is guaranteed—but not always. Having it in writing will help, but it is still no guarantee in itself. Your enlistment contract is binding on you, but the military has a lot of wiggle room.

8. Be wary of job "guarantees." If the military thinks it needs to fill a job you've requested, you'll probably get it. But nothing is set in stone. If needs and conditions change, your assignment may change, too.

9. Be prepared to lose some of your civil rights. You will be expected to follow orders, even when you think they aren't fair. Your right to free speech and expression, such as the way you dress and wear your hair, are going to be restricted. And keep in mind that the Constitution doesn't always apply in the military. It operates under rules of its own, and you will be expected to follow them.

10. Consider the benefits outside the *military*. Such things as cash bonuses, money for education, free food, housing, medical care, and job security that the military gives you are tough to beat. But before you take this big step, check out the alternatives in the private sector.

How to Deal with Recruiters

The first thing you need to know about recruiters is that they represent the sales department of the military. Selling is an honorable profession, though, and there is no reason to believe that you are going to get a fast shuffle when you sit down to have a talk with a recruiter.

It is his or her job to keep the ranks filled, of course. But the most important part of it is recruiting people who cannot only fill the jobs that are open, but will ultimately be happy in those jobs. Recruiters don't want to be responsible for creating malcontents down the line.

Yes, recruiters are salespeople. And yes, they have quotas to fill. But it makes a great deal of sense to think of them as the personnel department of the military. All of them are well trained in the field of human resources.

Don't Limit Yourself

Your talk with a recruiter is actually a job interview. All of the same rules apply that you'd expect if you were looking for a job in the private sector.

The secret for putting your best foot forward in any interview is to get some experience in interviewing itself. The way to do that is by applying for jobs you don't want. You'll be surprised at how easy it is to talk to an interviewer when you're not worrying about the outcome.

After three or four interviews, you're ready for the big one with all of the right answers and all the right questions. More important, you'll be more confident because you'll know what to listen for—you've been there before.

Make the Rounds

Even if you've already made up your mind that you don't want anything but an Air Force career, you ought to make it a point to talk with recruiters from all the other services first. If you're really determined to become an airman, those talks probably won't change your mind. But by talking with the others first, the experience is going to make you more relaxed when you get to the one you've actually been aiming for. Although it may seem like it, it isn't a waste of your time.

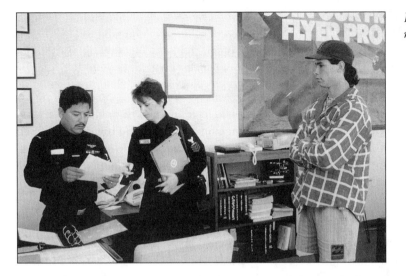

Don't talk to just one recruiter.

Among the things you'll learn when you make the rounds is that the services are more alike than they are different. You might find what you're looking for in unexpected places. For instance, if you're thinking of a career in aviation, you'll find that all of the services, from the Army to the Coast Guard, have jobs involving planes and helicopters. One of them might turn out to be exactly what you have been looking for.

If you were buying an insurance policy or looking for financing to buy a car, you know it's a good idea to shop around for the best deal. It's the same with enlisting in the service.

Take a Devil's Advocate Along

Your decision to join the military is one that affects your whole family. Recruiters are well aware of that, and they will probably encourage you to bring along one or both of your parents for your interviews. Take their advice.

It isn't a sign that you can't stand on your own two feet. On the contrary, it shows that your head is in the right place. And, after all, another pair of ears can't hurt.

Tip

Sometimes the thought of getting on a bus or a train and leaving your friends behind can give you the willies. But when you join the military, you can take a friend with you. All of the services offer what they call the "Buddy Deal." Two people who join together, and agree to share the same training and assignments, are guaranteed to stay together for at least a year. In some cases, taking advantage of it may even make you eligible for extra pay. It's the military's version of a finder's fee.

Talk with Someone Who's Been There

If it is at all possible for you to visit a military installation near where you live, by all means do it. It is the best possible way for you to get a feel for what military life is really like.

You should also have chats with men and women who have finished their military careers. It will give you a better idea of what your long-range future holds. And the stories of their experience of a few years in the military will help you know what to expect in your immediate future. But whatever you do, seek out people who have had the experience recently. If your father was in the service, he might not believe how much it has changed since his day.

Finally, take the advice you get with a grain of salt. Think about what you yourself might like or not like. You aren't looking for advice in this case, just a taste of the experience. You need to put it all together and decide for yourself. With that in mind, talk to as many people as you can catch up with. The more opinions you get, the better off you'll be.

No Such Thing as a Stupid Question

The recruiter's job is to answer your questions. But what questions should you ask? Obviously, you need to ask about all the changes your new life might bring. Some of those things, though, might seem silly. That doesn't mean they aren't worth asking about—even if you think you already know the answer.

Is there really a guy who blows a bugle in your ear at 5:00 in the morning? Can you go back for seconds during dinner? Can you make phone calls? Do you have to wear a hat all the time? Can men wear earrings? Can they grow a beard? Can women take their stuffed animals along with them? Do you get weekends off?

If there is anything at all that you have been wondering about, you'll get an answer. And the smile that goes with it won't be a condescending one. But first you have to ask. Sometimes you'll be pleasantly surprised by the answers.

Smart Questions

Just because you stepped into a recruiting office doesn't mean that your mind is already made up. The fact is, it shouldn't be. You are there to get answers. Until you are satisfied with them, you aren't under any obligation at all.

It's a good idea to write down your questions in advance. That way you won't forget to ask them. Think of it as a shopping list. Start it with these:

♦ How is this branch of the service different from the others?

♦ Why should I even think of joining?

♦ What steps are involved in the recruiting process?

♦ How much time do I have to sign up for?

♦ What special incentives are available right now?

♦ How can I be sure promises are going to be kept?

♦ What is Basic Training really like?

♦ Do you have to be in shape before Basic Training starts?

♦ Do women have to get GI haircuts?

♦ Why do men need those haircuts anyway?

♦ Can I really get the job I ask for?

♦ How much will I be paid?

♦ Will I have to buy my own uniform?

♦ Can I request overseas service?

♦ What kind of training comes after Basic Training?

♦ How good are those military schools? Who says so?

♦ Can I earn college credit while I serve?

♦ How can I qualify for tuition help?

♦ How often will I be promoted?

These, and others like them, are questions recruiters are asked every day. The most important one you can ask is that last one: how you can be sure the answers you're getting are on the up-and-up.

> **Tip**
>
> Make certain that you don't get just the answers that the recruiter thinks you want to hear. What you are looking for is straight-from-the-shoulder advice. You have a right to it.

Call Your Own Shots

Everybody in the military has a military occupational specialty (MOS). It isn't something that's pulled out of a hat, but is assigned based on a number of factors, beginning with your score on the aptitude test that everyone takes (refer to Chapter 3). The good news is that it's usually easy to get the MOS you want, but remember: You won't get a choice unless you ask for it.

Don't let a recruiter talk you into something that won't interest you. They have specific jobs that need to be filled, and they will try to talk you into them. But remember, this is your career. Your own goals are very important. If you express them, and stick to them, recruiters will generally bend over backwards to help you meet them. When all is said and done, they would prefer satisfied recruits over filling jobs that are short-staffed at the moment. But unless you are up-front with them, you may be taking a risk of not getting a job you want. Always keep in mind that the only way to get what you want is to ask for it.

Maybe you haven't decided what you want to be when you grow up. If that is the case, there isn't any better place to start than at a military recruiting office. Your visit to a recruiter can open your eyes to all of the things you can become.

Once you have decided on an MOS, training for it is generally guaranteed. It will begin right away after Basic Training and will last anywhere from 10 weeks to a year or more.

The most important thing to remember is that the choice is yours. If you sign up to learn computer-system design, you aren't going to be trained in vehicle maintenance. It's guaranteed.

Yes, there will be times when the military decides its needs are changing, and its needs always come first. That may change the promises they made to you. But these are never changes that are forced without careful consideration. The military's top need is to have personnel in jobs that they like. It makes sense that baiting and switching is going to result in some unhappy campers, and it is most often scrupulously avoided. Although "guaranteed" could be a word you might take with a grain of salt, the chance that the promise won't be kept is close to unthinkable.

On the other side of the coin, if you thought you'd like a particular field, and even show an aptitude for it, but then find that it isn't as wonderful as you thought once you get into the training, you can request a transfer to train for a different MOS. But this is another place where the word "guarantee" is a tricky one. Chances are pretty good that you can be transferred, but it depends on a lot of factors and often involves a lot of red tape. If it happens to you, the earlier you ask for something different, the better your chances of having your wish granted.

Keep in mind that once you've signed an enlistment contract, this isn't a job you can quit before you've served your time. But remember, too, that morale is important to the military, and if you feel like a square peg in a round hole, that could be a problem to them.

Warning

When you sign up under the Delayed Entry Program, you are actually enlisting, even though you don't have to show up for active duty right away. You won't have the option of changing your mind.

No Openings? No Problem

Among the hundreds of different career opportunities the military offers, some, obviously, are more popular than others. If training for the MOS you choose is all booked up when you sign up, you can put off reporting for duty for up to a year until there are openings.

The option, called delayed entry, is also useful for students who need to finish high school or college first. It can even allow you to take a vacation after graduation before you begin your new life.

One Career Leads to Another

At the same time you join the military for training in a specific skill, you can also apply for a related civilian job after your tour is over. An option called the Partnership for Youth Success works like an employment agency (without the fees) with hundreds of the country's biggest corporations that guarantee priority job placement down the road. In most cases, the program will set you on the career path you want with less concern about economic downturns in the future. Naturally, if you change your outlook, or even decide to make the military itself a lifetime career, you aren't obligated to apply for any of those civilian jobs. But it can be reassuring to know that there will be one waiting for you if you want it.

As for the future employers who are waiting to hear from you, they already know what you are going to find out for yourself. Military training and discipline are the most valuable kinds of training you can get when it comes to qualifying for the best civilian jobs.

The First Step Is Up

If you have more than 30 college credit hours before you start active duty, you can expect to be promoted to a higher grade right from the start. In order to qualify, you can sign up for the College First option. It will allow you to attend college for up to two years under the Delayed Entry Program or as a member of the reserves. With delayed entry, you'll collect an allowance of $150 a month while you're studying. If you are a reservist, you will also collect reserve pay at the same time (refer to Chapter 5).

When you actually report for duty, your starting salary will be higher because you'll start further up the pay-scale ladder. In addition, if you sign up after you've graduated from college, your rank, and the pay that goes with it, will be a good deal higher.

Experience in civilian jobs counts as well. If you have been working for a couple of years and don't think you've been advancing fast enough, the military is a great way to accelerate your pace. If your job has taught you a skill that the military thinks it needs, it's your ticket to a promotion before you even start.

And don't think that just applies to high-tech jobs. Suppose you've been working in a restaurant kitchen, for instance. The military travels on its stomach, remember, and every branch is on the lookout for culinary experience. Every branch will compete with the others to get you into their kitchens. That can result in a higher starting grade and probably an extra enlistment bonus at the same time. The pattern is repeated in dozens of areas, from auto mechanics to computer programmers.

Free Money

If you have all the right qualifications, you can find yourself richer by up to $20,000 just for passing Go. Some military enlistment bonuses are better than others, but in every case they are like getting free money just for signing on the dotted line.

One of the first factors to determine how much you'll get is how long you sign up for. Until quite recently, when the highest amount you could collect was $12,000, you had to sign up for at least three years. Now it's only two.

Another recent change allows you to collect an enlistment bonus even when you tap into the Army or Navy college funds, or take advantage of the scholarship money available from the Marine Corps and Coast Guard (note that the Air Force doesn't play the game).

Money for education and money for bonuses are two different things. Until the law was changed, a recruit could collect one or the other, but not both. But that is past history now.

How You Qualify

In order to qualify for the highest enlistment bonuses, you'll need to score in the top half on the Armed Services Vocational Aptitude Battery or ASVAB (you'll find out how easy that can be in Chapter 3). Then you'll be asked to take another test in one of the eligible occupational specialties.

There are more than 120 high-bonus-earning specialties to choose from. The key is picking the right one. The size of the bonus is based on the military's need for candidates in specific fields at specific times. The actual amount can vary from $1,000 all the way up to the $20,000 maximum. For instance, in the Navy's program, a recruit who volunteers for jobs in the nuclear field can expect a $12,000 bonus. The other services offer similar deals, depending on their individual needs. For the most part, they vary up and down depending on the number of recruits available to fill critical jobs.

"Critical Career" Choices

The basic idea behind enlistment bonuses is to encourage recruits to choose jobs the military calls "Critical Careers." The following are a few of the choices the Air Force puts into the category:

- Aerospace maintenance
- Air transportation
- Aircraft fuels systems
- Aircraft generation equipment

- ◆ Aircraft guidance control
- ◆ Aircraft hydraulics specialist
- ◆ Aircraft repair and reclamation
- ◆ Aircraft structural specialist
- ◆ Jet engine mechanic
- ◆ Security forces
- ◆ Supply
- ◆ Vehicle operations specialist

The list of critical jobs is similar in the other services. Recruiters can fill you in.

How You Collect

As generous as enlistment bonuses are, don't expect to start Basic Training with a bulging money belt. Payments are occasionally made as a lump sum, but more often than not, they are paid in segments. Usually, you can expect to collect half when you finish your skill training and the rest when your enlistment expires. It is a safeguard that you are going to keep your end of the bargain.

Also keep in mind that your bonus is going to be subject to social security and federal income taxes, just like when you win the lottery, which will be automatically deducted from your check.

The Last Mile

After you've done all your exploring, asked all the questions, filled out all the papers, signed all the contracts, and finally made up your mind which branch of the service is right for you, there is one last step for you to take. It begins at a military entrance processing station, affectionately known as the MEPS.

If you haven't already taken the required ASVAB, this is where you'll go through it. If you have already taken the test, be sure to let the administrator know and you probably won't have to do it again.

The physical examination also takes place at the MEPS. You'll also fill out a medical history questionnaire. It's a good idea to ask your parents in advance about diseases or other health problems you may have had when you were a kid and since forgotten.

Men and women take their physicals separately, and in both cases underclothing is required. Women are provided with a robe.

The preinduction physical examination consists of the following:

◆ Height and weight measurements

◆ Hearing and vision tests

◆ Urine and blood tests

◆ Drug and alcohol tests

◆ Muscle group and joint maneuvers (in underclothing)

◆ Complete individual physical examination and interview

◆ Specialized tests that may be required

There are processing stations in most major cities around the country. If keeping your appointment at one of them requires an overnight stay, your meals and hotel accommodations will be paid for. Usually candidates double up, two to a room. Extra costs, like phone calls and late-night pizzas, aren't covered. But your necessary expenses will be paid, even if you aren't accepted by the military.

> **Tip**
>
> Forget all the horror stories you might have heard about the preinduction physical. The game has changed in recent years with modesty in mind, and you won't be forced to walk naked past a long line of doctors. The changes have also resulted in a more thorough examination.
>
> When your father was a teenager, heart murmurs, flat feet, and punctured eardrums were about all that might make him ineligible to serve. These days, though, military physicals are looking for such things as severe allergies, diabetes, and alcohol or drug problems. These, among other issues that weren't always taken seriously before, can result in rejection in the new military.

The Final Step

Once you have passed the physical and taken the aptitude test, a counselor will explain the enlistment contract and go over the requirements of the job you have chosen one more time. If you think you've heard all this before, stay alert anyway. If something comes up that you don't remember hearing before, ask about it. This is your final step, and besides, you aren't going to get another chance to talk back to anybody for a long time to come.

Your final interview will be followed by a preenlistment briefing and fingerprinting for an FBI check. After that, all that remains to be done is taking the final oath. Your family is welcome, even encouraged, to watch that final phase, and to take pictures while it is happening.

Unless you have enlisted under the Delayed Entry Program, your last step will be out the door, where transportation will be waiting to deliver you to the beginning of your military career: Basic Training.

When an appointment is made for you to report to the MEPS for processing, you'll be given a list to help you get ready for it. Since you may be going directly from there to Basic Training, you should also take along the things you will need once you get there (see Chapter 3 for details). For the MEPS experience, these are what will be required:

- Bring documentation of any early medical problems.
- Bring your driver's license, your social security card, and your birth certificate.
- Persons of either sex should not wear earrings, which can interfere with the hearing test.
- Profanity on clothing is prohibited, as are offensive words or pictures.
- Hats are not permitted.
- Bring your eyeglasses or contacts with you, along with your lens case, and your prescription.
- Bathe or shower the night before.
- Get a full night's sleep.
- Wear neat, comfortable clothing, and underclothes.
- Leave stereo headphones, jewelry, and other valuables at home, along with all but a minimum of cash.
- Check with your recruiter about personal items you might need after you report for duty.

The Least You Need to Know

- Not just anyone can qualify for a military career; there are some restrictions and limitations you need to be aware of.
- Military recruiters are well-trained professionals who serve as the human resources department when you begin your military career.
- You can wait for a better offer before you sign up. It is easily possible to delay your enlistment.
- It is possible to combine enlistment bonuses or shop around for a better one.
- Your job choice will usually be guaranteed if you qualify for it.
- The military has changed, with more options, more benefits, and more attention to your personal needs. You should check out what they are before you decide on any other career.

Chapter **3**

Oh, No, Not Another Test!

In This Chapter

- Understanding the ASVAB
- How can you study for an "aptitude test"?
- Does taking the test carry any obligations?
- How the test is scored
- How your score affects your promotion chances

If you're a high school student, or young enough to remember when you were, the very word "test" probably turns your stomach. That may be why the military calls its aptitude test a "battery." But don't let that fool you.

The Armed Services Vocational Aptitude Battery (ASVAB), like any other test you've ever taken, requires a little skill along with a No. 2 pencil. You may be able to take the computerized version, but that just causes a callus at a different place on your index finger.

You'll be told time and again that you can't fail this test. Technically, that's true. But the numbers you score can follow you all the way through your military career. At the beginning, it will help determine what sort of specialties you might qualify for. As your military career goes along and you are being considered for promotions, your original ASVAB score will be taken into consideration, too. This is especially true when you cross the line toward becoming a commissioned officer. Low scores on the ASVAB can come back to haunt you, which is a good reason why you need to be careful to do your best in the first place.

What Is the ASVAB?

The battery is actually a sequence of 10 timed tests to determine your aptitude for different career areas. It will also give you a measure of your overall academic ability. It takes exactly three hours from start to finish.

The ASVAB format is broken down into 10 subjects; the number of questions and time limit are listed in the following table.

The ASVAB Format

Subject	Minutes	Questions
1. General Science	11	25
2. Arithmetic Reasoning	36	30
3. Word Knowledge	11	35
4. Paragraph Comprehension	13	15
5. Numerical Operations	3	50
6. Coding Speed	7	84
7. Auto and Shop Information	11	25
8. Mathematics Knowledge	24	25
9. Mechanical Comprehension	19	25
10. Electronics Information	9	20

Tip

Your school guidance counselor will be able to make the arrangements for you to take the ASVAB, or you can do it through a recruiter in any of the five services. The test is given year-round at hundreds of locations, usually recruiting stations and military processing centers, as well as through 14,000 high schools across the country.

You will spend three hours on the test. The time not devoted to the questions themselves is spent in a preliminary practice session and instructions.

You'll be given a score based on the number of correctly answered questions in each of the subjects. On top of that, your scores on some of them will be combined into separate scores reflecting verbal ability, math ability, and academic ability.

Military personnel administer the tests, and your scores are given to local recruiters, often all five services. If you take the test at your high school, as most do, your score will also be sent to the guidance counselor. Naturally, you'll get a copy as well.

Whether you take the ASVAB at school or at a recruiting office, you are going to need to do it at some point in order to qualify for enlistment. For purposes of enlistment, only 4 of the battery's 10 categories will make the difference. They call it the Armed Forces Qualifying Test score. (Call it AFQT and they'll treat you like a pro.)

The areas that make the difference are Arithmetic Reasoning, Mathematics Knowledge, Word Knowledge, and Paragraph Comprehension. Scores in the other six will have an effect on your advancement after you've signed up.

Can You Prevent Recruiters from Seeing Your Scores?

Many students take the ASVAB even though they aren't at all interested in enlisting in the service. It is a good idea because the scores can offer some insight on possible civilian careers, too.

When the results are forwarded to recruiters, though, they are also given your name and address. And they will be told other things you mentioned on the form that you filled out before you took the test. They will know, for instance, what your post-graduation plans are. But even if the military isn't one of the options you mentioned, they'll probably be in touch anyway.

Head Them Off at the Pass

Schools usually like to have their students take the ASVAB because it is a good tool to use in career guidance. Besides, it is administered for the schools, and it doesn't cost them anything. In most cases, in fact, guidance counselors usually schedule the test and require all juniors or seniors to take it. Sometimes, students themselves begin the process by requesting the ASVAB through their school administrators.

When school officials agree to allow the testers into the premises, they are given a list of options about how the results will be handled. Like most official government documents, the list is hard to read and sometimes harder to understand. To cut the red tape, as it were, the first option on the list is simply put as: "No Options." When that one is checked, none of the others on the list will matter. One that may matter to you, though, is Option 8, way down at the bottom of the list: "No Release to Recruiters."

It is up to school officials to consider the options. But they probably won't get to the bottom of the list unless you ask them to. If you don't, you can expect visits and phone calls from recruiters; it's supposed to be the other way around. If you're already considering a military career, you might welcome the attention, though. But it is probably better if you set the agenda with them yourself.

When and Why Take the Test

You can take the ASVAB as early as your sophomore year in high school. But if you are seriously considering joining the military, you should understand that for enlistment purposes the results won't be valid two years after you answer those 334 questions. It is a better idea to put off the ASVAB until you're closer to making the commitment.

If you are considering enlistment, the ASVAB is the first requirement. If you aren't, the test will be helpful to you in deciding on a civilian career. The results can guide you in your selection of college courses, or will let you know if you are on the right track in any job hunt.

The ASVAB has been developed over 35 years of matching people to the right jobs in the military and studying the outcome. It isn't a test that you either pass or fail. It is just a measure of how well you compare to a sampling of other students across the country.

Taking the ASVAB doesn't cost anything. It doesn't even obligate you to the military. Because of all the things it will tell you about yourself, it's silly not to take it.

Tip

Your score may be affected by a lack of experience in some areas because your school hasn't covered those things for you. But in the end, the ASVAB is going to give you some valuable insight about the pattern of your general occupational interests. It may even lead you in the direction of a field you never considered before.

Warning

If you have reason to think a recruiter has given you a wrong answer to any question, challenge it. Or get a second opinion from a different recruiter if you're still not satisfied.

Don't Do Well with Tests?

A lot of people freeze up in a testing situation. Maybe they didn't get enough sleep the night before. Maybe they have other things on their mind. Maybe the pressure is too much for them.

When you take the ASVAB, someone in the room will be looking over your shoulder with a stopwatch. In the Coding Speed section, for instance, you'll have to answer 84 questions in seven minutes. In Numerical Operations, you'll have three minutes to deal with 50. How's that for pressure? Don't worry about it. Everyone who takes the test has to deal with the same pressure, and your score is going to be compared to theirs.

Can You Take the Test Again?

Suppose you qualify for enlistment, but your score in Mechanical Comprehension is too low for you to make it in jet-engine maintenance. Does that mean you're going to have to settle for something else? Of course not.

Some recruiters may tell you that you can't take the test over again, more than likely because it represents more paperwork for them. (Recruiters are human, too.) But the fact is that you can, and sometimes it's a good idea. In this case, and at other times during the enlistment process, you have to stand up for your rights.

The Big Day

When you show up to take the ASVAB, you'll be given a booklet with 10 short tests made up of sample questions. Consider it your warm-up.

You'll also have a separate sheet of paper for your answers, and scratch paper for you to do your figuring. You'll be given complete instructions before you start, including the time limits for each section. And you'll be encouraged to ask questions of your own before you begin.

Here's a comprehensive look at each section of the ASVAB.

A. General Science

Most of the 25 questions here are usually covered in high school courses, so chances are you've already seen them on other tests you've taken. The areas this section covers are earth science, chemistry, biology, and physics. Pick what you consider the right answer to these multiple-choice questions and blacken the appropriate box on your answer form.

The following are a couple of sample general-science questions:

1. What kind of time does a sundial keep?

   A) Daylight saving time

   B) Solar time

   C) Sonic time

   D) Air time

2. A burning candle produces:

   A) Carbon monoxide and nitrogen.

   B) Carbon monoxide and water.

   C) Carbon dioxide and water.

   D) Carbon dioxide and nitrogen.

Answers: 1 B; 2 C

B. Arithmetic Reasoning

This test asks for answers to simple problems in arithmetic. Your score will be based on the number you get right, not the number you attempt to answer. You may use scratch paper to find your answer before you blacken the appropriate boxes. You are allowed to count on your fingers, but not to use a pocket calculator.

The following are a couple of sample arithmetic-reasoning questions:

1. If an airplane travels 1,000 miles in 2 hours and 30 minutes, what was its average speed in miles per hour?

   A) 200 miles per hour

   B) 300 miles per hour

   C) 400 miles per hour

   D) 500 miles per hour

2. A basketball player tried 320 shots and made 272 of them during a season. What percent of the shots were successful?

   A) 85%

   B) 80%

   C) 75%

   D) 70%

Answers: 1 C; 2 B

C. Word Knowledge

Every question in this subtest is a sentence with one word boldfaced and underlined. Pick the one from the options presented that is closest to that word's meaning and blacken the appropriate box on your answer sheet. You should try to answer all of these questions, but don't spend too much time on any one of them.

The following are a couple of sample word-knowledge questions:

1. The job was filled by a **<u>novice</u>**.

   A) volunteer

   B) expert

   C) beginner

   D) amateur

2. The drug will **<u>counteract</u>** any side effects.

   A) undermine

   B) preserve

   C) neutralize

   D) enhance

Answers: 1 C; 2 C

D. Paragraph Comprehension

The purpose of this section is to find out how well you understand what you read. You will read a short paragraph and then answer a question about it. Your score will be based on the number of questions you answer correctly. You should be able to answer all of them, but don't spend too much time on any one.

The following are a couple of sample paragraph-comprehension questions:

1. From a homebuilder's standpoint, three things that make a house livable are the client, the building site, and the amount of money a client is able to spend.

   According to this paragraph, to make a house livable:

   A) The piece of land makes little difference.

   B) The house must fit the owner's income and site.

   C) The plan should fit the designer's income.

   D) The house should have an attached garage.

2. Nucleic acids are found in all living organisms from viruses to man. They received their name because of their discovery in the nuclei of white blood cells and fish sperm by Miescher in 1869. However, it has since been well established that nucleic acids occur outside the cell nucleus as well.

   According to this paragraph, nucleic acids are found:

   A) Only in cells of man.

   B) Only in viruses.

   C) In all living cells.

   D) Only in white blood cells.

Answers: 1 B; 2 C

E. Numerical Operations

This is a speed test to find out how quickly and accurately you can solve arithmetic problems. You'll be given three minutes to solve 50 problems. You may finish before time runs out. If you do, go back and check your answers.

The following are a couple of sample numerical-operations questions:

1. 4 – 0=
   A) 4
   B) 2
   C) 3
   D) 0
2. 7 × 5=
   A) 45
   B) 40
   C) 35
   D) 30

Answers: 1 A; 2 C

F. Coding Speed

This section is to find out how fast you can accurately assign code numbers. It may look intimidating, but think of it as a puzzle, and it may actually turn out to be fun.

Each question is a word taken from the key at the top of rows of numbers. Look for the number that corresponds to the word in the answer section. Your answer will be the letter designation for the column where the number appears.

There are 84 questions in this series, but the answer charts each contain a number of them according to the number of words given at the top of each block. The challenge is to match the proper number from the columns with the word given at the left. You will be given seven minutes to match 84 words with their proper numbers.

The following are a couple of sample coding-speed questions:

Key					
Agile	6427	Humid	4903	Pit	6656
Beacon	8585	Jar	3059	Rest	7350
Data	9130	Overt	9845	Stun	7689

Questions	A	B	C	D	E
1. Pit	6656	7350	8585	9130	9845
2. Rest	9130	6427	7350	7689	4903
3. Beacon	6427	9845	7689	8585	7350
4. Humid	4903	9130	3059	6427	6656
5. Agile	8585	6427	9485	7350	4903
6. Overt	7350	7689	8585	9130	9845
7. Jar	8585	4903	3059	7689	9845
8. Data	3059	4903	8585	9130	7689
9. Stun	1317	4903	6427	7689	9845

Answers: 1 A; 2 C; 3 D; 4 A; 5 B; 6 E; 7 C; 8 D; 9 D

G. Auto and Shop Information

The questions in this section all have to do with automobiles. It isn't about makes and models, but what goes on under the hood, and the tools you use when you get out and get under. You will be scored on the number of correct answers, and you should make an attempt to answer all of the questions.

The following are a couple of sample auto and shop questions:

1. Synchromesh units are used in standard transmissions because they …

    A) Are stronger.

    B) Prevent grinding of gears.

    C) Are cheaper.

    D) Give the effect of overdrive.

2. The purpose of rubber cups in brake wheel cylinders is to …

    A) Push out the brake shoes.

    B) Prevent brake fluid from leaking out.

    C) Hold the springs in position.

    D) Absorb the shock when you slam on the brakes.

Answers: 1 B; 2 C

H. Mathematics Knowledge

This test is composed of basic mathematical problems. You won't come across anything that isn't familiar to the average high school student. Some of the questions will involve knowledge of algebra and geometry, but you won't need to know anything about calculus.

The following are a couple of mathematics-knowledge reasoning questions:

1. If $5x = 30$, then x is equal to ...

A) 150

B) 25

C) 6

D) 3

2. How many cubic yards of concrete are needed to make a cement floor that will be 9′ by 12′ and 6″ thick?

A) 2

B) 18

C) 54

D) 648

Answers: 1 C; 2 A

I. Mechanical Comprehension

The questions in this section are based on common mechanical and physical principles. Some of them will use drawings to illustrate specific principles.

The following are a couple of sample mechanical-comprehension questions:

1. The greatest mechanical power advantage is attained when an 11-tooth gear drives a ...

A) 29-tooth gear.

B) 11-tooth gear.

C) 47-tooth gear.

D) 15-tooth gear.

2. This instrument is used to test the specific gravity of battery electrolyte:

A) Voltmeter

B) Ammeter

C) Ohmmeter

D) Hydrometer

Answers: 1 B; 2 D

J. Electronics Information

This is a test of your knowledge of electrical, radio, and electronics information. Many of the questions have symbols and diagrams for you to decipher.

The following are a couple of sample electronics information questions:

1. One kilowatt is equal to …

   A) 1 watt.

   B) 10 watts.

   C) 100 watts.

   D) 1,000 watts.

2. Which of the following is an example of a transducer?

   A) Resistor

   B) Switch

   C) Diode

   D) Speaker

Answers: 1 D; 2 A

Think You Can Ace the ASVAB?

There isn't any reason why you can't earn a high score on this test. Most of the questions are based on things you've learned in school. A couple of hours of study will probably bring you up to speed.

Even though the ASVAB is an aptitude test, it isn't the square-peg-in-a-round-hole variety. You can study for it, and you should.

There are dozens of books that specifically address the questions you're going to find when you sit down to take the test. Many of them are in the form of workbooks with all of the questions. They give you the answers, too, so that you can practice the test itself and figure out your own score before you make it official. Taking those practice tests will show you where your weak points are. That will be where you should concentrate your study.

Many of the books on preparing for the ASVAB should be in your school library, or at least in the public library. There are also some preparation programs on videotape and CD-ROMs. You can find help on the Internet as well.

Most of these resources will explain in detail how to interpret your score for any career, not just for a military career.

Why Is Your Score Important?

Even without a lot of preparation, you can probably expect to rack up a decent score on the ASVAB. Students who have taken it usually report that it is a piece of cake. Some of them have even said that taking it was like getting three hours off from the batteries of tests that are thrown their way every day that they are in school.

Compared to taking the SAT or the ACT for college entrance, the ASVAB may seem like a walk in the park. But the score you earn may have a bigger impact on your future than either one of them.

If you are thinking about a career in the military, the score is not just the key to getting into the service in the first place. Those numbers will follow you through every promotion opportunity that comes your way. They will make a difference.

The Least You Need to Know

- You'll get a higher score on the ASVAB if you take the time to study. And there are a host of workbooks easily available.

- Your ASVAB results will follow you through your entire military career. It will turn up in promotion reviews.

- Taking the ASVAB in no way obligates you to sign up.

- Unless you don't mind if they do, you can ensure that recruiters won't see your score.

- You need to take the test in order to enlist.

- The ASVAB will open your eyes to what you are capable of doing, no matter where you plan to do it.

Part 2

You're Hired!
Now What?

Starting out in the military is pretty much like starting any new job. It's just a little more intense at the beginning. You can't avoid Basic Training, but it's easier when you know what to expect.

But it's what happens later that makes it all come together. It can all be summed up in one word: education. For openers, the military will pay for your education before you serve through ROTC programs. But it gets better. These are the only jobs available anywhere that offer college credit for time spent on the job—whether it's active duty in one of the five services, or time spent in the National Guard or the Reserves. And they're the only jobs that give you the financial means to get your degree in the end.

Chapter 4

The Part You've Been Dreading ... Shape Up!

In This Chapter

- ◆ The basics of Basic Training
- ◆ How you'll spend your days
- ◆ Is the drill instructor a sadist?
- ◆ Is Basic all hiking and dodging bullets?
- ◆ How to make those first weeks seem easy

George Washington once said, "Discipline is the soul of an army. It makes small numbers formidable; procures success to the weak, and esteem to all."

That was easy for *him* to say. He managed to skip Basic Training. But whether it's called Basic or Boot Camp, you can't avoid it. While you may not enjoy the experience, you'll be proud of yourself when it's over. Honest. It's a little like banging your head against a wall because it feels so good when you stop.

Marching in formation, doing push-ups, and running for miles into the sunrise are what Basic Training seems to be all about. But the bottom line is really discipline, that thing General Washington said makes small numbers of people formidable and makes the otherwise weak, successful. He was right that it builds self-esteem, too. And that may be the most important thing of all.

Basic may seem like torture when you're going through it, but it actually isn't. You'll understand that when it's over. Everybody loves to hate their drill instructor. But looking back on it, most people regard him as the best friend they ever had.

Basic is going to change your life, not just for your military career, but for all the years beyond. It's the fastest route to maturity known to mankind.

Tip

One of the most important things that Basic Training is going to do for you is to make you aware of other people around you. And not just aware of them, but close to them. Teamwork is at the heart of it, and knowing that in advance will make it easy. This is not something you are going to have to go through alone.

Who Needs It?

Of course, you yourself are different. You're over 18. You've already grown up. You can drive a car, vote if you feel like it, start a family, and maybe even buy a beer. But if you're an average guy or girl, there is a thing or two you need to know about yourself.

Remember how your mother used to nag at you to clean up your room? Remember how she sometimes wound up doing it herself? When was the last time you walked to school? Or walked anywhere more than a hundred yards away? Did you ever skip homework, then borrow someone else's and take the credit? Did you ever cheat on a test? Those are all little things, to be sure. Nothing that hurts anybody. But it's things like that, that add up to rough edges, and Basic is going to smooth them out for you.

How Long Does Basic Training Last?

The services are more alike than they are different. Apart from their basic missions, the pay scale is the same in all of them, and most of the rules don't vary much from one to the other. All of them require some form of initiation usually called Basic Training:

◆ The Marine Corps, which calls it Recruit Training, spends the most time at it. Its program lasts 12 weeks.

◆ If you live east of the Mississippi River, you'll be transformed into a Marine at Parris Island, South Carolina, not far from Charleston. Otherwise, you'll be shipped to Camp Pendleton, a short distance up the Pacific Coast from San Diego, California.

◆ The Army trains its recruits at various locations in different parts of the country. Basic Training at all of them takes nine weeks.

◆ The Navy turns recruits into sailors in eight weeks at Great Lakes Naval Training Center in Illinois, not far from Chicago on Lake Michigan.

◆ The Coast Guard's Recruit Training also lasts eight weeks. It takes place at a training center in Cape May, New Jersey.

♦ The Air Force has the shortest training program of all the services, just six weeks. It is conducted at Lackland Air Force Base in Texas, not far from San Antonio.

Do Women Have an Easier Time?

Except for the Marine Corps, which trains men and women in separate programs, all of the services make Basic Training a coed experience. But that doesn't mean that the Marines pamper female recruits. Marines don't pamper *anybody*.

Serving in the infantry is among the military jobs that women can't fill, yet the Army sends women recruits out for field training anyway. Generally speaking, they aren't exempted from any of the things that the men are required to do.

Basic Training is serious business—but not all the time.

It's the same in the Air Force and the Marines, which also include combat simulation in their Basic Training programs. In the Navy and Coast Guard, which don't concentrate on preparing recruits for fighting on land, women can expect a slightly easier time of it. At least in the physical sense.

All the services have minimum requirements for graduation from Basic Training. Allowing for the differences in the physical capabilities of the sexes, standards are usually slightly lowered for women. For instance, in order to graduate from the Coast Guard's training program, men are required to be able do 29 push-ups in 60 seconds. For women, the minimum is 23. Similarly, men must be able to do 38 sit-ups in a minute, and women just 32. The requirement extends to running. Men need to cover one and a half miles in 12 minutes, 51 seconds, but women can take 15 minutes, 26 seconds and still pass. There is no differential in swimming skills.

What to Take with You ... and What Not to Take

In every branch of the service, the first rule is to show up at the reception center with nothing more than the clothes on your back and one small bag. But what should be inside that bag?

- A three-day supply of comfortable clothing
- Three sets of white underwear
- Two padlocks, either with a combination or keys
- An eyeglass band, if you wear glasses
- An athletic supporter, if you are a man
- Six pairs of white calf-length socks, without logos
- Running shoes
- Disposable razors, or a safety razor with extra blades
- Shaving cream, if you are a man
- A toothbrush in a case
- Toothpaste
- Dental floss
- Soap and a soap case
- Two white towels and washcloths
- A hairbrush, or 6-inch black comb
- Shampoo
- Antiperspirant
- Prescription drugs
- A wristwatch

In your pocket or handbag, take the following:

- No more than $50 in cash; $10 should be enough
- An ATM card, if you have one
- Your social security card
- Your driver's license

For women only:

- Cotton underwear, in neutral shades, including one full slip
- Pajamas or a nightgown, and robe
- You may wear earrings, but only less than $1/4$-inch

There are several things you can't take with you when you leave for Basic Training. Some of them will be confiscated; others will be held and returned to you after graduation. The list includes the following:

- Weapons
- Knives of any size
- Drugs and narcotics
- Alcoholic beverages
- Tobacco products
- Food
- Pornography
- Over-the-counter drugs
- Gambling devices, such as playing cards and dice

There are other things you'll be better off without, such as jewelry. You will need a wristwatch, but it should be a simple, inexpensive one. Check with your recruiter to see what kind is considered best.

About That Haircut

One of the first things you'll do after you arrive at the reception center is sit down for a haircut. By the time you get out of the chair, you're going to look like a plucked chicken.

Waiting in line for that haircut will give you time to catch up on your studies.

But take heart, it will grow back. And you're never going to be quite as thoroughly shorn again unless you want to be. Oh, your hair will still have to be short, but not as severe as in Basic. The general requirement is summed up as "high and tight." For the rest of your military career, you are going to resemble a cross between a secret service agent and a body builder (from the neck up).

There are a couple of good reasons for GI haircuts. The most obvious is that you never waste precious time preening when there is a battle to be fought or work to be done. Secondly, it identifies you, in most situations at least, as a member of the military, even in civilian clothes. Right now, you may not much care. But after you've graduated from Basic, it is going to be a point of pride.

Female recruits don't need to worry about having all their hair shaved off. There are rules that will need to be followed, of course, but none of the services have any hard-and-fast requirements about hair length for women—as long as it's short.

Bet You Didn't Know

Military people have been sporting short haircuts since the Greeks and Romans marched off to war. But in the American military, it took on a special significance during the Civil War, when soldiers on both sides spent as much time scratching their heads as firing rifles. Hair lice and other vermin that collected in their longish hair was an enemy they all had in common.

Women in the military are not allowed to wear their hair extending below the bottom of a uniform collar. They must also be able to wear a military hat without their hairdo getting in the way. Some styles are forbidden, for example, ponytails, cornrows, and pigtails. That rule is summed up tersely as "no extreme or faddish styles."

Women are not allowed to use rubber bands to hold their hair in place, but they can use pins, combs, and barrettes. In that case, they need to match the person's natural hair color. Watch out for that word, "natural." Dyeing and bleaching are out of the question. There is a requirement that a woman's hair coloring must be complementary to her skin coloring.

Shaping Up in Advance

Nobody particularly cares what kind of shape you're in when you arrive at the reception center. The personnel there consider it their job to get you into shape, and they believe that there is plenty of time to do it. But that's no reason why you shouldn't try to be a couple of steps ahead of the pack. It will pay off in avoiding muscle aches and blisters. For example, here are some questions to think about:

◆ *How much running should you do?* You can't do enough of it. The Marine Corps will expect you to run 3 miles without getting exhausted. Both the Army and Air Force require a 2-mile run; and the Navy and Coast Guard want you to be able to run a mile and a half. But remember, that will be at the end of Basic Training, not at the beginning. While you're practicing your running before Basic Training, it's a good idea to swap your running shoes for boots every now and then. And it's also helpful to sometimes wear a backpack with about 5 pounds of books inside.

◆ *What if your muscles hurt?* That's a sign that you ought to slow down. If the pain doesn't go away, you should see a doctor. It probably will, though. Remember that you're doing this to get used to what's ahead. A few aches and pains along the way help guarantee that they won't slow you down at a time when you don't have the luxury of stopping to rest.

◆ *Should you change your eating habits?* Lay off junk food, at least for now, and stoke up on things you already know are good for you. And drink as much water as you can. A gallon a day is a good yardstick.

◆ *Is weight lifting the best possible training?* The truth is no. The military's program is centered around controlled calisthenics. The body you build with weight training will have a problem getting with the program. So put away the weights until you've come out on the other side of Basic Training.

◆ *Should you change your sleeping habits?* Get your body clock adjusted by getting to bed early, and then get up as early as you can and start exercising. Just about all of the physical training you're going to have to endure in Basic will take place first thing in the morning. And, of course, "first thing" to those people means the crack of dawn. It's a good idea to start getting up before the sun does.

◆ *Should you practice your push-ups?* Of all the things you'll be asked to do in Basic Training, push-ups are number one on the list. You'll be doing them in physical training, to be sure. But it's also the favorite form of punishment, even when you haven't done anything to deserve it. On average, you can expect to be asked to do about 900 push-ups a day. But you will build up to that. Going in, if you can do 20 without falling on your face, you won't have anything to worry about.

Tip

Get a copy of the physical fitness test (PFT) from your recruiter. It will tell you where the service you chose expects you to be in terms of physical condition by the end of Basic Training. You won't have to be anywhere near that point when you show up, but with a bit of practice at your own pace, at least your muscles won't scream at you during those first few days of Basic.

Can't get a copy of the PFT? Don't worry; maybe you're better off not knowing at this point. But there are a few things that you can expect even if you don't check it out beforehand: push-ups, sit-ups, pull-ups, swimming, and running.

Making Basic Easy

The most important thing you should know about Basic Training is that it is geared for your success. Nobody is ever going to ask you to do anything that you can't do. If you think you can't, they'll show you how. That's why it is called "training." There are, though, a couple of things you can do to make the experience a little easier:

♦ Get that chip off your shoulder. If you get the idea that you're too good to play these games, keep it to yourself. Just remember that all this *is* a game, and the way to win it is to go with the flow. Put your feelings on hold for a couple of weeks.

♦ Don't forget that Basic Training is a team sport. Watch out for your buddies and help when you can. Not only will it be noticed and make you look good, but that's the whole point of this exercise.

♦ Remember that your military career isn't always going to be like this. At the most, if you're in the Marines, Basic Training lasts only three months. More often it is less. There is a future in what you're doing. This experience is intended to get you ready for it.

♦ Blend in with the team. Of course, you want to stand out in the crowd, but save that for later.

♦ Don't take it personally. Whatever anyone says to you while you're going through Basic isn't a personal attack. It may feel that way sometimes, but remember that it's all part of the game.

♦ Don't try to prove that you are the best. If you are, it will come out anyway. But attitudes of any kind are going to work against you.

♦ Remember that there is no such thing as pride when you're going through Basic Training. Leave it at the door.

Your First Day

What happens right after you join the reception battalion is going to surprise you. The people will be friendly, even gentle. The routine will seem relaxed. There won't be anything at all to square with your notion of what Basic Training was going to be like. That's because it hasn't started yet.

The Basic Training experience is nearly the same in all the services, but we'll use the Army's program as an example of what you might expect.

Your first day will be spent getting used to the idea of military life. You'll find out what it's like to sleep in a barracks, to eat in a mess hall, and to do what is expected of you. This includes such things as saluting and calling everybody "sir."

Your time in the reception battalion will be spent establishing your military records. The files that are created, from medical to financial, will follow you through all of your military career. This is the time you'll be issued the gear you need, including uniforms, and someone will be on hand to make sure they fit you. You'll be given another dental and eye check. You'll get immunizations. You'll be given a battery of tests, sit through personal interviews, and attend lectures. You'll be issued an ID card and collect your initial pay.

Your actual military experience will begin a day or so after you graduate from Basic when you are assigned to your training battalion. Chances are that the people who arrived when you did will be with you through all of Basic. Although it isn't guaranteed, it's a good idea to start right away to make as many friends as you can. The buddy system works. Besides, misery loves company.

Here's what you can expect during a typical day in the life of Army Basic:

5:30 A.M.	Wake up
6:00	Physical training
7:00	Breakfast
8:30	Training
Noon	Lunch
1:00 P.M.	Training
5:00	Dinner
6:00	Drill Sergeant time
8:00	Personal time
9:00	Lights out

> **Tip**
>
> You are going to be paid twice a month, but you'll never see a check. The military prefers to pay you through a direct deposit into your bank account. If you don't have one now, open one. And don't forget to take all the details with you when you report for duty. Down the road, a monthly statement will be mailed to your home address.

Week One

You'll probably be transported by bus from the reception battalion to your next stop. When you get there, a team of drill sergeants may swarm all over it. They'll all be shouting at the top of their lungs for you to get moving on the double (English translation: running), and then one of them will probably block your way. That, or some variation on the same theme, will mark the real beginning of your Basic Training experience.

Expect to spend the next several weeks running everywhere you go. Be prepared for long days and short nights. Get used to eating on the fly. And understand that you are expected to be on time, even early, for everything. All the time.

Push-ups are among the activities that never seem to stop in Basic Training.

During your first week of actual training, you are going to be indoctrinated with more of the basic rules of military life and the values that will be expected of you. You are also going to learn how to march in formation, and you will spend a good deal of your time practicing what you learned. The Army calls this "Drill and Ceremony," D&C for short. This is also when you'll be shown how to get your barracks in shape for inspection.

If you can see your face reflected from the toes of your boots, they may be shiny enough to suit the drill instructor (DI).

You are going to be given your first physical fitness test early in this first week. It will be a snapshot of your condition at the start. Every day, first thing in the morning, you'll join the rest of your company in a round of exercises. The daily dose is going to start changing the results of future fitness tests.

Finally, you will be issued an M-16A2 rifle. You will be shown how to take it apart and put it back together again. You'll learn how to keep it clean, too, and you'll be taught how to sight and fire it. But you won't actually pull the trigger. Not yet.

Week Two

Although you have been issued a rifle, you won't do much with it this week except practice taking care of it. The second week of Army Basic Training concentrates on unarmed combat. It includes such things as first aid and learning how to read a map. Apart from the daily calisthenics, physical activity this week is limited to a visit to the Victory Tower.

You're going to go there quite a few times before you're finished, but on your first trip to the Victory Tower, you are going to rappel down to the ground from a platform 30 feet high.

Even if you're bigger than he is, never forget that the drill instructor is the boss.

In the weeks ahead, your experiences with the Victory Tower will progress to things like climbing rope ladders, crossing rope bridges, and swinging, Tarzan-style, across deep open spaces.

Week Three

You are finally going to get to fire that M-16A2 rifle you've been cleaning for nearly two weeks. In this third week, they'll teach you the basics of marksmanship. They are also going to issue you a bayonet and show you the moves that will allow your rifle to do double duty for you. Among other basic skills that are taught in week three is dealing with chemical warfare attacks. Your classroom time will be spent learning about history and tradition.

Week Four

During this week, you will learn some things about respect. Not just for the officers over you, but for your buddies. Respect for other members of your team is the most important lesson of Basic Training. This is where you are going to find out, if you haven't already, that you aren't the center of the universe. It can mean the difference between life and death in combat. Just as important, it will change your entire outlook on life.

Your physical training will continue every morning. And at some point during this week, you'll find out how much good it is doing when you take your second physical fitness test. You are going to be pleasantly surprised at the results.

Tip

If you wonder whether you will really get good at shooting, the answer is … probably not. Everybody gets one of those medals (marksman, sharpshooter, expert) even if an "expert" possibly isn't really one. But everybody does need to get at least "pretty good" at it, although a badge that says "pretty good" wouldn't carry much pride.

Week Five

The fifth week of Army Basic is the time for qualifying with your rifle. During the week, you will fire 40 rounds of live ammo. At the end of it, you'll be tested and given a badge identifying you as a marksman, sharpshooter, or expert.

Week Six

It's time for another physical fitness test, your third. During the sixth week of Basic, you are going to learn about other weapons at your disposal. And before the week is over, you'll take part in a combat exercise using live ammunition.

Physical training never stops during Basic. You'll get used to it.

Week Seven

Although daily physical training isn't going to stop this week, this is when you'll take your final physical fitness test. If you can still remember the first week, it will be fascinating to compare the results of this one to the one you took back then.

Week Eight

This is the big one. It's the week they've been preparing you for. You will participate in a 72-hour concentrated exercise the Army calls Victory Forge. Basically, it is a war game. The battalion is broken down into squads to do specific tasks, usually against one another. Everyone faces tactical obstacles and challenges geared to building teamwork. The situations are as realistic as they can possibly be.

Sometimes you may get the feeling that you'll never make it to the top of the wall. But once you do, you'll be at the top of the heap.

Week Nine

At last! Graduation. This last week of Basic is the fun part. Sure, you'll still have to do push-ups and sit-ups. There are still some lectures to attend and inspections to endure. But it all ends with a military revue and issuing of the badges and insignia of a full-fledged soldier. You'll still have to salute a lot and call everybody "sir." But by the end of the week you'll have your own name again, and the rest will be second nature to you.

In order to graduate from the Army's Basic Training, you must be able to do all the following:

- ◆ Qualify with the M-16A2 rifle
- ◆ Pass the final physical fitness test

- Throw two live hand grenades
- Negotiate all of the Victory Tower events
- Complete gas chamber exercises
- Complete a series of foot marches up to 10 miles
- Participate in a buddy team under live fire
- Negotiate the night infiltration course
- Participate in unarmed combat training
- Demonstrate an understanding of and a willingness to adhere to the Army's core values
- Demonstrate adherence to the Army's standard of conduct
- Participate in teamwork development
- Negotiate the obstacle course
- Pass a field gear and uniform inspection
- Take part in Victory Forge

The Moment of Truth

The culmination of the Army's Basic Training program, Victory Forge, and the Air Force's version called Warrior Week, were both modeled on what the Marine Corps calls the Crucible.

As you might expect, the Marine version is the toughest that the services have to offer. The exercise lasts 54 hours, during which time recruits get less than a total of 8 hours of sleep.

They will march close to 40 miles in two and a quarter days. And they will be given only two and a half MREs (meals ready to eat), which they will have to ration out for themselves. And that's just for starters. The physical demands seem impossible. The participants have to figure out every problem as they go along without any input from higher-ups.

The exercise revolves around four, four-hour "events." Sometimes it might be getting through a minefield and across a rope bridge with all their gear. Sometimes they may be surprised by pop-up targets that need to be mowed down before they can advance. And sometimes they experience ambushes by other squads that are taking part in the Crucible.

The Army's Victory Forge isn't quite that tough, but it's far from a walk in the park. The Air Force's Warrior Week falls between the Army and Marine Corps rite of passage in terms of toughness.

Like Basic Training itself, the best part of these intense programs comes at the end after you realize that you lived through it after all. The end of the Marine Crucible begins at four in the morning, after about four hours of sleep, with a nine-mile march. They reach the Parade Deck back at the base at about sunrise, and gather around as the American flag is raised.

After a brief ceremony, the drill instructors each present their recruits with the corps' insignia, the eagle, globe, and anchor. And for the first time since they arrived ready for training, they are addressed as "Marine." It wasn't easy earning the title. But in that moment it all seems worth it.

Who Is That Guy?

One constant in everyone's Basic Training experience is the drill instructor. They are father figures and mother figures, symbols of authority, and all the teachers you've ever known rolled into one. You'll probably dislike them on first sight, and as the weeks go by, dislike is going to turn into something resembling hate. But somewhere along the line—more often than not after it's all over—the emotion is going to turn to respect. And much later, when you look back on the experience, you're going to find yourself wondering why anybody would want that job anyway.

A few days after graduation, the drill instructor will report for duty to begin training another group of recruits, and the process will start all over again.

It is as punishing an experience for them as for any of those new recruits. Are they sadists? Or masochists? The answer is neither. With very few exceptions, they have volunteered for the job, and most wouldn't trade it for any other in the military.

The Navy calls its trainers Recruit Division Commanders (RDCs). In every case, no matter how much experience they have, and it's usually considerable, each of them is required to go through Boot Camp over again before they can qualify for the job.

They are also required to participate in a 13-week program of intensive training. During this time, they will "shadow" a working RDC. When they finish, they will work in tandem with an experienced RDC through at least one Boot Camp tour.

Navy RDCs begin the day at four in the morning. The recruits are still asleep, and it's part of the job to switch on the lights and wake them up. After they fall in line, the next part of the job is to lead them through the morning's physical training session.

While they are taking their showers and getting their compartments ready for inspection, the RDC is busy with paperwork. There are individual progress reports to prepare and daily schedules to coordinate. Then comes the inspection. All this happens before breakfast.

As the recruits march off to the mess hall, the RDC, who got them into formation in the first place, checks on every step they take. And so it goes all day long.

In the evening, after a long session of working with all of the recruits to help build their skills, the lights finally go out and everybody goes to sleep. Everybody, that is, except the RDC. There is still a lot of paperwork to be done, including filing daily reports with the barracks officer.

The job is essentially the same in all of the services. It doesn't always seem to be the case to the people in their charge, but these people are dedicated professionals. The person who will watch over you, and harass you, too, during your first weeks in the military is probably the most dedicated teacher you've ever had.

Think about it. There are literally hundreds of easier jobs that they could be doing in the military. Right after your graduation from Basic Training, you'll head off to a school to be trained for one of them.

The Least You Need to Know

- ◆ Basic is no piece of cake, but it's not as bad as you might have thought. And remember that everybody around you is in the same boat.

- ◆ You'll have fewer problems if you consider it a game, and fewer still when you consider yourself part of a team.

- ◆ You won't ever be asked to do anything you can't do. Every step in Basic Training builds on steps that went before it.

- ◆ A lot of Basic involves physical training, but a great deal of it is training for life in the military. It's about attitudes.

- ◆ Don't take anything anyone says personally. The goal of Basic Training is to make you think like part of a team. Individual personalities have nothing to do with it.

- ◆ This is the world's fastest route to real maturity. Your outlook on life is completely transformed in a few short weeks.

The Reserves, National Guard, and ROTC

In This Chapter

- ◆ Why the reserves might be a better option
- ◆ Part-time job, full-time benefits
- ◆ Can you lose your job if you're called up?
- ◆ The difference between the reserves and the National Guard
- ◆ One option that makes a real difference every time you show up
- ◆ A college scholarship worth aiming for

Within hours of the collapse of the World Trade Center's Twin Towers, Operation Wingfoot moved into high gear. Men and women from the 101st Cavalry, New York National Guard, were deployed to Ground Zero.

A Military Police (MP) company augmented the battalion's mission, but the majority of these soldiers were trained as tankers. They had to learn the ins and outs of traffic and crowd control virtually overnight. Even the NYPD was impressed that they were able to do it.

Until they were replaced three months later, the 101st was responsible for guarding all the entrances to New York City. That included not just bridges and tunnels, but railroad and bus terminals as well.

In their capacity as homeland defenders, the members of the National Guard patrol airports, guard nuclear power plants, and keep an eye on reservoirs. They were even assigned to guard athletes at the Winter Olympics in Salt Lake City, many of them National Guard soldiers themselves.

It's all in a day's work for members of the National Guard ... and that's exactly what this chapter is about.

At Your Service

One of the lines in the Marine's Hymn says that "if the Army or the Navy ever look on heaven's scene, they will find the streets are guarded by United States Marines." Yes, of course, they just might. But here on earth, it's more likely to be the National Guard.

All the services have reserve corps, and the Marine Forces Reserve may possibly be the most formidable. But when it comes to keeping peace on the streets of America in an emergency, it's the National Guard that does the job. They show up after hurricanes, snowstorms, earthquakes, and floods. They are, in fact, on the spot whenever they are called into action to cope with any kind of emergency.

There isn't any way for them to be trained in advance for every job they're going to be asked to do. But all of them are trained to turn on a dime. And they do it elegantly.

Who Are These People?

When you sign up for any of the services, the total length of your enlistment will be divided between active and reserve duty. When you become a reservist, you'll be available for recall in the event of war or other emergency defined by the federal government. It is still, technically, your employer.

It is the National Guard, on the other hand, that serves the Army and the Air Force in their stateside missions. It may help to think of it as the active reserves. You can join without first having served in the military.

As a member, you'll report to the governor of the state or territory where you live. As a citizen-soldier, you will be called out whenever the governor determines that public safety is threatened. When national security is threatened, the National Guard may be federalized and activated to provide trained combat and support units in a hurry.

How Will Your Boss Take It?

Generally speaking, service in the National Guard is a part-time job. But sometimes it will take precedence over your full-time job. Is your boss going to like that? Possibly not, but you are protected.

You can't be refused a job when you reveal that you're a member of the National Guard. If your unit is activated, your employer is required to hold your job open for you for up to five years. During your absence, you are entitled to pensions and other benefits as though you had actually been on the job. You are not required to report for work within the first eight hours after the end of your weekend drills or your annual training period.

Your two-week training period is considered a leave of absence, somewhat like jury duty. But your employer may choose to consider it as vacation time. Most, however, do regard it as service to your country and do not use it as a substitute for a vacation. Remember that the training and experience you will get as a member of the National Guard is going to make you more valuable in your regular full-time job. Most employers know and appreciate that.

How Guardsman Are Trained

If you've been thinking of joining the National Guard as a way of joining the military while avoiding Basic Training, forget about it. As a guardsman, you get to go home after you graduate from Basic; however, you are still going to have to take that first step of intensive training.

Just as you would in the regular Army or Air Force, you will get to choose a military occupational specialty (MOS). And, like recruits in the full-time forces, you will be expected to follow up Basic with advanced individual training. The time it takes varies according to the MOS you pick.

Time on Duty

During your tour of duty, you'll be required to spend one weekend a month at a nearby drilling location. Usually, the weekend means Saturday and Sunday, but from time to time you may be asked to report on a Friday night. That way, you'll be bright-eyed and bushy-tailed for training the next day.

You will also be expected to attend one two-week intensive training course each year. It is usually scheduled in the summer, and it will be at a facility not far from where you live. That's one of the advantages of being part of an organization that is based in your home state.

What's It Worth?

Most members of the National Guard think of it as a part-time job. You are paid for every day you show up, including weekend drills, summer camp, and special duty. The pay is competitive, and is usually better than you might expect in a part-time job that makes more demands on your time.

There are also such benefits as help with your education expenses, a retirement plan, and low-cost insurance—in short, most of the financial benefits you'd get in the regular Army or Air Force. You will also be eligible to take courses in special military schools.

Air National Guard

Although they are sister organizations with the same requirements and benefits, the Air National Guard experience is often slightly different than the Army's version.

The Air Guard's personnel are divided into two groups: military technician and active duty. Technicians train with their units on weekends once a month and in a two-week training program once a year. Active duty members serve full-time.

The difference between the Air Guard and regular Air Force officers and airmen is that they serve under the authority of their state or territorial governor. Both technicians and active air guardsmen are subject to transfer to federal authority and mobilization in the event of a national emergency.

The Air National Guard has total responsibility for providing the air defense interceptor force for the entire United States. Its members also serve as air traffic controllers, fly in the general-purpose stateside fighter force, and participate in rescue and recovery operations.

The Air Guard mans weather flights, and transports people and supplies around the world in C-130 Hercules aircraft. It conducts air refueling operations, flying KC-135 Strato-tankers, as well as other jumbo aircraft, and its bomber units fly B-1s. Its rescue and recovery squadrons fly lifesaving missions with HH-60 helicopters.

The Air National Guard sometimes handles heavy equipment, which they transport in the cargo bays of C-17A Globemasters.

The Air National Guard also has civil engineering squadrons trained and equipped to repair and maintain airbases.

Coast Guard Reserve Force

Except when they pull special duty in civil emergencies, part-time guardsmen and reservists spend their time honing their skills for events they all hope will never happen. But there is one branch of the reserve force whose members are ready to perform every time they report for duty: the Coast Guard Reserve.

If you live near one of the coasts, your one weekend a month and the two-week annual training period will more than likely involve port security. You may board ocean-going vessels looking for safety violations and contraband. Or you might be assigned to monitor cargo operations.

In areas where there is pleasure boating, along the coasts or on big lakes, you could be involved in search-and-rescue work. You might be sent out to maintain buoys and other aids to navigation. Or you could conduct safety checks on those pleasure boaters.

The Coast Guard Reserve is also active in duties as diverse as enforcing fishing laws and hunting down pirates. (Yes, they still exist.)

The Coast Guard considers its reservists an integral part of the team. And because of its unique mission, the only way to keep them trained is through hands-on experience.

You can join this branch of the reserves without signing up for active Coast Guard duty. The basic and advanced training takes about 30 weeks, but if you're a student, it can be spread out over two summers and one weekend a month, for which you will be paid.

The Coast Guard Reserve also offers three rates not otherwise available in the regular Coast Guard: port security, data processing, and investigation. Its benefits include money and credits for college, a retirement and insurance plan, and medical and dental insurance (not to mention travel on military aircraft).

The best part is that you get to spend your monthly weekend of duty where the action is. And you get to be part of the action as well. Of course, like the other branches of the reserves, you get paid every time you show up.

Marine Forces Reserve

There isn't any easy route to becoming a Marine. You can't join its reserve force without first having served out an enlistment in the regular corps. It is the largest component of the Marine Corps, though, with more than 104,000 members.

Generally speaking, Marines sign up for eight-year tours of duty, with four of those years spent in the reserves. After that, their status changes to "Individual Ready Reserve." But,

Bet You Didn't Know

The Marine Forces Reserves regularly drill together and participate in such activities as the annual Toys for Tots campaign just before Christmas each year. Its members believe that it makes them "Twice the Citizen" by being prepared to serve their country in time of war while also serving their communities.

especially after the start of the war in Afghanistan, thousands routinely signed up with local reserve units to continue their availability for call-up when they are needed. They do this completely on their own. It's all part of the tradition of the Corps. Once you're a Marine, you'll always be one … and proud of it.

Naval Reserve

The Navy's so-called "citizen sailors" are officially called the Naval Surface Reserve Force, with operations in each of the 50 states—even landlocked ones—as well as in Puerto Rico.

It is possible to become a citizen sailor, and qualify for the educational and other benefits, without first having served in the Navy. Like other reserve outfits, you will be required to spend one weekend a month and two weeks a year in training.

Training usually takes place at Navy or Naval Air Reserve centers. After you sign up, you will also be expected to take part in a Non-Prior Service Accession Course (NPSAC) at some point during the first year of your enlistment.

NPSAC takes place at the Naval Training Center at Great Lakes, Illinois. The program lasts 14 days, during which you will learn about naval customs, history, and tradition. There is also some physical training, but the Navy expects you to keep in shape on your own.

The Navy also offers a program it calls Accelerated Initial Accession, which will give you on-the-job apprenticeship training in some specialized skills. This leads to advanced training in occupations like aviation, electrical and mechanical systems, shipboard propulsion and repair, administration, and logistics.

Naturally, you will be paid for every day you serve in the Naval Reserve. But if your experience in a civilian job is comparable to a Navy field, you can join at a higher rank, Petty Officer Second or Third Class, and you will collect four day's pay for your two days of weekend service every month.

The pay scale in the reserve is exactly the same as in the regular Navy. And the chances for promotion, along with still higher pay, are also the same.

What Is ROTC?

The Army, the Air Force, and the Navy (whose program also serves the Marine Corps) established Reserve Officer Training Corps (ROTC, pronounced "rot-see") scholarship programs as far back as World War I to help these branches educate and train young men and women for service as commissioned officers.

Right now, there are some 47,000 students enrolled in these programs. About 6,500 are commissioned each year. Applicants for ROTC programs are awarded scholarships after a very competitive selection process. But taking part in the competition is well worth it. The scholarships include full tuition, books, fees, and other financial benefits.

> ### In Their Footsteps
>
> Back in the 1960s, military Reserve Officer Training programs were a flash point for antiwar demonstrators on university campuses. Most of the rebelliousness was heartfelt, considering their opinion of the war. But some of it may also have had something to do with some resentment of the big scholarships ROTC students earned—not to mention the fact that they had good-paying jobs waiting for them when they graduated.
>
> The good news is that the benefits are better now than they were then, and the job at the end offers better pay, too. Better still, even on campuses like Columbia University in New York, where the protests of the '60s were unusually nasty, ROTC participation is now considered "cool." It's something people who have participated in the program have known all along.
>
> As General (Ret) Colin Powell, United States secretary of state, put it, "The order, the self-discipline, the pride that had been instilled in me by ROTC was a tremendous companion to my basic liberal arts education and prepared me well for my Army career, or for that matter, any career I might have chosen."

The Navy and Marines ROTC Program

The naval ROTC offers the most flexibility in choosing schools. Students can attend any one of 67 NROTC universities across the country. The participating schools may be either public or private. Whatever school they pick, they can also choose their major, but they will need to complete one year of calculus and one year of calculus-based physics.

The Navy's four-year scholarship includes full tuition, books, and class fees, plus $150 a month for living expenses, but not room and board.

To qualify, you will need to meet minimum SAT scores of 530 verbal and 520 math. If you take the ACT test instead, your minimum score needs to be 22 in both English and math.

The Navy ROTC (NROTC) also offers two-year full-tuition scholarships, which cover books and fees as well, and sweetens the deal with $200-a-month subsistence during your junior and senior year. It offers a four-year scholarship, with the higher subsistence allowance for students pursuing a Bachelor of Science degree in nursing as well.

When they graduate from college, NROTC students are commissioned in the unrestricted line Naval Reserve or Marine Corps Reserve.

In Their Footsteps

Naval Lt. Commander Heidemarie Stefanyshyn-Piper is an astronaut. Her journey began as a naval ROTC student at the Massachusetts Institute of Technology (MIT), where she earned her B.S. and M.S. in mechanical engineering. After graduating, she completed her naval training as a basic diving officer and salvage officer. Among her assignments was the destranding of the tanker *Exxon Houston* off the coast of Hawaii.

She joined NASA in Houston seven years after graduating from MIT, and today she is the lead astronaut for payloads, working with developers ensuring that payloads can be operated successfully onboard the International Space Station.

Air Force ROTC Programs

In order to qualify for an Air Force ROTC (AFROTC) scholarship, you must first be interviewed by a selection board. It will rate you on what it calls a "whole person" concept. The criteria includes a review of your high school academic records and your score on college entrance exams. The board also assesses your leadership potential, your work experience, and your record of extracurricular activities. Before ranking your merits, the board will also interview officials at your high school.

Once your application has been accepted, you are free to chose any school you want. But that school must offer AFROTC and have a scholarship major that has been approved by the Air Force. There are dozens of them, ranging from electrical engineering and meteorology through foreign languages and mathematics. And the range of colleges on the Air Force list gives students a wide-range of choices.

The Air Force offers scholarships for either four or three years. The different options are as follows:

- Full tuition paid for four years, plus most lab fees and $510 a year for books.
- Tuition and fees up to $15,000 a year for three years, along with a $510 annual allowance for books. Any tuition beyond $15,000 is paid by the student.

◆ Full tuition, and an annual $510 allowance for books, but only at college or universities where the amount comes to less than $9,000 a year, which limits the choice, but also guarantees that there aren't any out-of-pocket tuition costs.

These scholarships are open to any major a student chooses. But 75 percent of them are granted in majors that the Air Force considers important to its mission. The most important of these are electrical engineering and meteorology, but the preferred list includes such things as foreign languages and architecture among the sciences.

In every case, Air Force ROTC students are also paid a nontaxable stipend of $250 a month during the school year.

Army ROTC Programs

The Army's ROTC (AROTC) program is the oldest of its kind, dating back to 1916. Its participants take part in a military curriculum that integrates classroom work with some field training. Cadets can also volunteer for such special summer training as airborne, air assault, and mountain warfare.

The Army awards hundreds of ROTC scholarships every year. Most pay full tuition, and can be worth as much as $60,000 a year, sometimes more. They are awarded on merit, determined through academic achievements, extracurricular activities, and personal interviews. Scholarship winners may apply to up to three schools from the more than 600 that accept AROTC students. The Army will have the final say, but it is usually sympathetic to a student's individual needs.

In addition to its regular four-year scholarship program, the Army ROTC also offers two- and three-year scholarships for students already in college, but who didn't enroll in ROTC at the beginning.

All of these scholarships pay full tuition and most fees along with a $150-a-month allowance, as long as you are enrolled in a military science course.

Like other ROTC programs, you need to be enrolled in a college that accepts it. But in the Army's version, there are no special requirements for a major. The only requirement is participating in the military science course. The first two years of the classroom work cover the Army's role in the overall society, and provides an introduction to the principles of management and leadership. During the junior and senior years, the course focuses on ethics, situational leadership, and American defense policy.

Some students consider this coursework worthwhile, and participate in the program as "nonscholarship" ROTC students.

Tip

You might expect that if you are thinking of a military specialty like flying helicopters, you'd have to wait to get the specialized training that follows college. The Army ROTC can help you do it sooner.

A unique program offered by the University of North Dakota (UND)—the only one of its kind—offers helicopter training as part of its AROTC program. That means that when you graduate, you'll have the necessary certification for FAA private or commercial ratings as a professional pilot. Oh, yes, you will also have a college diploma. Credits from UND's helicopter program apply to that, too.

You Don't Have to Be a Scholarship Winner

Every branch of the ROTC is available to both men and women. You can join at any time before your junior year. The courses involved during the freshman and sophomore year explore the contemporary military and its relationship to society in general. They also teach management and leadership skills.

The advanced portion in the second two years concentrates on situational leadership and ethics. Together, they build special skills that are as important in civilian as military life.

If you don't qualify for a scholarship but join the ROTC program at college anyway, you aren't putting yourself under any obligation to the military, ever. It is simply an elective, for which you'll receive credit toward graduation.

Scholarship winners aren't under any obligation at all to serve in the military if they drop out of the program after their first year of college. Once you've graduated from a college ROTC program, your obligation varies according to the branch of the service that has been paying the bill.

- ◆ If you earned an ROTC scholarship through the Army, you will graduate as a second lieutenant and will serve in either the regular Army or the Army Reserve or National Guard.

- ◆ Naval ROTC midshipmen who received scholarships are commissioned as officers in the Naval Reserve or Marine Corps Reserve.

- ◆ Air Force ROTC scholarship winners take a special professional officers course during their junior and senior years. They also take part in a six-week field-training course at an Air Force base. On graduation, they serve as pilots, navigators, missile engineers, and in other technical specialties as commissioned officers.

The whole idea behind ROTC is to provide the services with recruits who are college graduates, the first best step to a professional officer corps. Although for the most part, these graduates enter the service with little or no specific military training, they have accumulated the background skills that in the end make better officers.

The Least You Need to Know

◆ You can serve your country without committing to a full-time military career, and in fact, start a military career by going directly to college.

◆ The military offers full-tuition scholarships, and most offer wide choices of both schools and courses. Most of the programs pay a small living allowance, as well as the cost of books.

◆ Each service puts its own spin on defining "citizen soldiers." Some reservists are only required to make themselves available in an emergency. Others are required to make a minimum commitment of their time.

◆ As a reservist, you can be as active as you choose.

Chapter 6

Yes, We Are Collegiate

In This Chapter

- Benefits of the new GI Bill
- College on Uncle Sam's time
- Wiping out student loans
- Big-time benefits without full-time service
- The best deals to pay for college

Back before World War II, the majority of the people who went to college were rich kids and those who were planning professional careers. You needed a college education if you wanted to be a doctor or a lawyer or a teacher. If you had a family fortune behind you, it was a way to build contacts with others like yourself. Everybody else was expected to educate themselves at the school of hard knocks. Then along came the Serviceman's Readjustment Act of 1944—the GI Bill of Rights.

The idea of giving veterans money to go to college wasn't an easy one to swallow back then. Some of the strongest critics, in fact, were college officials themselves. It would bring overcrowding, they said, and it would lower standards.

But when all was said and done, college classrooms became more relevant to what was going on out in the real world.

The New GI Bill

The original GI Bill of Rights was intended just for World War II veterans, and it was gradually phased out. It was reinstated in 1985 for the benefit of Vietnam vets and military personnel serving in time of peace. Congressman G.V. Montgomery, whose name was given to the new law, created it.

The original law gave GIs an outright grant of $500 a year for education, but the new version is a voluntary program requiring a small upfront contribution.

Everybody who enlists in any of the armed services, including the National Guard and Reserves, can agree to have $100 deducted from their paychecks every month during their first year of service. That adds up to $1,200. But when their tour of duty is over, they can collect up to $650 a month for tuition and other educational expenses.

The total GI Bill educational benefit adds up $23,400, paid over 36 months. Based on the initial contribution of $1,200, accumulated a little at a time during the first 12 months of service, that represents a 19.5 to 1 return. There aren't many ways to make your money grow that well. No wonder more than 90 percent of all service personnel are signed up for Montgomery benefits.

You Can Have It Right Now

The GI Bill doesn't kick in until after you've served your time in the military. It's a veteran's benefit. You can get a college education and get money for it during the time you're serving. You can take advantage of these benefits and still qualify for the GI Bill when you become a veteran yourself.

In Their Footsteps

The new breed of college student that the GI Bill produces has the big advantage of having learned discipline while they were in the military. They know what they want and, thanks to their military experience, they know what it takes to get it. Self-discipline has always been the key to college success, but for the first time, this isn't a lesson students have to learn after they arrive on campus.

The new veteran-students who went to college on the original GI Bill made demands on the system that completely changed the whole concept of higher education. They asked for, and got, new degree programs in fields like business and accounting. Literally thousands of new courses were created in the late 1940s and early 1950s.

On top of that, they broke down age-old barriers to race, social status, and even religion that had denied the fathers of many of them the opportunity to improve their lives.

Every branch of the service, and the National Guard as well, offers college programs to help you continue your education while you're serving. The majority of them let you earn credits that are recognized at colleges and universities across the country. You build college credit during the time you serve.

About 30,000 active duty members of the military services earn their degrees every year, while they are still serving.

Making College Indispensable

These days, everybody regards a college education as the only way to go, no matter where their life is headed. Yet, in the memory of many people living today, it was once an experience open only to the privileged few.

The military changed all that. And today, it is still doing the job of making higher education possible for hundreds of thousands of students.

Military School Credits

The military has more than 300 of its own schools that offer some 10,000 courses. The classes at these schools are intended to train you in the skills you need for about 4,100 different occupations in the military.

There is a side benefit, though. The American Council on Education has certified about 60 percent of these courses as eligible for credits in civilian colleges.

Servicemember Opportunity Colleges

Studying on your own, in classrooms, over the Internet, or by mail is possible through 1,418 schools of higher learning that have signed on to the Servicemember Opportunity Colleges program—SOC for short.

If the military reassigns you to another location (yes, they sometimes do that), all of those schools and colleges have agreed to transfer earned credits among themselves for service members. No matter where you go, you can still do the coursework and accumulate credit for it.

Career Degrees

The Army's version of SOC, which is similar, but with more varied opportunities to the programs the other services offer, will guide you through the options that will lead you to the right choices for a Bachelor's degree in different fields. It breaks them down into

Army career degrees, specialized degrees, and general-purpose degrees. The list of general degrees, which of the three programs are more like typical civilian programs, includes college-level study in these MOSs (Military Occupational Specialities):

- Fire Support Specialist
- Chemical Operation Specialist
- Helicopter Repairer
- Aircraft Electrician
- Aircraft Armament/Missile Systems Repairer
- Avionics Mechanic
- Armament Electrical Systems Repairer
- Information Systems Operator-Maintainer
- Telecommunications Operator-Maintainer
- Personnel Services Specialist
- Information Systems Technician

The military-related degree-builder programs include:

- Satellite Communications Systems Operator-Maintainer
- Journalist
- Broadcast Journalist
- Helicopter Repairer
- Legal Specialist
- Recruiter
- Career Counselor
- Medical Equipment Repairer
- Medical Specialist
- Patient Administration Specialist
- Medical Laboratory Specialist
- Hospital Food Service Specialist
- Radiology Specialist
- Pharmacy Specialist
- Preventive Medicine Specialist
- Respiratory Specialist
- Mental Health Specialist
- Automated Logistical Specialist
- Unit Supply Specialist
- Air Traffic Control Operator
- Military Police
- Internment/Resettlement Specialist
- Intelligence Special Agent

The specialized MOSs that come under the Army's career degree program are:

- Intelligence Analyst
- Imagery Analyst
- Common Ground Station Operator
- Ground Surveillance Systems Operator
- Counter Intelligence Agent
- Interrogator
- Signals Intelligence Analyst
- Cryptologic Linguist
- Communications Interceptor/Locator
- Electronic Intelligence Interceptor/Analyst
- Signal Collection/Identification Analyst

The list is a long one, and it is growing all the time. It is based on the courses offered in the Army's own schools. The learning experience and the on-the-job experience is transferable to civilian schools for degree credit.

Testing Credits

Just about every military base has an education center, and all of them are qualified to administer exams in nearly any subject you can think of. The results of these tests are recognized throughout the academic community, and colleges and universities will give you credit for things you have learned on your own outside of traditional classrooms through distance learning programs. If you pass one of these tests, it will be worth three full college credits per subject. There isn't any limit to how many different subjects you can test for.

Concurrent Admissions Programs

When you graduate from high school, the most perplexing decision you'll be faced with is whether to go right on to college or to look before you leap. Sometimes it's a matter of money. Sometimes you may want some breathing space to get your act together.

Consider this option: You can enlist in the military. There simply isn't a better way to get your act together or to find a way to pay for an education and make your college plans at the same time. All the services participate in the college admissions program known as CONAP.

If you are accepted by the college you select and it is one of the 1,500 that participates in CONAP, your full-time college career can be deferred for up to two years after you are discharged from the service. By that time, your military education benefits are going to give you the money you need, and you will be able to start your full-time college career with a few credits already under your belt. You can stop worrying about your future.

Learn and Earn Credits While You Serve

In the meantime, you can begin your college studies while you are serving in the military. Most colleges offer distance learning for people in the service. Many conduct traditional classes at military installations.

If you begin your college work while you are on active duty, you can take courses from a different institution than the one you have chosen for future study. One of the big advantages of CONAP is that credits are generally transferable.

Under the varied CONAP options offered by all of the services, you can earn credits that will be applied when you begin your full-time degree program. The participating colleges give credit for the courses you take for your military job. Many also award credits for your experience on the job.

> **Tip**
>
> The military offers tuition help for active duty and reserve members who learn while they serve. The Army, for instance, will pay 75 percent of your tuition or expenses, up to $197.50 per credit hour. In some specialties, it pays 100 percent. The maximum is $3,500 a year.
>
> The program applies to both graduate and undergraduate courses. The other services offer similar deals when you take courses on your own time during your active duty tour.

Community College of the Air Force

Air Force enlisted personnel can earn an associate degree in more than 80 fields of study ranging from computer technology to paralegal and information management. Community College of the Air Force (CCAF) is the only program of its kind in the service. It works with Air Force training schools, regional accrediting agencies, and hundreds of different colleges and universities.

CCAF also operates a full-time community college program at Maxwell Air Force Base in Montgomery, Alabama. It is the biggest community college in the world. Since it was established in 1972, it has awarded associate degrees to 200,000 students. All of them studied there as part of their active duty in the Air Force.

The degrees CCAF grants are recognized by most professional, industrial, and governmental entities that issue licenses and certifications in the civilian world.

Opportunities in the Navy

The Navy's Associate Degree Completion Program allows you to get paid and qualify for all the benefits the Navy offers while you're a full-time college student. You need to have finished a year or more of college before you sign up. And you'll need to be taking courses that will eventually qualify for jobs in the nuclear field. If you meet the requirements, you can sign up and go on to finish college on the Navy's payroll. This is a brand-new program, and chances are it will be expanded into other fields.

Check with your Navy recruiter—other opportunities may already be available. The Navy, whose submarines and carriers rely on nuclear power, is especially interested in recruiting people trained in managing atomic power. But there are other critical fields such as medical specialties that more than likely will be added to the Associate Degree Program.

Guard and Reserve Opportunities

The National Guard and military reserves have hundreds of thousands of part-time soldiers who are serving to be able to learn skills that can help them move ahead in their regular jobs—or find a better one.

You don't have to have been a full-time member of the active services to qualify for the educational benefits.

In addition to your drill pay as a member of the National Guard or active reserves, you will qualify for veterans' benefits offered by the Montgomery GI Bill.

National Guard student benefits vary from state to state, but most states offer tuition waivers at state-supported colleges and universities. Some offer a specific amount per semester. It's a good deal either way, and many part-time guardsmen are full-time students.

As a guardsman or reservist, you aren't limited to enrolling in a school that is on the regular military's list of institutions in the Servicemember's Opportunity Program. You are free to go to any accredited college or university, vocational or technical school. It is entirely up to you.

Tip

If you are in the National Guard or reserves, you may be eligible for a "kicker" on top of your regular GI Bill benefits.

If you sign up for six years and actively drill with your unit, the kicker will add $100 to $350 a month to the payoff for your education. It all depends on your occupational specialty, but the list of those that qualify is a long one.

More Than Just College

A college degree is the most obvious goal of the National Guard's educational benefits program, but it isn't the only one. The list of opportunities includes …

- ◆ Cooperative training.
- ◆ Correspondence courses.
- ◆ Vocational and technical training.
- ◆ Remedial, deficiency, and refresher training.
- ◆ On-the-job training and apprenticeships.
- ◆ Independent study programs.

Among those, if you take a training job as a welder, a mechanic, or a cook, for instance, you'll qualify

Tip

Most of the educational benefits offered by the National Guard take effect the day you enlist. And before you enroll for higher education, the Guard helps by paying for the tests you'll need to take, such as the SAT.

for educational benefits. If you are an apprentice in a job that involves related technical instruction, such as an electrician or a plumber, you can collect your benefits while you're working full-time and collecting pay.

Got Student Loans?

If you are like most college students, the bills seem to pile up faster than the credits. Chances are, you've been tiding yourself over with student loans. But the bills for those pile up, too. There is a way out. Continue your college career in the military.

All of the services have programs to help you repay your outstanding student loans. Among them, the Army offers the highest amount, up to $65,000. By contrast, the Navy and the Air Force cap the benefit at $10,000.

But as you have already learned, there is no such thing as a free lunch. So don't think you can show up at the recruiter's office with a shoebox full of unpaid loans and expect them to automatically be lifted from your shoulders.

The Army's Loan Repayment Program

Although the benefit varies from one service to another, the procedure for getting help with your education loan debt is roughly the same for all of them.

The Army's eligibility standards include these rules:

- You can't be a veteran of any other service.
- You must have a high school diploma when you enlist.
- You must have an ASVAB score of 50 or higher.
- You must enlist in a critical military occupation specialty.
- Your student loans must have been made, insured, or guaranteed under the Higher Education Act of 1965, after October 1, 1975.

Tip

In the Air Force version of the Loan Repayment Program, you will need to enlist for four or six years, and you will need to complete your initial skills training before payments can begin.

That's just for starters. Among the other rules that apply is that the program is open only to enlisted personnel. If you become an officer during your first year of active duty, you will be disqualified.

The most important rule of all is that the repayment benefit is denied for any loans that have been defaulted.

Army enlistees earn $33\frac{1}{3}$ percent or $1,500, whichever is greater, toward the unpaid balance of student loans for each year of active duty. The maximum allowed is $65,000.

The payments are made directly to the lender starting at the end of the first year of your enlistment. You will be liable for federal and local income taxes in the year they are made.

The Fine Print

If you've done any research on the loan-repayment programs, you may have heard that if you accept college-loan repayments, you will lose your GI Bill benefits. Until not very long ago that was true. But the law has been changed to open up a loophole.

In programs like these that are tied to length of service, the Department of Veterans Affairs is forbidden by law to pay benefits for more than one program using the same period of service as the baseline. That's the bad news.

The good news is that the rules have been altered slightly. The VA will now allow you to use the loan repayment program against your first enlistment, and the GI Bill for your second. In other words, if you want to qualify for both kinds of benefits, you're going to have to reenlist.

Distance Learning

It has been possible for active members of the military to get a college education in their off-hours for years. But new procedures have made it easier today than it has ever been.

When the secretary of the Army announced the Army's new way of doing things, which is also becoming standard in the other services, he said that the initiative called "Distance Learning" would give 165,000 first-term soldiers the means of earning college degrees. It pays off with a two-year associate's degree during four years of service. It once took as long as seven years.

Better still, distance learning doesn't cost a dime. The Army picks up the tab for laptop computers, Internet service, books, and tuition. The program also opens up more free time for soldier-students to keep up with their personal studies.

How Distance Learning Works

Basically, what the Army likes to call Army University is an online correspondence course. Students access it with laptop computers, which are issued like M-1 rifles to anyone who participates. Their laptops go wherever they go, and there is never an interruption in the learning process, no matter where that might be.

Their first step is often learning how to use the computer, and that is part of the program, too. The Army itself considers that one of its own best benefits. It has an almost desperate need for computer-savvy people, as digital systems and computer-controlled weapons systems are becoming the heart of its mission.

Students begin by logging on to eArmyU.com, and a group of participating colleges takes it from there. The Army itself has no input in the course content. It just provides organization and technical support. And, of course, the student body.

Participating students receive their credentials from a single college. But during the course of the program, they will receive input from a dozen or more of them.

High School, Too

When the distance learning concept was developed, the Army also included an element that helps potential recruits earn high school equivalency diplomas.

Technically, you need to finish high school before you enlist, but the requirement is considered on a case-by-case basis and is often waived.

With these new methods of speeding up the process, the Army is ready, willing, and able to help dropouts turn their lives around and get their GEDs before Basic Training begins.

The Least You Need to Know

- The GI Bill is back, and better than ever. It is making college educations possible for thousands who couldn't otherwise afford it.
- The military will pay for your education while you serve when you take courses on your own time during active duty. The military can also help pay off your student loans. There are limits, but most programs are generous enough to get you out of debt.
- Many colleges will give you credit for many courses you take in the service while you're learning your military specialty.
- National Guard members are eligible for educational benefits, too. Many part-time soldiers are full-time students, collecting pay and tuition help.
- You can begin your college career in uniform. Under some programs, you can qualify for military benefits while you're still a student.
- You can qualify for a degree while you're serving. Colleges and universities will grant you full credit for courses you take while you're on military duty.

Part 3

Special Opportunities

Can you picture yourself at one of the service academies? No reason why you shouldn't. Of course, it isn't easy to get accepted, but nothing worthwhile ever is. And, as you'll see, there isn't much you can do that is more worthwhile than this.

There are some military careers that are closed to women, but not very many. The list is getting smaller all the time. And if you come from a minority background, you're not going to find any barriers anywhere in the military. The only color anyone sees is the color of your uniform.

And while you're serving, you are going to get all sorts of benefits that private employers never offer, from free housing and meals, to travel, to a free education, to free medical care. It gets even better when your tour has ended. You can go to college, buy a house without a down payment, and get medical care for yourself and your family. The best part is that your retirement begins when you're still young enough to enjoy it.

Chapter 7

Top of the Heap: The Service Academies

In This Chapter

- ◆ The traditions of America's service academies
- ◆ How to qualify for enrollment
- ◆ How they are different from regular colleges
- ◆ Daily life on campus
- ◆ Where the experience leads

Of all the things you may have heard about America's service academies, something that may not have been mentioned is that they are the very best business schools anywhere in the country. Make that anywhere in the world.

Since World War II, the U.S. Military Academy at West Point, the Naval Academy at Annapolis, and the Air Force Academy at Colorado Springs have produced 1,530 corporate CEOs. Their graduates include more than 2,000 corporate presidents. There are more than 5,000 vice presidents among their alumni. And thousands more became entrepreneurs, running their own successful companies.

The Secret of Business Success

It isn't uncommon for military academy graduates to eventually go on to elite business schools to earn their MBAs. The purpose, usually, is to learn the language of the business world. But, as one Naval Academy graduate explained it, "[At business school] leadership was a class we took. At the academy, leadership was a way of life."

The 105mm howitzers on the plain at West Point are often used to salute important visitors.

Leadership is something business schools sometimes overlook. Yet without good leadership, even the best-planned business venture is going to fail. In fact, a good leader can even make a poor plan work.

Along with other valuable lessons like honor, teamwork, and discipline, the major goal of the military academies is to produce leaders.

From the first day at West Point, plebes are required to reply, "No excuse, sir," when they are called out for even small mistakes. It changes their outlook on life real fast. A business run on the principle of "no excuses" can't miss.

By the time they become seniors, these cadets are put in charge of up to 100 underclassmen. They make sure they toe the mark in every way. These upperclassmen don't have any special powers, but they do wield a lot of responsibility. And by the time they graduate, they know very well what it means to be a leader.

Naval Academy midshipmen are trained to become masters at leadership.

Graduation day at West Point is an experience cadets never forget.

How to Get In

Because their goal is educating the best students America has to offer, getting accepted at one of the military academies is tough. But if you have the right stuff, it isn't an impossible dream.

The basic eligibility at all of them begins with your age. You need to be older than 17 and younger than 23. The process is a long one, though, and if you've set your sights on one of the academies, it's a good idea to begin working toward your goal when you start high school.

Got the right stuff? You can find out at Annapolis.

You must be an unmarried U.S. citizen. You shouldn't have any dependent children (nor any on the way). And you'll need to pass a tough battery of medical examinations, including a physical aptitude test.

Except for the Coast Guard Academy, which accepts students just by merit, you will be required to have an official appointment to enter a service academy. Every U.S. senator and every member of Congress can appoint five candidates to each of the academies every year. The president has the power to appoint 100 and the vice president, five.

You should not limit your search for an appointment to just one of these officials. The appointment process assumes maximum strength, that is, the number of students matches the official number of openings. But the reality is that the number actually fluctuates from year to year, and there are never as many openings as anticipated when the appointment process began. The bottom line is that only about one third of the appointees actually enter the academies.

Go for as many appointments as you can. Contact your senator, your representative in Congress, the vice president, and even the president. Their offices will guide you through the application process.

Money Matters

Considering the ultimate rewards of an academy education, you'd expect to be faced with a high tuition. But the fact is, there isn't any.

All the academies require an advance deposit to cover the first cost of uniforms and supplies, but after that, everything is free.

Not only is there no tuition, but room and board are free, too. On top of that, cadets and midshipmen get free medical and dental care. They even get a monthly salary to pay for supplies and clothing with enough left over for personal expenses. In an average year, the numbers in the following table reflect the numbers of students at West Point, Annapolis, and the Air Force and Coast Guard Academies.

The Stats

Branch	Enrollment	Annual Admissions	Percent Female
Army	4,000	1,200	15
Navy/Marine Corps	4,000	1,200	16
Air Force	4,000	1,200	12
Coast Guard	850	265	30

Academic Requirements

Like other colleges, the military academies are looking for high ACT/SAT scores. But they look for a whole lot more. Your class rank in high school is important. They are also interested in recommendations from your faculty. And they expect to see a high percentage of your school's graduates enrolled in four-year colleges. They use these statistics as a handy yardstick to measure the relative quality of the education your high school offers to all of its students.

They will consider the kinds of courses you have taken in high school. The emphasis will be on four years of English and math. They expect you to have studied composition, literature, grammar, and speech. In math, you should have a solid foundation in algebra, geometry, and trigonometry.

The mix of your high school courses should also include two years of a foreign language, as well as two years of a laboratory science like chemistry or physics.

Although they aren't among the basic requirements, your chances of being accepted will be better if you take courses in geography, government, and economics.

Personal Requirements

In order to get accepted at any of the military academies, you will be expected to be in good physical and mental shape. They are looking for candidates with above-average strength and agility, too. But there is another quality that makes all the difference: leadership.

You should participate in as many extracurricular activities as you can—not only athletics, but every opportunity where you can shine. The admissions departments of the military academies will be looking not just at participation, but whether you rose to responsible positions, whether in sports, clubs, or class activities. It extends to church, to scouting, and to community organizations.

If you stand out in your school and community, chances are you are going to stand out when you apply to one of the academies.

 Bet You Didn't Know _____

There are more than 20,000 students at Virginia Tech University in Blacksburg, Virginia. About 600 of them are enrolled in its Corps of Cadets. Those students live in a military environment, but take academic courses along with civilian students.

The first year, once known as the "Rat Year," is about as tough as it gets. All ROTC students must be in the Corps, but it is possible to be a cadet without joining the ROTC program.

The Other End

All the military academies grant a Bachelor of Science degree after four years of work. In every case, you'll be required to follow it up with five years of military service, although most stay in longer. Your active duty begins with a commission. West Point graduates go into the Army as second lieutenants. Annapolis turns out Marine Corps second lieutenants and Navy ensigns. Air Force Academy graduates are second lieutenants, too, and four years at the Coast Guard Academy earns a rating of ensign.

Air Force Academy cadets who become pilots are committed to 10 years in the service. Navigators must stay in the service for six years. All others commit to five years of active duty.

Of course, it doesn't end there. Before they retire, academy graduates can count on regular promotions—sometimes all the way to the top.

Life at West Point

"When do we get a minute to catch our breath?" At the U.S. Military Academy a fair answer might be, "the day after graduation." West Point cadets take a perverse kind of pride in saying that they are studying on the busiest campus in America. They don't take the Naval Academy, the Air Force Academy, or the Coast Guard Academy into account, though. There is never a dull moment at any of them.

Naturally, academy officials take a different view. "There is still time for fun and relaxation," says their official catalogue for prospective students.

West Point offers more than 100 extracurricular activities. They range from 24 intercollegiate sports to intramural sports that include rugby and crew. Cadets are expected to participate in them.

On the less strenuous side, there is a glee club, a fine arts forum, and a cadet drill team. There is a student-run radio station, too, and a regular program of dances and other social functions.

Time Off

There is also a bit of time off. Cadets get to go home for four days at Thanksgiving, two weeks at Christmas, and 10 days (including weekends) for spring break. Summer leave is about four weeks, but special training assignments often shorten it.

During the academic year, upperclassmen get more weekend leaves than cadets further down the line. But nobody gets every weekend off. First-year students, known as plebes, can count weekend passes they get in a whole year on the fingers of one hand.

Plebes have no privileges at all during cadet Basic Training. Here, too, the folks who run things say that isn't quite true. They're allowed to phone home once during each weekend, they point out. And you can bet that when they do, they're going to call their father "sir."

Living Conditions

Most of the gray stone buildings at West Point are more than a century old, but the cadet barracks are surprisingly modern, if not a little Spartan. Two or three cadets bunk together in a single room. There is space for desks as well as beds for all of them, plus a generous amount of closet space. Every cadet has a personal computer, and usually bunkmates share a single printer. The barracks also all have recreation rooms, lounges, and study rooms.

All cadets march together for meals in a single mess hall. Breakfast is at 6:55 A.M., lunch is at noon, and dinner is at 6:30 P.M. It is optional, except for one day a week, usually Friday, when it is mandatory to break for dinner. For anyone able to keep awake that long, lights out isn't until midnight.

The Student Hierarchy

The typical West Point cadet graduated in the top 10 percent of his or her high school class. About 25 percent of the students are nonwhite, and 15 percent are women. The student body has been carefully selected so that everybody who makes it was a leader of the pack back home. What is amazing is how they are all able to leave their individuality at the front door.

During their first year as plebes, West Pointers learn what it means to follow. Then in the second year, when they are known as yearlings, they are given complete control over two plebes. They are completely responsible for their performance.

Tip

Originally formed to train the local militia in Charleston, South Carolina, the Citadel's Corps of Cadets includes more than 2,000 students preparing for careers in the Army, Navy, and Marine Corps. Its graduates have served with distinction in all of America's wars since the Civil War. The Citadel is one of several independent colleges whose training closely resembles the military academies.

The yearlings are under the thumbs of third-year students, designated "cows." They are each responsible for squads of three yearlings and the six plebes who are under them.

At the top of the heap are the "firsties," the senior class. During their final summer, they run the traditional eight weeks of training for the incoming plebes and yearlings. At the end they have become the commissioned officers of the cadet corps. They answer to company commanders, who in turn report to battalion commanders and on up the line through regiments and brigade.

But in the end, it is the students themselves who make the difference. Everyone on the West Point campus is made responsible for being a leader and a follower at the same time. And it pays off.

Military Training

For most of its years as a military school, West Point (and Annapolis, too) was a civil engineering school. During World War I, Superintendent Douglas MacArthur started a change in emphasis, first by expanding the physical fitness and athletic programs.

Over time, the academic program was expanded to include more than a dozen fields of study, from the sciences to the humanities.

But when all is said and done, it is still a military academy. The first day you arrive there, you begin to learn military standards, courtesies, and traditions. Then the training starts. It begins with a six-week Basic Training program, affectionately called the Beast Barracks by the ones who have survived it.

The training involves long foot marches and mountaineering, marksmanship, and tactical maneuvers. It has all the elements of the regular Army Basic Training, but intensified.

During the second summer, cadets go through eight weeks of field training, either on the West Point reservation or at Fort Knox, Kentucky. Some of them work with drill instructors at regular Army training centers. Still others undergo troop leader training at Army bases around the world. The rest take part in the academy's own recruit training.

Academic Training

The basic curriculum is rooted in the sciences and the humanities. It includes 31 mandatory courses. Every cadet is required to complete 40 one-semester courses—plus physical education and military development, naturally. At the end of the second year, a student decides on a major and chooses elective courses.

Classes are small, usually with 12 to 18 students. The overall student-faculty ratio is about eight to one. About three quarters of the faculty and military personnel have completed graduate work at some of the country's top universities. More than 30 percent of them have doctoral qualifications. This pattern is repeated at the Naval and Air Force academies as well.

Bet You Didn't Know

Texas A & M, at College Station, Texas, has had a military presence on its campus since its founding in 1876. Today its Cadet Corps numbers more than 2,000, the largest uniformed body of students in the country after the military academies themselves.

Its members routinely outshine their civilian counterparts academically because they take part in mandatory daily study periods. They also have access to volunteer academic assistance and the Corps' own computer facilities.

Basic Training

All the service academies have Basic Training programs that for the most part put regular military Basic in the shade. Cadets and midshipmen who go through the first rite of passage swear that theirs is the toughest there is. And at the other end, they usually say it with pride.

Air Force Academy—"The Beast"

At the Air Force Academy in Colorado Springs, they call the six-week program "The Beast." It begins with the freshman cadets—who will be known only as "Basic" until it's over, begin the experience standing in formation and being asked to take a look at the person on each side of them. Then they are told that one of those people won't make it to the end. OK, it's an exaggeration—the fact is that about 10 percent don't cut it—but it puts them in the proper frame of mind for what's to come.

Basic at the Air Force Academy starts with a bus ride to a place called the "Bring Me Men" ramp. After marching up the ramp, the day becomes a blur of haircuts, physicals, blood tests, and equipment issue.

While they're waiting in line after line, the Basics use the time to memorize the ranks and names of the cadre who will be over them. (Cadre, here, as at every military training facility, refers to the permanent staff of instructors and administrators.) Every time they see one of them over the next six weeks, they will have to shout those names. They themselves will not have a name.

Meals are served on the run. Basics must sit at attention while they eat. Their eyes must be cast downward, their fists clenched in their laps. They must chew their food seven times, no more, no less. (No apparent reason, either.)

If they want to make any movement, scratching their nose, for instance, they have to ask permission. And so it goes. Any infraction of any rule results in punishment, usually push-ups, not just for the offender, but for everyone.

The emphasis of the program is on physical fitness. The majority of the new cadets aren't used to exercising in the thin air 7,000 feet up in the Rocky Mountains. But, of course, they grow accustomed to it, and quickly. They'd better.

The program is broken into two parts. After 17 days of intense training, the Basics get a day off. Then they come back for the "Second Beast," 20 days of even more intense training.

The Air Force Academy's statistics for a typical class (AFA Class Of 2004):

♦ Applications: 9,547

♦ Acceptances: 1,341

♦ Male: 1,142

♦ Female: 199

♦ White: 1,087

♦ African American: 81

♦ Hispanic: 82

♦ Native American: 18

♦ Asian: 60

♦ Average High School Grade Point Average: 3.8

Making It Past "The Beast"

Every day is tough in the belly of The Beast, but the most punishing of all are the final two; together, they are known as "Recognition." After all those weeks as a nameless cipher at the beck and call of the cadre, there is finally some light at the end of the tunnel.

The challenge starts at 5:00 in the morning with intensive physical training until noon. Then the day begins. The would-be freshmen are taken to an obstacle course that puts six challenges in their way, each tougher than the one before it.

There is no mincing of words from the officials at the Academy itself. As one officer explained it, "We make it hard …. A lot of these kids were superstars in high school. We need to give them a challenge so they feel a sense of accomplishment." In other words, the idea behind it all is to wear down every cadet.

The final day is highlighted by a 2-mile run that is something like a scavenger hunt. The squadrons search for painted rocks that they are required to carry back over the 2-mile course. These are no ordinary rocks. They weigh 200 pounds or more.

Bet You Didn't Know

Notorious for its thorough training of freshmen students, Virginia Military Academy, located in Lexington, Virginia, has a small student body. The result is that everyone knows everyone else. It has only recently begun accepting women to its cadet corps, but the nearby Mary Baldwin College has the only all-woman Corps of Cadets in the country. MBC students in ROTC programs take related courses at VMI.

A Surprise Ending

When they get back to their barracks, which they had been allowed to leave a shambles when they left it that morning, they find their beds made, their uniforms pressed, and their shoes shined. It is the work of upperclassmen, a kind of welcome to the Corps of Cadets.

Then they walk a gantlet. Upperclassmen line the hall, and as the recruits walk between them, they salute. It is then that the recruits hear their names spoken for the first time since the ordeal began.

At the end of the line, they walk under crossed sabers and are given the prop and wings, the symbol of a full-fledged cadet at the Air Force Academy.

Coast Guard Academy

The experience at the Coast Guard Academy, at New London, Connecticut, is a little bit different from the other service academies. The first big difference is that you don't need an official appointment to be accepted.

The barque USS Eagle *is the pride of the Coast Guard Academy and America, too.*

As with other service academies, the Coast Guard is looking for students from the top 25 percent of their high school graduating class. About 62 percent of those who actually make it are in the top 10 percent.

Summer Training

Except for three weeks of vacation, students spend their summers in military and professional training. The first seven weeks of the pre-freshman summer, called "Swab Summer," are devoted to physical and military training for incoming cadets. The last week of the program is spent aboard the square-rigged barque, *Eagle*, America's tall ship.

Cadets spend five weeks of their sophomore summer aboard the training ship. They also spend three weeks serving with an active Coast Guard unit, and two weeks handling small boats.

Juniors spend their summer in leadership training, rifle and pistol training, and aviation. The final summer in a cadet's training involves 10 weeks serving as a junior officer aboard a working Coast Guard cutter.

The academy requires athletic participation in at least two of three seasons. It offers such intercollegiate sports as basketball, football, cross-country, and swimming. It also, appropriately, has a sailing team.

Academic Training

Coast Guard cadets graduate with a Bachelor of Science degree in one of eight majors. Every graduate completes at least 126 credit hours. The emphasis is on engineering disciplines, including marine engineering and civil engineering, but it also includes environmental science and management.

The instructor-to-student ratio is one to eight. Class size varies from 10 to 20. All students live on campus, although upper-class students with a high academic level often take elective courses at nearby Connecticut College, which is also in New London.

The academy also has a bridge/combat simulator, a radar trainer, 65-foot training vessels, and, of course, the queen of them all, the 295-foot-tall ship, *Eagle*.

After graduation, cadets are commissioned as Coast Guard ensigns, and are required to serve for at least five years.

Bet You Didn't Know

There aren't any registration fees at any of the service academies, and the Coast Guard Academy is no exception. Like the others, it requires an initial deposit for uniforms and equipment, in this case, $3,000. But there are no other costs. Tuition is free, and cadets are paid monthly stipends to cover their expenses. Every student is also issued a laptop computer bundled with professional software.

Merchant Marine Academy

Often overlooked in the roll call of America's service academies, the Merchant Marine Academy at Kings Point in Long Island, New York, is the newest of them. It was established in 1943.

Its 950 students earn Bachelor's degrees in four years of study. They are also awarded a license as a merchant marine officer and a rating as an ensign in the Naval Reserve.

Under a new program, Kings Point graduates can receive commissions as second lieutenants in the Marine Corps. In order to qualify, they spend two six-week summer sessions at the Marines' platoon-leader classes at Quantico, Virginia.

There is no tuition at the Merchant Marine Academy. Candidates for admission need to secure nominations from their U.S. senator or representative in Congress. Nominations are governed by a quota system based on population and by individual scores on college entrance exams.

Although this is a military academy, the Merchant Marine is not a military organization. It is the fleet of American ships that carry imports and exports during peacetime and becomes an auxiliary of the Navy in time of war.

Midshipmen at the Merchant Marine Academy spend one of their four years as students serving aboard a merchant ship for hands-on training. When they graduate, they are qualified to take command of almost any seagoing vessel, from cruise ships to tugboats.

Unlike the other service academies, apart from reserve duty, they have no military obligations to fulfill. By and large, they go on to take important jobs with companies engaged in the maritime trade.

The Least You Need to Know

◆ Acceptance at a military academy is a challenge in itself. You need to be able to demonstrate that you are an outstanding student, at the top physically, and you need to show talent as a leader.

◆ Qualifying for this free education is not impossible. There are hundreds of openings every year, and although competition is stiff, you shouldn't dismiss it as unattainable.

◆ The benefits go far beyond a military career. America's most successful businesspeople are frequently academy graduates.

◆ It is an experience that marks you as the best of the best, not only in a military career, but anywhere you go in life.

◆ Academic programs at military academies are the best you can find anywhere. All of them rank near the top in academic excellence.

An Officer and a Lady: Opportunities for Women

In This Chapter

◆ The surprising history of women in the military

◆ What women still can't sign up to do

◆ How segregated *are* the sexes?

◆ Progress since the Gulf War

For most of America's history, women were second-class citizens. A girl might think of becoming a nurse, but it was rare for one to plan on being a doctor. She could be a teacher, but it was men who became principals. Many young women became stenographers, typists, and secretaries, but almost never the boss.

All that has changed, of course. Women are on an equal footing with men in just about every corner of society. But they still, apparently, are lagging behind in terms of how much they are paid for what they do, compared with men who have the same jobs.

The military hasn't always been welcoming to women, but that has changed, too. They are still shut out of jobs that might involve going into combat, but there are no bars to promotion based on sex, no "women-only" jobs, and unique among career paths, there is no difference between what men and women are paid for the same responsibilities. To find out more about opportunities for women in the military, keep reading.

Better Go in Disguise

Women fought side by side with men in every American military action right up through the Spanish American War at the end of the nineteenth century. But most of them did it disguised as men. Sometimes they managed to march off into history with the brass none the wiser to the fact that the troops they led into battle weren't always what they seemed to be.

Others, like Deborah Sampson, a Massachusetts volunteer who served through the entire Revolutionary War, were found out when they were put into hospitals. Although Sampson had been hospitalized for wounds twice earlier, nobody noticed until her third trip that she wasn't the man she claimed to be—which may say something about the quality of hospital care that was given to the minutemen.

Although the Marine Corps denied it for years, Lucy Brewer served as a Marine aboard the USS *Constitution* during the War of 1812. These days, they are rather proud to note that a woman served the Corps that long ago. The Army today points with pride to Sarah Borginis, who received a battlefield promotion to colonel in 1846 during the Mexican War in Texas. Both were firsts in the American military, but there were still more to come.

There are several instances of women serving on both sides during the Civil War, although the majority of them passed themselves off as men. But among those who didn't bother, more than 60 women are officially listed among the war's casualties.

Making It Official

In 1898, when the Spanish-American War was being fought in Cuba, troops were more often felled by tropical diseases than by enemy bullets. As a way of coping, Congress authorized the Army to recruit female nurses, but carefully avoided giving them military status. More than a thousand women signed up as civilian employees at the less-than-generous salary of $30 a month.

Over the next several years, the Army and the Navy each formed special Nurse Corps units, but the women who joined them didn't have any rank and didn't share equal pay and benefits with men in the service.

When the country entered World War I in 1914, it was already obvious that women could make a difference in the military. The Army worked with Congress to figure out a way to enlist women, but while the debating was going on, the Navy began recruiting them without a special law, and the Coast Guard followed its example.

Almost overnight, some 13,000 women signed up for duty. They were given equal status with their male counterparts, and they were issued specially designed uniforms and insignia. Including the membership of the Army and Navy Nurse Corps, more than 30,000 women served the war effort before it was over in 1918.

WACs, WAVES, WASPs, and SPARS

By 1945, the military brass were still arguing the point that women might have skills they needed. Some of them had noticed that a lot of women were better qualified for a great many jobs than their male recruits.

In response to that, the Army organized what was called the Women's Army Auxiliary Corps (WAAC), later shortened to the more familiar Women's Army Corps (WAC). Many members of Congress, and some in the military, were horrified by the idea, but not long afterward, the Navy followed suit. Its women's division was called WAVES (Women Accepted for Volunteer Emergency Service).

The Marines didn't come up with a fancy name, calling its female recruits Women Marines, even if that did seem like a contradiction in terms to most career officers in the Corps. The Coast Guard, meanwhile, drew on its motto, *Semper Paratus*, meaning "Always Ready," for its new division, which it called SPARS.

In the mid-1940s, when the Air Force was still part of the Army, many women were serving as civil service pilots delivering supplies and new aircraft to Army bases. They became known as WASPs (Women Air Force Service Pilots), and after the Air Force became an independent service in 1947, they changed their name to WAF (Women in the Air Force).

More than 350,000 women served in one or another of those branches during the World War II years. The public still wasn't ready for the idea of women serving in the military, and the stated purpose of these auxiliaries was to free men to go off and fight the war.

Indeed, many of them did stay close to home, banging away on typewriters and covering telephone switchboards. Many others handled such unfamiliar jobs as packing parachutes and repairing equipment. Some worked as teachers in military schools, and some directed air traffic. But although they had equal status with their male counterparts, and collected equal pay and benefits, their jobs weren't very different than if they were holding civilian jobs.

Bet You Didn't Know

Nearly all of the action-adventure movies made during World War II had women in their casts. Although it was probably partly a matter of giving work to female contract stars, and of adding a bit of sex appeal, it did reflect a reality. By the time the war ended, there were more than 57,000 Army nurses and 12,000 Navy nurses on active duty. They served in more than 1,000 Army hospitals and 350 Navy installations in more than 50 different countries. Many of these women participated in the D-Day invasion of Normandy, and followed the troops all the way to Berlin itself. One out of every 40 of these women who served their country received medals or citations for their bravery.

Down, but Not Out

The women's auxiliaries were phased out when the war ended, and once again, the only way a woman could aspire to a military career was as a nurse.

It had been demonstrated that women had a place in the military, though, and in 1948, after a long, impassioned debate, Congress passed the Women's Armed Services Integration Act. It was a start, but the idea still had a long way to go.

The new law restricted the number of women in each branch of the service to 2 percent of the total. It specifically prohibited women from becoming generals and admirals, and only one woman in each branch could be a colonel or captain. A woman could manage to become a commissioned officer, though she couldn't command male units. The enlistment age for females was higher and their mandatory retirement age lower.

The bars were raised to prevent women in the Navy or Marine Corps from serving aboard anything but hospital ships. They were also forbidden to fly combat aircraft in any branch.

Among other things hidden away in the law's fine print was a rule that women were not entitled to the family support that was routinely given to men. Women were also given an automatic discharge if they became pregnant or if a child lived in their home for longer than a month in any year.

Changing the Playing Field

The rules were changed slightly, but hardly noticeably, through the efforts of a civilian group that called itself the Defense Advisory Committee on Women in the Service. It endeared itself to the military by calling itself DACOWITS, but its real impact wasn't felt in the Pentagon until 1973, 22 years after it began making its recommendations.

The moment of truth had come with the elimination of the draft and the establishment of the all-volunteer force. To relieve the resulting manpower shortage, the government turned a friendlier eye toward women. The result was that over the next three years, the number of women in the American military almost tripled to nearly 120,000.

Female college students were allowed to enroll in college ROTC programs for the first time, and before long they were being accepted at the military academies, too. But if their gains had been dramatic, women weren't out of the woods yet.

In Their Footsteps

The Defense Advisory Committee On Women In The Services (DACOWITS) was formed in 1951 with the blessing of Secretary of State George C. Marshall, who had formerly been the military's chief of staff. At the time, there were no women in military leadership positions, and its mission was to bring about change.

The committee, which still exists, is composed of 30 to 35 members, nearly all civilian women. The secretary of defense appoints a third of its members (the others are recommended by the individual branches of the service) for three-year terms. They visit military installations looking for "issues" that they raise with the Defense Department and the various services in written reports. DACOWITS has come under fierce attack by conservative groups who charge that it is a tax-supported feminist lobby that has outlived its usefulness. Nevertheless, its work as a watchdog for women in the military continues, especially with its effort to open combat units to women.

Changing the Rules

Among the details that were overlooked in the rush to sign up more women was that men and women were not treated as equals when it came to family benefits. They were quick to drop the rule that married women couldn't enlist, but it took a decision by the Supreme Court for their husbands and children to be entitled to the same benefits as those of men in the service.

A few years later, a federal court ruled that discharges on the grounds of pregnancy were unconstitutional. The Army responded by making such separations voluntary, and the Navy reserved the right to deny requests for discharges among pregnant women who had special skills. For its part, the Coast Guard solved the problem by allowing new parents of either sex to take a leave of absence for up to a year without losing their ratings or specialties.

Changing the Numbers

Naturally, the new openness attracted women to the military in huge numbers. In fact, so many signed up that some die-hard traditionalists among military planners began calling for a new draft to reduce the need for so many women.

Instead, the Carter administration called for doubling the number of women volunteers in 1977. President Reagan kept up the pressure, and so did President Bush. By 1989, the number had reached 232,823.

Opening New Jobs

During the 1970s and 1980s, the last barriers to meaningful jobs for women were eliminated. They were no longer being relegated to clerical and health-care jobs, and many were moving closer to all-male roles behind, but still close to, lines of combat.

Recruit training is just one of the jobs women are filling in today's Army.

The Navy traditionally refused to allow women aboard its ships, but in 1993, Congress responded to its request for a change in the law. The following year, women were assigned to the crew of the aircraft carrier USS *Eisenhower*, and today, except for submarines, there are few ships in America's fleet that don't have women aboard.

All the services, except the Marine Corps, opened aircraft training to women in the early 1970s. During the Gulf War, they served as helicopter pilots and flew refueling missions over Iraq itself. The policy was broadened in 1994, and for the first time women were allowed to compete for assignments in aircraft that fly combat missions.

At the same time, women were excluded from jobs that might involve ground combat, but the military opened the door to make many of those previously closed job options available to women. Today, about 90 percent of military occupation specialties are open to women and men on an equal footing.

It wasn't easy getting this far, and there are still some problems to be solved. But there hasn't been a time in American history when women were given so many opportunities. And they owe it all to a bunch of women who knew how to fight for their rights.

Bet You Didn't Know

When 415 women, including nine pilots, reported for duty aboard the nuclear-powered carrier *Eisenhower* in 1994, the ship had been refitted to make their lives easier. More heads ("bathrooms," to landlubbers) had been installed and sleeping quarters had been modified. The ship's barbers were given a crash course on cutting women's hair. The laundry was adjusted to accommodate their lingerie. Menus were changed to include more low-fat items. The male members of the crew were indoctrinated on new rules for dealing with women aboard their ship. They didn't stop cursing like a bunch of sailors, of course, but they did tone it down. When the *Ike* went back to Norfolk after its first cruise as a coed ship, its commander noted that the women in his crew had improved the carrier's efficiency.

What Women *Can't* Do

Even the Israeli army, which has been drafting women into its ranks for more than half a century, draws the line at sending women into combat. The American military has also made that its policy.

But it isn't so easy to define front lines in modern wars, where most of what might be called combat takes place behind computer screens miles away from the action. There are still some specialties that could lead to physical contact with the enemy, though, and they are still off-limits to women.

In today's American military, you won't see a female Green Beret or Navy SEAL. You won't find women driving tanks, nor will you find them wading ashore in a company of Marine combat troops. There aren't any women in airborne combat units, either.

Although most of the Navy's ships have women among their crews, there aren't any aboard submarines. But that isn't because it is considered more dangerous duty than, say, aboard a destroyer. It's because the living space for the crews of even the biggest nuclear submarines is too cramped. There simply isn't enough room to divide it up so that women sailors can have some privacy.

What Women *Are* Doing

During the war in Afghanistan, a male soldier told a reporter, "We just came back from an assignment and the crew chief was a female and no one batted an eye. It's the norm here now."

Among women serving there who were interviewed, most reporters noticed that their answers weren't a lot different from the ones they were getting from the men who were serving alongside them. They all missed hot showers, for instance, and they missed the computer access they had at their home bases. But they missed those things in just about equal numbers.

What was missing was a difference between the sexes. It is small and getting smaller.

Bet You Didn't Know

Many women served their country alongside their male counterparts in ground operations during the war in Afghanistan. But they have also been represented in roles that would have been previously unthinkable in every conflict since the Persian Gulf War in 1991. For the most part in recent wars, women have served in traditional behind-the-scenes activities such as medical care. But every recent war has found them at the controls of helicopters and fighter aircraft.

Training

The Merchant Marine Academy and the Coast Guard Academy led the way in admitting women into their cadet corps, but now all of the service academies have large female contingents.

In general, the women have consistently outperformed their male counterparts in the academic part of their training, especially in foreign languages and English. They often lag behind in science and engineering courses during their first two years, but almost always catch up during the last two.

Because of that, the academies haven't changed their academic programs to accommodate women. But they have taken a closer look at their physical fitness standards. While women still have to push themselves hard, on paper, at least, it looks like they might have it easier than the guys. That isn't the case. The comparison might be similar to what would happen if a junior high school kid went out for the high school football team.

All the services, except the Marine Corps, train women and men together, but allowances are made for the physical differences. Still, if a woman isn't required to run as far, and often can wear running shoes rather than combat boots, that doesn't take away from the fact that training isn't actually any easier for them than for the men who train with them. It's all a matter of pushing yourself to the outer limits of your ability. It is at the heart of all military training, regardless of sexual differences.

Among the things female recruits learn in Basic Training is applying a different kind of makeup. The results are sometimes surprising.

Bet You Didn't Know

Within NATO, Italy and Germany are the only countries that don't allow women to carry weapons, but there is pressure to change that. In the Norwegian military, women have been serving on submarines for more than 25 years. And in Denmark, women are encouraged to compete for any job the military offers.

Israel is the only country in the world where women are drafted into the military. It is against policy for them to serve in combat, but they do serve as border guards, and many go with patrols deep into Palestinian territory.

Breaking the Mold

No one will deny that a career in the military opens new options for women that their mothers never dreamed of. But many of the technologies use equipment that was designed for men. Most of it has been changed, but it is easier said than done sometimes.

When women began applying for flight training, for instance, the cockpits of the trainers needed to be redesigned. Women are shorter, as a rule, and have shorter arms and legs than the men the trainer was originally designed for. The project also brought benefits to shorter men, too. Not every candidate for flight training is a 6-footer.

To do the job, the Army's Research Development and Engineering Center created a database of the dimensions, from head to toe, of almost 10,000 military personnel. This field (known as anthropometrics, by the way) is one of the fascinating military specialties almost unknown in the private sector, which usually relies on the military for that kind of research.

Others in the military take advantage of the same research. The Navy used it to figure out how to build bunk space and shower facilities aboard its ships.

But flight trainers and shower stalls aren't the only things that are changing around military bases now that women are there. Some weapons systems are lighter than they were a decade ago, and even uniforms are slightly different as the services try to downplay the differences between the sexes. It is probably most pronounced in the PXs, where women's clothing is taking up more and more shelf space. Anthropometrics notwithstanding, though, nearly all of the sizes marked are larger than in civilian department stores. It is one of the things military women say they have the biggest problem adjusting to. Here they are in better physical shape than they've been in years, but they are buying larger-sized jeans and dresses.

When the Women's Army Auxiliary Corps was formed during World War II, the government hired Hattie Carnegie, one of the top fashion designers of the day, to create its uniform. Then they staged fashion shows at war-bond rallies to draw in more recruits.

Whether military uniforms are making a fashion statement today may be open to debate. Especially after Operation Perfect Freedom in Afghanistan, though, the military look took on a new significance. And when the Marine Corps recently changed the camouflage pattern in its uniforms, it trademarked the new pattern and set up a unit to market it for commercial use.

The Other Woman—Military Wives

Since colonial times, women married to men in the service have discovered that they are just as much married to the institution as to the man. The same, of course, is true of men married to women in the military, although a large percentage of them are part of the military themselves.

Right now, more than 60 percent of all military personnel are married, and most of them have families. Married people get extra pay for spouses and children and, statistically, the officers among them stand a better chance of promotion to senior ranks than single officers.

If you are a married man considering a military career, you need to also consider the life your wife is facing as well.

Nearly every woman we categorize as a military wife faces the same general restrictions on her life. Everything she experiences is directly related to her husband's rank—the housing she gets, the clubs she belongs to, and even the friends she makes.

Every military base is a self-contained unit with no need for contact with the world outside its gate. Families living there get free medical care, schools for their children, discount shopping, theaters, and churches. Most facilities also include family counseling centers.

Wives all have their own social pecking order, too. It closely follows the position of their husbands in the chain of command. The Department of Defense issued a regulation to prevent that, so that there would be more equality in the social lives of military wives. But it is generally ignored.

In most cases, no one ever dominates a social circle for too long. It is a fact of military life that the family is going to move at least once in three years, sometimes even more often than that. When a transfer takes place, wives and children are forced to make new friends and establish new support systems in each new home.

The Least You Need to Know

- Although they were once treated as virtually unacceptable, women are more welcome in the military today than they ever have been. Better still, they are routinely promoted to higher ranks during their tours of duty.
- Women are mastering jobs in the military that the civilian world is still slow to make available to them.
- Restrictions against women are falling fast. Specialties that were restricted as recently as a few years ago are now widely available.
- Pay and benefits are the same for men and women in the military, unlike in many civilian occupations where women often take on the same responsibilities as men, but don't reach the same pay level.

An Equal Opportunity Employer

In This Chapter

- ◆ Ending discrimination in the military
- ◆ How the military gives minorities a leg up in the civilian world
- ◆ Special educational opportunities for minorities
- ◆ No English? No high school diploma? No problem
- ◆ Getting ahead like nowhere else
- ◆ Minority women in the service

As recently as 50 years ago, blacks were no better off in the military than they were anywhere else in society. Then, in 1948, President Harry S. Truman said, "Enough is enough." He signed an order that did away with racial discrimination, in any form, in the armed services.

By the time blacks began fighting seriously for their civil rights in the 1950s and early 1960s, the Army, and the other services as well, had already become completely integrated. Nobody was questioning the rights of any minority to compete on an equal footing with whites and with each other.

Yes, there were some glitches along the way. But right now, the military is light years ahead of the private sector in terms of equal opportunity.

Getting Better

In the early phases of creating this military meritocracy, racism in the county as a whole was still a visible open wound. In response to what was going on outside the gates of its bases, the Army stepped up its efforts to bridge the gaps.

Among the first changes was a requirement that every soldier needed to take courses in black history as part of Basic Training. More important in the 1970s, race-relation skills became part of the efficiency reports required for officers and Non-Commissioned Officers (NCOs). These evaluation reports are crucial to future promotions, and the new addition was not only mandatory, but rigidly enforced.

Black troops aren't relegated to serving behind the lines anymore. You'll find them leading the way these days.

The result was that more blacks began receiving promotions. At the same time, officers whose efficiency reports even hinted at racism were relieved of their commands.

It set a pace that has, if anything, been intensified in the years since. It is unlikely today that any officer or NCO in the military isn't sensitive to the issue of race. And it has become second nature to them, not something they need to keep reminding themselves of.

Bet You Didn't Know _____

The overlapping of the civil rights movement and the Vietnam War brought charges that blacks were being relegated to the status of "cannon fodder" in Southeast Asia. While it appeared to be true that middle-class whites were going to great lengths to avoid the draft and that black draftees seemed to be filling the gaps, the numbers tell a different story.

During those years, blacks of military age accounted for 13.5 percent of the population. But, according to Department of Defense statistics, only 9.7 percent of the military were blacks. In the actual fighting, blacks accounted for 10.6 percent of the Americans there, and of the total deaths, 12.5 percent were black. Whites accounted for 88.4 percent of the Vietnam fighting force, and 86.8 percent of those who died there.

Changing Times

Over the years, the Hispanic population, as well as other minorities, have been underrepresented in the military. Although Hispanics between the ages of 18 and 44 account for more than 12.5 percent of all Americans, only 8 percent of military personnel in that age group are Hispanic. Whites account for 70.5 percent of the same age group in the civilian population, but only 63.7 percent of the military population is white.

About five percent of 18- to 24-year-olds in the general population are classified as "other" minorities. The grouping includes Native Americans, Asians, and Pacific Islanders, among others. Of that group, the percentage serving in the military is as high as 10 percent in the Navy, with slightly smaller percentages in each of the other services. Overall, about 6 percent of military personnel represent these "other" ethnic groups.

The numbers vary for each of these minority groups from year to year, but they have been relatively static for several generations ... with one striking exception.

The end of the draft in 1977 increased, rather than diminished, as many had expected, the number of blacks in the military. In the last year of the draft, the Army was about 17 percent black, but the percentage more than doubled over the next 10 years. Today, 3 out of 10 enlisted Army personnel are black. Economics had everything to do with it. A combination of enlistment bonuses and higher pay, not to mention a guaranteed job, plus equal opportunity, has made the military a career that no one in the private sector comes close to matching.

Making It

In today's world, blacks and Hispanics who have served out their enlistments are much more likely to find a welcome in corporate personnel offices. Even among those who didn't end up with skills that are directly transferable to civilian jobs are finding that they have a leg up when they go job hunting.

The reason, experts say, is because the military teaches underprivileged young people how to cope with the kinds of bureaucracy they're going to find in the corporate world.

Most human resources people say that there is another factor as well. Any minority job candidate who has served in the military has competed against whites. And they have discharge papers to prove that they were successful at it.

A Crack at College

Because the rest of America still hasn't caught up with the military, a great many young blacks and Hispanics are still graduating from substandard high school systems. Even if they could afford to go on to college, which most can't, they usually hit a stone wall at the admissions offices where the track record of their high school is as closely studied as their own record.

If that experience sounds familiar in your life, the military can solve the problem for you. Start your career at a recruiting office, and chances are good that you're going to get where you want to go.

Getting Academic Skills

Suppose that you didn't do all that well in a high school that doesn't do very well, either. That doesn't mean it's too late to turn your life around.

The military, these days, isn't just a bunch of people sitting around waiting for a war to happen. It has become an institution where learning virtually never stops. But it isn't like any school you've ever seen before. Classes are small, the spirit is high, and the teachers really care whether you pass or not.

A lot of the things you'll learn at these military schools will count as credit toward college after you've finished your enlistment. There are even opportunities to take college-level courses in your spare time while you're still serving, and Uncle Sam will pay for 75 percent of your tuition. Plus, all your room and board is free.

Or if you'd rather wait, thanks to your military experience, you'll have the money you need to go on to college after you retire in a couple of years. (Get more details in Chapter 6.)

Getting an education while you're serving is one of the big advantages of today's military.

Building a College Fund

Anyone who serves in the military for at least 36 months—just 3 years—is entitled to collect $28,800 for more education. You can use it for college or for technical schooling. Combined with that benefit, called the Montgomery GI Bill, the Army or Navy college funds will boost the total up to $50,000. The Marine Corps and Coast Guard college funds will raise it to $30,000.

Could you put away that much in a college fund in just three years?

The ROTC Advantage

As you've seen in Chapter 6, you might not have to wait to go to college. The military is interested in finding more officer candidates, and the Reserve Officer Training Corps is the biggest source of scholarships there is. And like everything else connected to the military, discrimination based on race or ethnic background simply doesn't exist.

ROTC scholarships are based strictly on merit—your achievements in high school—and not on financial need.

If you have been thinking of going to a so-called historically black college or university, there is something new you should check out. The Army has recently added a new program that can give you a full four-year college scholarship. Not only that, but it is prepared to kick in another $750 a year for books and supplies. It'll also give you $3,150 a year, tax-free, for your living expenses.

Preference goes to students looking for degrees in nursing, physical sciences, or engineering. But you can choose any field that interests you and still qualify.

Naturally, qualifying isn't easy, but it isn't impossible, either. Basically, you'll be judged on how you score on college entrance tests, as well as your high school grades and extra-curricular activities. If you had to take a part-time job during your high school years, that experience counts as substitute credit.

During your college career, you'll be expected to take an ROTC class, which involves a couple of hours a week. And when you graduate, you'll serve in the regular Army. But you'll go in as an officer, and every step you'll take after that will be up.

In Their Footsteps

In all of America, there isn't a better role model, for whites as well as blacks, as Secretary of State Colin Powell. His career started on the mean streets of the South Bronx in New York City (CUNY). His father was a shipping clerk foreman and his mother a seamstress. Both were Jamaican immigrants.

As a teenager, young Powell was an average student, at best, and when he enrolled at the City College of New York (CUNY), his grade point average hovered around a low C. But he "found himself" through the school's ROTC program. He liked the structure and the discipline, but most of all, he loved wearing a uniform. Powell earned a Bachelor's degree at CUNY, but more pleasing for him, he also earned a commission as an Army second lieutenant.

After he came home from Vietnam, he enrolled at George Washington University and the National War College and got an MBA. He got straight A's, too. His military experience had changed his attitude about academics. Over the next several years, he served as a White House military assistant, then secretary of defense, and then national security adviser.

By the time the Gulf War started in 1990, he was chairman of the Joint Chiefs of Staff. Before the war ended, he was a national hero. When he retired three years later, he was offered a $6 million advance for his memoirs. The book, which became a best-seller, was called *My American Journey*. It had been a long journey up from the South Bronx.

Building a Career

Statistically, blacks are nearly twice as likely to reenlist when their first tour is finished. It is partly because of the racial climate in the military. Who would want to leave a job where he or she is well treated for one where the boss might have an attitude? But there is more to it than that.

In civilian life, the road to promotion for any high school graduate often begins in the mailroom. And there are few guarantees that you are going to move up as fast as you expected.

In the military, on the other hand, a new recruit can expect to be promoted at least to an E-4 in a three-year enlistment. In the Army, that is a specialist, fourth class. In the Air Force, it is senior airman; the Marines call their E-4s corporal; and the Navy, petty officer third class. The basic pay scale in that grade is close to $1,500 a month.

Getting Ahead

Close to a third of all staff sergeants and sergeants first class in the Army these days are black. About a quarter of first sergeants, master sergeants, and sergeants major are black, too. There are nearly 94,000 of these noncommissioned officers in the Army right now.

Many of them move up in the ranks beyond that, but it takes time for those promotions to come. One reason is that most black NCOs aren't going for training in combat specialties, where there are more promotion opportunities. Another is the level of education that is required. The majority join up right out of high school, and although they are continuing their education in uniform, it takes time.

Time is on their side, though, and most are making good use of it. Right now, blacks hold more management jobs in the military than in any business institution in America.

In Their Footsteps

Edward A. Carter was an Army sergeant when World War II broke out. But as a black man, he was relegated to duty behind the lines, so he gave up his stripes and joined an infantry unit as a buck private so that he could get into the fight. He got his wish. After just 11 days in his new outfit, Carter found himself pinned down, alone, with five bullets in his body and the enemy bearing down on him.

There were eight men in the German patrol, and Carter kept his cool until they were right on top of him. Then he opened fire with his machine gun and six of the enemy fell to the ground. Grabbing the other two and using them as shields, he rejoined his company. When his prisoners were questioned, they paved the way for a major Allied advance. Carter earned a Distinguished Service Cross that day, and 42 years later, a belated Medal of Honor.

But his short tour with the infantry wasn't his only military experience. As the teenage son of a missionary in Shanghai, he fought in the Chinese Nationalist Army against Japanese invaders. Later he joined the Abraham Lincoln Brigade, American volunteers who were fighting against the fascists during the Spanish Civil War.

Opportunities for Hispanics

All the services have been working to recruit more Hispanic volunteers, and both sides are coming up winners.

Out of a population that accounts for 11.7 percent of all Americans, the Department of Defense says that Hispanics make up 8.7 percent of the Army's current roster; the Navy's, 9.4 percent; the Marines', 12.9 percent; and the Air Force's, 5 percent.

But the numbers are growing fast. As recently as a decade ago, the overall percentage of Hispanic enlistees was less than 4. It has since grown to 8 percent, almost double what it was. One reason, of course, is the low level of discrimination in the military. But Hispanic teenagers are finding that enlisting is the best way to get an education, and to find a career. It is a way to turn their lives around.

You May Not Need a High School Diploma

Officially, the military won't accept enlistees without a high school diploma. The hard fact of life is that nationwide, about 30 percent of Hispanics are high school dropouts, according to a 1999 report in *National Journal* magazine. But there is a way around the rule. It is called a GED (General Educational Development) certificate.

The GED was developed with the military in mind, in fact. The American Council on Education established it in 1942 to help draftees during World War II. It has since become accepted in the civilian world, and about 80,000 people take the test every year.

The Pentagon has ruled that GED-holders can't account for more than 10 percent of the total number of enlistees. There is pressure to make the number bigger and to open the door wider. It will likely happen sooner than later.

The attitude of the services is that not everyone drops out of high school because they can't cut it. Many need to quit to help support their families, they point out, and they believe that shouldn't be a mark against them.

Simply put, they are working to turn people they can't recruit into people they can.

For now, the military will pay for GED enrollment for anyone who is drug-free, has no criminal record, and scores reasonably well on the Armed Services Vocational Aptitude Battery. The only other requirement is that you must enlist once you've picked up that piece of paper that calls you qualified.

Language Is No Barrier

You probably have noticed that a lot of military recruitment advertising, and forms as well, are in Spanish as well as English. For the most part, that is because Hispanic families tend to be close-knit, and almost always interact with one another when it comes time to make an important decision. Most of the younger generation of Hispanics speaks and understands English, but their parents and grandparents sometimes don't.

The military makes English a requirement. All of the training and education is conducted in English, and there is no time to wait for translations.

But understanding another language is an asset as far as the military is concerned. The Army even offers a bonus of $100 a month to anyone who is fluent in a second language.

All the services have special language programs to teach English to recruits who might not understand it before they report for Basic Training. The course takes about 14 weeks. As a course in English as a second language, it doesn't just concentrate on Spanish-speakers, but a host of Asian languages, and many from Central Europe as well.

You Don't Have to Be a Citizen

If you are a legal resident alien or if you have a green card, you are eligible to join the U.S. military. Even without citizenship, you will still be able to claim all the educational and retirement benefits. The only special requirement is that you will need to become an American citizen before you can reenlist at the end of your first term of service.

Minority Women

Although more than half the population of the United States is female, women account for only about 15 percent of the military. More than 30 percent of them are black women.

Even in times of full employment when the economy is strong, black women are twice as likely to be without a job as their white counterparts. The military, which has become more like the civilian workforce—but without racial discrimination—represents an opportunity like no other.

Their success in military careers varies a bit from one service to another. black women are more likely to become officers in the Army and in the Navy.

The number of officers in the categories of 0-1 to 0-3—second lieutenant to captain in the Army, ensign to lieutenant in the Navy—has been high among black women over the last several years and the percentages have been steady. Higher up, though, the percentage of 0-4s and 0-5s—major and lieutenant colonel in the Army and lieutenant commander and commander in the Navy—has been growing at a steady rate.

In terms of base pay, an 0-1 earns a minimum of $3,228 a month with three years of service; 0-5 pay is $4,228 a month or more with the same amount of experience.

In recent years, there has been an increase in the number of minority women who are serving as tactical officers. But most women in the military are concentrated in two occupational categories: administrative/support and medical services.

The number of minority women in administrative/support jobs actually fell a bit during the 1990s. The reason seems to be that women already in those jobs were staying in them, and there were few new openings.

In the years since, as more openings came along, the numbers began growing again. But it served as a sign that women who had those jobs in the first place were happy in them and not generally looking for transfers. Even now, openings are more likely to be the result of promotions and not transfers.

The number of minority women in medical jobs in the military is almost always growing. The reason is that there are more opportunities for promotion within medical specialties. These are also specialties that are least likely to be affected in the unlikely event of military downsizing, like the so-called "draw-down" in the 1990s when the size of the military was reduced.

The Bottom Line

When discrimination was driven out of the military more than 50 years ago, there was a lot of hand wringing over the idea that it would lead to an all-minority fighting force.

That prediction was dead wrong, as it turned out. In general, the percentage of each minority group in the military isn't much different from its representation in the overall population:

Minorities in the U.S. Military

	Blacks	Hispanics	Other	Overall
Army	26.4%	7.9%	6.5%	40.8%
Navy	18.3%	8.9%	8.3%	35.6%
Marine Corps	15.5%	12.4%	4.6%	32.4%
Air Force	15.9%	4.8%	4.7%	25.4%

Source: Department of Defense, Fiscal Year 2000

What the changed attitude did accomplish was more opportunity for all minorities. It has spilled over into the private sector, but it took the military to prove to America that discrimination is an old-fashioned idea that doesn't work anymore.

The Least You Need to Know

◆ The military is one of the few institutions anywhere in America that is completely color-blind.

◆ Blacks hold more management jobs in the military than in any of America's corporations, and most of its integrated institutions.

◆ There are no bars to promotion for minorities and no limits to available jobs.

◆ Educational opportunities have never been more open to minorities than they are in today's military.

◆ The military is less interested in what you are than in who you are, and it works at helping minorities to succeed.

Chapter 10

Perks, Perks, and More Perks

In This Chapter

- ◆ The Montgomery GI Bill's benefits
- ◆ Home loans with no down payment
- ◆ Life insurance for less than a dollar a month
- ◆ Lifetime medical benefits
- ◆ Pensions

Historically, the world's fighting forces have been made up of slaves, the destitute, or the unwary dragooned into service. Right up until modern times, the men who led these often-reluctant soldiers and sailors were from the upper classes. They were men in search of glory and the social status that went with it. Through it all, though, wars were usually something that happened on the other side of the world from where people who were sometimes affected by them lived—in places nobody ever heard of and everybody would soon try to forget.

In more recent conflicts, when the general civilian population started finding itself closer to the action, the concept began to change. People began joining the military to defend their homes, their families, and their country. There was a word for it: patriotism.

It is still the best reason for joining. Thousands sign up for the military every year with nothing more in mind than serving their country. They are rewarded with pride. But now, in the twenty-first century, there are other rewards to consider. And those rewards, also known as "perks," are the subject of this chapter.

Yours for the Taking

It begins the day you sign a contract for military service: Many enlistees collect bonuses of up to $20,000 just for signing on the dotted line.

There are qualifying circumstances, to be sure. The amount you can collect for passing "Go" depends on your education, your experience, and your qualifications for a job that needs to be filled. Nobody is ever going to hand you a bunch of money based on your good looks. But this is as close as it comes.

If you have a college degree, you can probably start your military career as a commissioned officer. If you had to drop out of college, the military can give you the means to pick up where you left off. It will even pay off your student loans if you had to leave because you couldn't afford to stay.

The military will also give you a chance to earn your degree while you're serving. And it will help you pay for it.

Everything you need—the clothes on your back, the roof over your head, the food you eat, the medical and dental care you get—is all provided free. The computer that keeps you in touch with the college that will grant you a degree won't cost you anything, either. Neither will the Internet access.

Along the way, you are entitled to cash benefits and special add-on compensation. You can earn extra money for things like flight pay, sea pay, and hazardous or overseas duty. You are also eligible for tax-free payments to cover off-base housing and subsistence for yourself and for your family.

There are about 70 separate pays, allowances, and benefits available to military personnel beyond their basic pay. Nobody can access all of them, but during your career, you'll probably be able to tap into half a dozen of them.

You and your family will be entitled to free travel, too, and the military maintains resorts around the world where you can get away from it all without paying high resort prices. You'll have time to enjoy it, too. No matter which branch of the service you choose and what your job or rank might be, you are going to get 30 days' paid vacation every year. And you'll get weekends off, too, or at least the equivalent in time off.

That, however, is only the beginning. It gets better.

Bet You Didn't Know

Military personnel are offered deep discounts at the resort hotels at Walt Disney World at Orlando, Florida. But they have a much better option. A military-only resort called Shades of Green (SOG in military-speak) on the Disney property offers rates as low as $66 a night for military personnel, their families, and retirees. The rate goes up according to rank, but nobody pays more that $109 a night. What they get for their money is two championship golf courses, lighted tennis courts, a swimming pool, and free transportation to the Disney parks up the road.

The military also operates similar facilities at Hale Koa on Waikiki Beach in Hawaii, the Dragon Hill Resort at Seoul, South Korea, and Rocky Mountain Blue, a ski resort in the Colorado Rockies. Coming soon is a luxury hotel at the foot of a Bavarian Alps in Germany. There are also dozens of less elaborate vacation spots run by, and for, the military around the country and the world.

A Typical Nonmilitary Scenario

If you take a job with a private company, you aren't going to get any of those benefits or anything closely resembling them. And even if you stay with that company for the rest of your working life, what you're going to find at the other end isn't going to compare with the payoff at the end of a military career.

Suppose you're a college graduate entering the workforce. You'll probably be 22 years old. You'll start out in an entry-level job (no hiring bonus), and start working your way up. Along the way, you're going to have to dress for success. In case you haven't looked lately, a necktie alone can cost 40 bucks.

Assuming that you have star quality, you might make junior management in another 5 to 10 years. Then, while you're watching your back, you'll inch slowly on up.

Assuming that there is no economic downturn and you don't get laid off, you might work for that same company all your life. Even if you bounced around from job to job, you might want to get out early and get on with your life.

You will be able to collect Social Security when you hit 62—unless the law gets changed in the meantime. The benefits will be reduced, though. You can't collect full benefits until you hit 65. But you've already slogged through 40 years of working. You're tired, and it may seem worth it to retire early even if the monthly check is smaller.

On the other hand, you could wait until you're 65 to collect all of the Social Security income that you're entitled to. But by then you will have worked for 43 years.

Sure, you may have managed to save some money over those years. You'll probably have it invested in the stock market. But what will happen if you picked the wrong stocks? Some people put their money in bonds so they can live out their old age on the interest. But every drop in interest rates is like a stake through their hearts.

You will probably have had medical insurance while you worked at that job. You may even have had it for a low premium cost. But even if you can keep it after you retire, it's going to cost a lot, and you may eventually find yourself priced out of coverage. That leaves Medicare. It's good, but not great, and you're going to be surprised at how much comes out of your pocket for things like prescription drugs and procedures that Medicare won't cover.

Compare that to a career in the military, and the choice is a no-brainer. Keep reading to find out more.

Not a Retiree, a Veteran

You don't usually think of the end of the road when you're at the beginning of it. But American men born in 1984 can expect to live at least to the age of 71. Women in the same age group will probably live to see their seventy-eighth birthday. But those are just average numbers. The Census Bureau projects that the population over 85 is going to quadruple over the next 50 years.

How much of that time would you like to spend following a career? In the private sector, expect to spend more than 40 years. In the military, though, it's 20. That means that if you enlist when you are 22, you'll be retired at 42 with almost half your life still ahead of you. But you will be more than just retired. You will be a veteran.

Being a veteran, like these men who served in the Korean War, is an honor that never leaves you.

There are about 25 million people in the United States today who fit into that category. Most of them are too young to be called senior citizens. They get more respect than the average senior, too—most of all from the government they served. It spends more than $50 billion a year showing its gratitude.

Basic Veterans' Benefits

Some former military personnel fit the description of retiree, but not all. The majority are just plain vanilla veterans. These are people who enlisted for a tour of active duty or two and then went back to civilian life.

But they all went back with a package of benefits. Every veteran who has fulfilled a military contract is eligible for …

- ◆ A thorough physical and dental examination.
- ◆ Paid time off to go house hunting or job hunting.
- ◆ Job counseling.
- ◆ Moving expenses.
- ◆ 26 weeks of unemployment insurance.
- ◆ GI Bill educational benefits (if you signed up and contributed to the program).
- ◆ GI Bill home loans.
- ◆ Low-cost life insurance.
- ◆ VA medical and dental care.
- ◆ Supplementary health insurance.
- ◆ Small business loans.

These benefits are available to all veterans after two years of active duty. In nearly every case, you will also be entitled to collect 26 weeks of unemployment insurance while you're looking for a job after your tour of duty ends. Most of the details of your entitlements will be spelled out for you. You can get answers to specific questions form your local office of the Veterans Administration or through any of the veterans' organizations in your area.

Disabled Veterans

The government offers special benefits for veterans who need continuing care for medical conditions related to military service. The qualification doesn't mean that you are restricted to help with combat injuries. Far from it.

The medical condition that puts you in the ranks of the "disabled" doesn't even have to be caused by military service. Suppose you developed tendonitis playing tennis or football in high school. It wasn't serious enough to slow you down, but it began to bother you when you were playing sports while you were in the service. If it needs treatment, it is classified as a military-related disability, and you can get free treatment at VA medical facilities for the rest of your life, if you need it.

As a disabled vet, you are also entitled to other special benefits, such as ...

- ◆ Cash grants to remodel your home to accommodate a disability.
- ◆ Vehicle allowances if your disability makes it necessary to modify your car.
- ◆ Up to $500 a year to cover the cost of artificial limbs.
- ◆ Priority preference for government jobs.
- ◆ Free VA medical and dental care.
- ◆ Vocational rehabilitation.
- ◆ Disability compensation in lieu of a pension.

In short, you may be a disabled veteran and not know it. Check it out though the Veterans Administration medical facilities near where you live.

Tip

There are veterans' care facilities in every state, from full-sized hospitals to clinics. All of them are supported by the individual states, and operate under rules established by the U.S. Department of Veterans Affairs, which frequently inspects them. They charge for their services, but the fees are dramatically lower than those charged at private medical centers. The VA also operates nursing homes for patients who need daily care, and "domiciliaries" for those who can take care of most of their own basic needs.

Low-Income Veterans

If you aren't able to work because of a medical condition that isn't related to your military service, or because of your age, you will be able to draw a special VA pension. There are other benefits available, too:

- ◆ Special vocational training
- ◆ Preference for government jobs if you're a combat vet
- ◆ Free VA medical and dental care

These benefits have nothing to do with what you did while you were in the service or what happened to you during that time. They are intended to offer a helping hand to veterans who can't work, but don't qualify for a service-connected disability benefit.

Tip

VA Pensions for low-income veterans apply only to vets who have served during wartime. Recipients can't serve in the reserves while they are drawing a VA pension. They get high-priority free medical and dental care, although they can't collect a disability pension at the same time. Their widows or widowers, and their dependent children are entitled to continue getting the pension after they die. Their survivors are also entitled to educational benefits.

Discharge Status

The basic package of veterans' benefits aren't available in a few discharge categories. These include separations "under conditions other than honorable," such as dishonorable discharges and bad-conduct discharges. There are also discharges ordered by a court-martial, those involving conscientious objectors who refused military obligations, and personnel who were absent without leave for more than 180 days. A few benefits might still be available, but always on a case-by-case basis.

The first piece of advice regarding those kinds of discharges is to avoid them. It isn't worth the trouble.

Altering Your Discharge Status

An adverse discharge doesn't have to follow you all your life, either. You can request an upgrade at any time. The first step is to file an appeal with the discharge review board connected to your branch of the service. You can present them with documentation of your case, or you can call witnesses to testify for you. You have the right to an attorney, or you can call on a veterans organization or your state's veterans affairs department for help.

You will be required to state your case, either by mail or in person, and be able to prove that your original discharge was unfair, or even illegal.

The boards always consider these appeals based on current standards. If you were being discharged today with an honorable or general discharge with the same infractions in your records, the upgrade will probably be granted.

Voluntary Separations

If you are joining the service today, you won't qualify for the Voluntary Separation Incentive or the Special Separation Benefit. But the law that created them isn't dead. It is only sleeping.

These benefits were added in the 1990s when the military was going through a post–Cold War "drawdown." People who were "downsized" were asked to take voluntary discharges. That made them eligible for special separation pay. They are also entitled to commissary privileges, and can visit clinics on military bases. They are also still eligible for all the other basic veterans' benefits.

At the moment, there isn't any military drawdown looming on the horizon. But there is no way of knowing whether it will happen again during your military career. Keep in mind that if you get hit with one, the landing is going to be soft.

Military Retirees

"All the sugar is at the bottom of the cup," they say, and it is no more true than in the case of men and women who have retired from a military career.

There are still thousands of World War II veterans enjoying the benefits of their service almost half a century ago.

Generally speaking, the term "retiree" applies to people who have served a 20-year tour of duty. In some cases, though, it is possible to qualify after just 15 years in uniform. But that isn't automatic. The shorter term is based on a long list of qualifying factors.

Those with shorter terms get smaller retirement checks, but every career retiree can expect ...

- ◆ A final physical and dental checkup.
- ◆ Paid time off for job hunting or house hunting.
- ◆ Job counseling.
- ◆ Cash payment for unused leave time.
- ◆ Moving expenses to anywhere you want to go.
- ◆ Unemployment compensation in most states.
- ◆ GI Bill educational benefits.
- ◆ GI Bill home loans.
- ◆ Low-cost life insurance.
- ◆ On-base medical care.
- ◆ VA medical care.
- ◆ Lifetime commissary privileges (for spouses and children, too).
- ◆ Small business loans.

Retirees are also generally eligible for veterans retirement homes and burial in national cemeteries, a right that also extends to their spouses and children.

Tip

For more than a century the government has provided for elderly veterans at the U.S. Soldiers and Airmen's Home in Washington, DC, and the U.S. Naval Home at Gulfport, Mississippi. Both provide a complete range of medical and recreational facilities. Each of them accepts veterans from every branch of the military, including the Coast Guard, and each accepts women veterans as well as men.

To be accepted, veterans must have served in an enlisted capacity or as a warrant officer during their entire career, a minimum of 20 years. They must be at least 60 years old and have a service-connected disability. Those with disabilities not connected to military service must have served in one of the country's wars. Their spouses don't qualify for admission, but there are dozens of similar facilities across the country that fill the gap. Most of them are also open to widows and widowers of veterans.

Health Care

The Department of Veterans Affairs runs the biggest medical care program in the country. There are more than 175 VA medical centers and more than 800 clinics. You'll find them in every state.

In the rare event that they can't handle your medical problem, you can use your health-care benefits at a private hospital. But it is far more likely that it will be those civilian institutions referring their special cases to VA hospitals, rather than vice versa.

Basically, the system is in place to care for veterans with service-related medical problems or those who are too poor to pay for medical care. But its services are available to all veterans, usually for a nominal fee. You'll find the fee laughably low compared to the co-payments private health insurers ask you to cough up.

Any honorably discharged veteran with at least two years of service, or a member of the National Guard or reserves who was called for active duty, can enroll in the VA health care program. The number of people who have taken advantage of it has been growing by leaps and bounds, as private doctors have been refusing to accept elderly patients on Medicare. HMOs have been abandoning retirees as well, and many company-sponsored health plans have increased the cost for retirees beyond their ability to pay for it.

Because of that, the VA has become the health provider of last resort for retired people who have served in the military. The number has doubled since the mid-1990s to about six million today. It's a safety net that doesn't exist for those without military service in their past.

The rules are constantly changing, but for a snapshot of what medical benefits are available right now, log on to the VA's website at www.va.gov.

Pensions

Chances are that by the time you are ready to retire from the military, the way you will calculate your pension will have changed. Congress loves to tinker with programs like this.

Its latest tinkering, the Fiscal 2000 Defense Authorization Bill, made it necessary to have a calculator handy to figure out what your pension will be. Before then, it was a pretty simple formula: Serve for 20 years, retire, and start collecting half of your base pay.

The new plan, called High-3, gives you a better bottom line, but arriving at it is almost as complicated as filling out an income tax return. It applies to everyone who has entered the service after September 8, 1980.

To figure it out, you start by multiplying your years of service by your base pay when you retire. But your base pay isn't the amount you collected during your last month. It is an average of your highest 36 months of active duty pay. You will receive 55 percent of that amount as your pension.

Your basic pay in the military, by the way, is more than just your salary. Usually called regular military compensation (RMC), it is the total of your salary, your cash or in-kind allowances for housing and subsistence, and other allowances. Not all of your RMC counts, but a 20-year retiree can use nearly 70 percent of it for the calculation.

After you start collecting your pension, you will get regular cost-of-living adjustments along the way. Unlike the cost of living adjustments you get while you are serving, which are based on government estimates of general salary levels, your pension will go up according to the annual Consumer Price Index. But your actual increase will be 1 percent less than the index.

Not Your Average Retirement Plan

The basic difference between civilian and military pensions is vesting. In a civilian job, you are eligible to collect retirement benefits if you stay on the job for a minimum number of years, whether you stay until retirement age or not.

In the Army and the Navy, you are considered retired after serving for 20 years. If you walk out the door even a couple of days before your time is up, your pension will be reduced.

The Navy and Marine Corps don't consider their members retirees until they've put in 30 years. But 20-year veterans are transferred into the reserves, where they collect retainer pay. It's still a pension.

Anyone who retires from any branch of the service is subject to recall to active duty. Even in today's world, when the Guard and reserves have been activated during the war on terrorism, there haven't been many instances of retirees being among them. The exceptions depend on needed skill levels. In any event, the odds of retiree recall are highest during the first five years. After that, they virtually disappear.

 Bet You Didn't Know _____

Although 20 years of service is the traditional benchmark for military retirement, the law was amended in the 1990s to allow a military career to come to an end after just 15 (but less than 20) years. This isn't an option you can ask for. You will be selected on the military's current needs for someone with your rank and skill level. The monthly payment to 15-year retirees is determined by basic pay without other pays such as a housing allowance included.

The rate is based on the average base pay over a three-year period, multiplied by 2.5 percent for each year of service. Then it is reduced by $1/12$ of a percentage point for each month short of 20 years of service. (Remember, these retirement formulas were devised by the same kind of people who write the income tax laws.) Otherwise, 15-year retirees have all the same benefits as people who have put in the additional five years.

Finally, your 20 years of service includes all active service and training. It also includes time in the active reserves.

A New Retirement Choice

The new retirement scheme also gives another option to anyone who joined up after August 1, 1986. It is called REDUX.

It allows you to decide at the 15-year point in your career whether you want to go for the established 20-year retirement program, or take an immediate taxable cash advance of $30,000.

When you actually retire, you will collect in the neighborhood of 43 percent of your highest 36-month pay. Each cost-of-living increase will be reduced by 1 percent, but when you reach the age of 62, those percentage points will be added back.

In order to collect the bonus, you'll need to agree to serve out your 20 years. If you don't, you are going to have to give the money back at the rate of $6,000 a year.

VA Pensions

Many military people sign up for pensions through the Veterans Administration. But they are not for everyone. And they can collect one or the other, but not both. They are intended to offer an option to veterans with special needs.

In general, VA pensions are given to veterans with low incomes or poor health. Their disabilities can't be connected with their military service. Those with service-related problems can collect VA disability compensation. Age isn't a qualifying factor either.

The size of VA pensions varies, and if you have other income, the benefit is reduced dollar for dollar from that other source.

The basic yearly rates are …

- ◆ $9,000—Single, without children.
- ◆ $12,000—With one dependent (spouse or child).
- ◆ $15,000—Without dependents, but unable to care for oneself.
- ◆ $18,000—With one dependent and unable to care for oneself.
- ◆ $11,000—Housebound with no dependents.
- ◆ $14,000—Housebound with one dependent.
- ◆ $12,000—A married couple, both veterans.
- ◆ $1,500—Additional for each child.

The numbers aren't large, pensions rarely are. But they can make all the difference in the world to people who need them.

Life Insurance

Years ago, GI insurance meant term insurance that was in effect for only five years after you left the service. Today, you can keep it going for the rest of your life.

Called Veterans' Group Life Insurance, it is available in any amount, at $10,000 increments, from $10,000 to $250,000. Each block of $10,000 worth of insurance costs 80 cents a month if you are under the age of 29. Even at the age of 50, it is only $6.50 a month for $10,000 worth of coverage. And if you pay annually, you get a discount.

The same low rates apply while you are serving in the military, the reserves, or the National Guard. In that case, the coverage is called Servicemember's Group Life Insurance.

While you are actually serving in the military, you will be able to buy low-cost life insurance under the Servicemember's Group Life plan. When you retire, it becomes known as Veterans' Group Life Insurance. But when you switch, the amount of insurance you can buy can't be more than you had when you were on active duty. The rates are based on blocks of $10,000 worth of coverage, and in 2000, these were the monthly premiums for each block:

- Age 29 or younger—$.80
- Age 30-34—$1.20
- Age 35-39—$1.60
- Age 40-44—$2.40
- Age 45-49—$4.20
- Age 50-54—$6.50
- Age 55-59—$8.80
- Age 60-64—$11.25
- Age 65-69—$15.00
- Age 70-74—$22.50
- Over 75—$45.00

The beneficiary can be anyone you name, even your own estate, and doesn't have to be a relative. And you can change them anywhere along the line.

Home Loans

Most benefits for servicemembers, reservists, and veterans involve direct payments from Uncle Sam. In the case of home loans, all the government does is guarantee that if you default on your mortgage payments, it will cover the lender's loss. The government won't give you money to pay off your mortgage, but because it will step in if you should stop paying, it eliminates the necessity of paying for mortgage insurance (if you put less than 80 percent down on the home).

The lender will have the final say whether you get a mortgage or not, no matter what the government promises. But if you are turned down, the Department of Veterans Affairs will go to bat for you.

There is no time limit on when you can use this benefit, and there isn't any limit on how often you can use it, as long as you don't buy more than one house at a time. Many veterans recently have been using their loan privileges to refinance their homes.

In order to qualify for a government-backed loan, the house itself needs to pass inspection by the VA. Its appraisers will be looking to see if the house is worth its price and what condition it is in. That, by the way, won't guarantee you that you haven't picked a lemon. All that interests the government appraiser is the government's financial risk.

In most cases, VA home loans will be granted without down payments. A down payment might be required for a mobile home or for the land to put one on, or they might be required if the loan is higher than the value of the house. Sometimes a lender might require some money up front, and the government won't stand in its way.

Whether you have to make a down payment or not, you will have to come up with a funding fee to cover the government's costs. It is usually 2 or 3 percent of the mortgage, an amount most lenders will include in the loan for you.

Apart from education benefits, this chance for home ownership is most often cited as the best veteran's benefit the government offers.

The Montgomery GI Bill and Top-Up

If you sign up for a couple of tours of duty, but don't stay in for 20 years to qualify as a retiree, you certainly aren't left out in the cold.

In the first place, if you served on active military duty or in the reserves and have an honorable discharge, you are entitled to the education benefits of the Montgomery GI Bill. Get details on it, and its history in Chapter 6.

You are going to have to sign up in advance for this benefit within your first few weeks of active duty. You won't get a second chance.

After signing up and having $100 deducted from your pay every month for 12 months, you are also going to need to meet one of these requirements:

◆ Three years of continuous service if you originally signed on for three years or longer.

◆ Two years of continuous service if you signed up for a shorter enlistment. Reduced benefits apply.

◆ Continuous service of at least two years, followed by four years in the selected reserves.

Selected reserves are reservists or National Guard members assigned to units and members of the trained manpower pool.

Even without serving on active duty, reservists and guardsmen are eligible for Montgomery GI Bill benefits. While active-duty personnel don't usually use the benefit until after they have left the military, and can take up to 10 years to start, selected reserve eligibility ends when an enlistment period does.

The basic Montgomery benefit varies by length of service:

◆ $536 a month for 36 months after three years of active duty

◆ $536 a month for 36 months after two years of active duty and four years in the selected reserves

◆ $436 a month for less than three years on active duty

People who enlisted in hard-to-fill jobs can collect an additional $5,000, known as a "kicker."

Reservists and guardsmen who don't contribute to the program up front get $255 a month. If they are full-time students, the benefit lasts 36 months.

It isn't possible to double-dip—that is, the government won't pay for the same class more than once. But reservists who also served on active duty can, and often do, use the benefits of both at different times. It's all legitimate, but it has to be done within 48 months.

In order to receive payments under the program, you need to enroll in classes or courses that have been approved. There aren't many restrictions. The approved list includes…

◆ College or university courses leading to associate, bachelor's, or graduate degrees.

◆ Independent study leading to a college degree.

◆ Cooperative training programs.

◆ Certain correspondence courses.

◆ Apprenticeships and on-the-job training.

- Business, technical, or vocational schools.
- Advanced pilot training for veterans with pilots' licenses.

Active-duty personnel who have contributed $1,200 to the Montgomery program during their active-duty service can't get the money refunded if they decide later not to go to college after all.

A new law passed in October 2000 makes it easier to go for your college degree with the Montgomery GI Bill (MGIB) while you're still on active duty. Now the amount of the educational benefit is equal to the difference between the total cost of a college course and the amount of tuition assistance the military had been paying for that course.

In order to qualify, you need to be approved for tuition assistance and also be eligible for benefits under the Montgomery GI Bill. The program, called Top-Up, can kick in after you have served at least two years in any branch of the service.

The actual amount you can get is the same as you would get if regular MGIB benefits were being paid. The difference is that you don't have to wait until you are discharged. If you claim a Top-Up benefit, your Montgomery benefits will be reduced accordingly.

It doesn't apply to members of the selected reserves in the GI Bill program.

Keep an Eye on Those Discharge Papers

Not every veteran is eligible for every available benefit. Some depend on where you served, some on how long, and others on when you were on active duty. Most are keyed to other income you might have. Just about all of them depend on the type of discharge you have.

The rulebooks keep changing, most often for the better. But it will be up to you to keep track of any new wrinkles. Unless the payout on a benefit you're already getting goes up and you start getting bigger checks, no one is going to call you with any good news. It's up to you to keep in touch with them.

In order to qualify for any new benefits—or existing ones, for that matter—you're going to need your discharge papers. It may sound silly to say that you should put them in the safest possible place since they represent 20 years of your life, but you'd be surprised how many people lose track of them. Your family should also know where you put them. They are eligible for military benefits, too.

For insurance, county clerks in most states will file a copy of your discharge papers for you. It doesn't cost anything.

You'll be handed that piece of paper (yes, the "papers" are all on one sheet), technically known as DD Form 214, on your last day in the service. It will be your ticket to *any* veterans' benefit. Although the government already has your records, it insists that you show them the paper before they'll show you the money. It's a way of reducing fraud.

When you become a military veteran, you join the company of such men as Lt. John Finn (USN-Ret.), who earned the Medal of Honor during the 1941 attack on Pearl Harbor.

The Least You Need to Know

- ◆ Military benefits don't stop when you are discharged. When you retire, you are a veteran and eligible for a host of benefits that you didn't qualify for while you were still on active duty.

- ◆ As a military retiree, you'll qualify for such things as medical care and the option to buy a house with no down payment.

- ◆ Nearly all of your needs are taken care of, from housing to hospitalization to nursing home care when you can't take care of yourself.

- ◆ Military retirement benefits keep getting better; the laws are constantly changing to improve the amount of your pension.

- ◆ The government will pay for your college education, after you've served for as few as three years.

Part 4

Life in the Military

Even before you picked up this book, you probably already had a good idea which branch of the service you'd prefer to be part of. But remember, there are five of them.

And keep in mind, too, that some of the things you grew up believing may not be quite true. Not everyone in the Air Force pilots an airplane and not everyone in the Army is an infantryman.

Some of the specialties that may interest you might be available in all five branches of the military. There are other similarities from one branch to another, as well. In many cases, your choice might be based simply on lifestyle. In some, it may come down to jobs open at the time you're job hunting. But before you jump into it, compare the life as well as the opportunities. After all, it's how you're going to be living for a couple of years, at least. There's no reason why you shouldn't enjoy it.

Chapter 11

Making Up Your Mind

In This Chapter

- ◆ Choosing a branch of the service
- ◆ Who's in charge?
- ◆ Civilian jobs in the military
- ◆ Serving your country as well as yourself
- ◆ Military honors

There are five branches of the American military. All but one of them, the Coast Guard, reports to the Department of Defense. A sixth, the Merchant Marine, is under the wing of the Department of Transportation, but it can become an arm of the Navy in time of war. The Coast Guard is also a unit of the Department of Transportation.

Both the Coast Guard and the Merchant Marine are separate from the Pentagon because, technically, neither of them is an integral part of the country's defense system. Both deal with matters of security on the high seas and in coastal waters, and their missions are essentially the same both in peace and war.

The top brass of the other four services are combined under an umbrella organization called the Joint Chiefs of Staff. It is composed of the commander of the Air Force, the chief of naval operations, the Marine Corps commandant, and the Army's chief of staff. Its fifth member, the chairman of the Joint Chiefs, is appointed by the president.

Serve Without Joining Up

The Joint Chiefs' staffs are career military people, of course, but they work side by side with civilian employees of the Department of Defense (DOD).

The DOD has about 800,000 civilian employees. That represents about a quarter of all military-related careers.

The jobs they fill are as wide-ranging as those available to men and women in uniform. They develop and maintain sophisticated computer programs and websites, they are trained to become systems experts, and they take care of the routine business of feeding and housing military personnel. It is usually the civilian employees who make sure that everybody gets paid on time. And they are the ones who keep track of the other benefits that come with putting on a uniform.

Their job classifications include scientists, lawyers, engineers, and linguists. About 75 percent of the DOD's civilian component work for the government in clerical, professional, and administrative capacities.

There are civilian employees assigned to virtually every military installation, both stateside and overseas. (For more details on these opportunities, see Chapter 20.)

Bet You Didn't Know

Just as the term "White House" is interchangeable with the presidency, military pronouncements are often credited to "the Pentagon." More formally, it is the headquarters of the Department of Defense, located across the Potomac River from Washington, D.C. It is an amazing place, with 23,000 employees—a large percentage of men and women who have made the military a career.

The building itself is among the world's biggest office buildings. It is twice as big as the Merchandise Mart in Chicago, and it has three times the floor space of the Empire State Building in New York. The Capitol across the river could fit into any one of its five wedge-shaped sections with room left over. The Pentagon has 17.5 miles of corridors, but you can walk between any two points inside the building in less than seven minutes without breaking into a run.

This model of efficiency was opened in 1943 after just 16 months of construction. The military people who moved into it had been spread out over 17 different buildings in the early years of World War II. The Pentagon was one of the targets in the September 11 terrorist attacks on America, but although a large section of the building was destroyed and hundreds killed or injured, the machinery of the military didn't stop for a second. The war on terrorism that began soon afterward was planned and coordinated in the wounded building.

A Level Playing Field

Civilians working for the military are paid according to salary levels established by the Civil Service Administration, and don't vary within job descriptions across the entire government.

All of the pay scales are the same in all of the branches of the service, too, and most of the jobs available are the same, if not similar, in all of them. You're as likely to become a helicopter pilot in the Coast Guard as in the Air Force, even more likely in the Marines or the Army, both of which have much larger inventories of helicopters. In fact, the Army flies more of them than the entire military components of most NATO countries.

The main differences among the services are their basic missions. The choice you make about which branch of the service you should join is usually entirely personal. For example:

- If you like the idea of being part of an elite fighting force, the Marine Corps might be your best bet.
- If world travel is high on your list, the Navy will take you to places you've been dreaming about.
- For a wider choice of career options, the Army has what may be the most impressive list.

Many people join a branch of the service to follow a family tradition. If your father was in the Air Force, for instance, you're probably leaning in that direction yourself.

Sometimes, the decision can be based on something as simple as how you'll be fed. Navy food seems to have the best reputation, although all the services compete with one another in the quality of their chow. But there is another factor. One recruit said he chose the Navy because he didn't like picnics.

"In the Army or the Marines, you might have to eat your dinner on the ground somewhere," he said, "but in the Navy, you get to sit down at a table."

A silly reason for making the choice? Maybe. But it's as good a one as any. The services are more similar than they are different, and the one you choose is completely up to you—whatever reason you come up with.

Following a Tradition

In spite of the list of benefits—from education to impressive bonuses—that's as long as your arm, a great many people join the military for the same reason men and women always have: to serve their country.

One measure of where you can serve the United States best might be determined by the number of Medal of Honor winners in the history of each branch.

The Army wins that contest hands down. More than 2,300 of its soldiers have won the medal since the Civil War. Many of those went to members of the Army Air Corps in the two world wars, but the Air Force accounts for 16 of the medals on its own. Members of the Navy have been awarded 744 Medals of Honor, and Marines have claimed 300 of them.

The Medal of Honor is granted for "gallantry above and beyond the call of duty." Each of the armed services has its own regulations for qualifying. But in every case, there must be at least two eyewitnesses to an action that clearly represents something much more than ordinary bravery in combat.

The Army and the Air Force, each of which has a separate Medal of Honor, requires recommendations within two years of the date of the deed, and the award must be made within three years. The Navy allows for a little more time. Sometimes, but rarely, exceptions have been made.

The medal is presented by a high official, usually the president himself, "in the name of the Congress of the United States," which is why it is sometimes called the Congressional Medal of Honor.

Apart from the lifetime acclaim that obviously goes with the honor, recipients are also given a special pension. They get free travel on military aircraft and front-row seats at presidential inaugurations. Their children get priority consideration in the competition for acceptance at the service academies.

The Pyramid of Honor

Although soldiers in the Continental Army could earn a medal called the Purple Heart, instituted by George Washington, the American military had no way of recognizing its heroes until 1862, when the Medal of Honor was established for Civil War soldiers and sailors. In the years since, other awards for bravery have been added. Their precedence is represented as a pyramid with the Medal of Honor at its apex. The Purple Heart is awarded to anyone who sustains wounds in battle.

The following is a list of honors for the Army and Air Force:

1. Medal of Honor
2. Distinguished Service Cross/Air Force Cross
3. Distinguished Service Medal
4. Silver Star
5. Superior Service Medal

6. Legion of Merit

7. Distinguished Flying Cross

8. Soldier's Medal/Airman's Medal

9. Bronze Star

10. Meritorious Service Medal

11. Air Medal

12. Army/Air Force Commendation Medal

13. Purple Heart

In Their Footsteps

In the spring of 1968, Marine Captain Jay Vargas and his unit began marching on the Vietnamese village of Dai Do. Enemy fire was intense as they crossed the open field, and most of the officers in the company stationed nearby were killed. A green second lieutenant took charge and barked an order into his radio for Vargas to pull his men back. He chose to ignore the order, and before long, Vargas and his men had taken Dai Do.

Eventually a counterattack pushed the Marines into a graveyard on the other side of the village. They improvised foxholes by pulling bodies from new graves and established a perimeter for the night. At the same time, AC-130 gunships were circling overhead, and artillery shells were exploding all around them. They were in as much danger from friendly fire as from the enemy that had them surrounded. At dawn the next day, they were still pinned down, but Vargas decided that he'd had enough. He launched a counterattack of his own and retook the village. Then the enemy swept in on them from the jungle. The Marines were low on ammunition by then, and they grabbed anything they could find to use as weapons in hand-to-hand fighting.

Captain Vargas was hit by shrapnel and wounded for the third time in the three-day action, but that didn't stop him. When three of his men were wounded, he carried them back behind the lines, although the only weapon he had was a pistol and the enemy was everywhere. During the rest of the day, he fought his way back and forth through enemy lines, getting six more wounded men out. When his Medal of Honor was awarded for his actions at Dai Do, he had his late mother's name, M. Sando Vargas, engraved on the back instead of his own.

The following is a list of honors for the Navy and Marine Corps:

1. Medal of Honor

2. Navy Cross

3. Distinguished Service Medal

4. Silver Star

5. Superior Service Medal

6. Legion of Merit

7. Navy and Marine Corps Medal

8. Bronze Star

9. Meritorious Service Medal

10. Air Medal

11. Navy Commendation Medal

12. Purple Heart

Getting the MOS You Want

Whatever your reason for choosing one branch of the service over another, look before you leap.

Yes, all of the branches are similar. And, yes, the benefits are all pretty much the same. But it is important, even critical, that you check out all of them before you sign an enlistment contract.

The reason for that is a thing called an MOS—your military occupational specialty.

Even more so than choosing a specific branch of the service, the MOS you choose is the most important decision you're going to make when you start out on a military career. And there are plenty of them to choose from—the Army alone offers 212 broad categories, and each of them breaks down into long lists of subdivisions. Altogether, the military offers more than 2,000 different MOSs.

In some cases, the specialty you select may have a big enlistment bonus that goes along with it. Some have a better track record than others in terms of promotion opportunities, too. And some reflect exactly what you think you'd be happiest doing.

Qualifying for one MOS or another starts with your score on the Armed Services Aptitude Battery. Beyond simple aptitude, your experience in a civilian job might be what it takes. Your education, even if you've just taken a course or two after high school, can count as well.

But suppose, for instance, that you want to get military training in advanced telecommunications. You may qualify based on your ASVAB score. You may have worked as a computer programmer, and you might even have a college degree in the field. It is a field of obvious importance to all the branches of the service. They should be begging for you to sign up, right? Maybe not.

Getting the MOS you want is sometimes a matter of getting in line for it. It all depends on the number of openings there are when you go down to the recruiting office. You could sign up with the delayed entry option and wait for up to a year for an opening. But you're not guaranteed that one is going to come along.

Your best option would be to check out the other branches. One of them might have a shorter waiting list. Or none at all. Like everything else, it's largely a matter of being in the right place at the right time.

If you qualify for an MOS that one of the services considers important enough to offer special incentives to fill, chances are pretty good that they will have openings. But don't count on it as a guarantee.

Don't count, either, on signing up for a related job in hopes that the one you really want is going to come along later on. A recruiter might guarantee you a choice of a military occupation, and most of the time the promise will be kept. But there are no guarantees beyond the original commitment. Yes, you might get lucky. But the military is no place to trust to luck.

Assume Nothing

There are so many job opportunities throughout the military that you can pretty much take your pick. Getting what you want is a matter of your qualifications, and sometimes they may not be as obvious as you think.

You need to consider the assets you can bring to the job. Signing up for the military is no time for modesty.

Think about the things you've done and the things you want to do, and you may be surprised at how you might look through a recruiter's eyes. Like any other job you apply for, or anything else you do in life, for that matter, all anybody knows about you is what you tell them. Don't lie, but don't overlook anything, either. You don't always know exactly what people are looking for. And you don't usually think of little things that may turn out to be important.

You may be surprised to find out what a real catch you are as far as the military is concerned. And how it may pay off big time in the MOS they're willing to offer you.

If you slept your way through high school and spent all of your spare time lost in the world of computer games, what do you think your prospects might be against the guy who quarterbacked the football team and got straight A's in every class?

The logical answer is that he ought to be far, far ahead of you in the pecking order—but in reality, you might be in a position to leave him in the dust. It's because of those computer games. Your parents probably nagged at you to give them up for something more productive, but then, they didn't have the whole picture.

In today's military, there is more need for recruits who have developed the nearly perfect hand-eye coordination that you get by playing computer games. The computerized nature of modern warfare has made it a much bigger asset than physical endurance.

The military still needs jocks, to be sure, but right now, they're looking for a few good nerds as well. And some of the most interesting MOSs are wide open for people who have gathered their skills down at the video arcade.

The important point is that you never know what's important. Before you go for an interview, whether it's with a military recruiter or a corporate human resources manager, make a list of your good points. Then make another one of your bad points. Take both lists with you because there may be things on that second list that aren't so bad after all.

The Least You Need to Know

- The uniformed services are more alike than different. The pay scales are the same and many of the specialties are the same, too. The difference is in their individual missions and how they appeal to you.

- You can serve the military without actually enlisting. There are thousands of civilian jobs available, and they exist on virtually every military installation around the world.

- Benefits aside, patriotism is still important. Serving your country in these times may be the best statement you can make about what America means to you.

- You need to choose your military job carefully. You are going to be working at least for a couple of years, and given the number of choices you have, there isn't any reason why you shouldn't be happy doing it.

- If you've been thinking that a military career is just for jocks, you're dead wrong. Those ex-football players are still in demand, but even more-so are people who have developed skills with such things as computer games.

This Man's Army

In This Chapter

- ◆ The biggest and oldest of the uniformed services
- ◆ How life in the Army has changed
- ◆ Opportunities within opportunities
- ◆ How the Army is structured
- ◆ A preview of your days as a soldier

Considering the amounts of money in base pay, benefits, and bonuses that recruits can expect to collect in today's Army, it is hard to believe that they originally had to struggle along without pay. They even had to supply their own uniforms and rifles.

It wasn't as though the Continental Congress didn't have the best of intentions. They knew it was going to take money to fight a revolution. In fact, they appropriated $2 million to do the job.

Paul Revere engraved the printing plates, and Benjamin Franklin headed a committee that signed each of the notes individually. The problem was that the money wasn't worth the paper it was printed on. The British were amused, but the minutemen were not. But the cause was worth more to them than money, and the fledgling U.S. Army went to war anyway.

The Army was officially organized in June 1775, by incorporating the Massachusetts Militia as the core of the Continental Army. George Washington, a member of Congress, was unanimously elected its commander in chief. He agreed to serve without pay (as if he had an option).

Washington's command was bolstered with four major generals and eight brigadier generals. Their troops consisted of 16,000 men. Other colonies augmented the force and together they fought, and won, the Revolutionary War. Then, after it was over in 1783, everybody went home. America had no army. But it did have local militias, and they were called back whenever the country was threatened.

Before the outbreak of the Civil War, the number of available troops was still hovering at around 16,000. But as the U.S. Army became the Union Army during the war between the states, the number went up to well over a million.

The Army was completely reorganized in 1903 with the establishment of a general staff and a new emphasis on officer training. During previous wars, experienced officers from professional armies in Europe had been hired to serve as advisers.

In 1914, before America became involved in World War I, the Army's strength had reached 98,000, nearly half of whom were stationed overseas. The National Guard, 27,000 strong, kept things quiet on the home front.

The Draft

In the 1860s, troops had been raised for the Union Army through conscription. It was a polite name for compulsory military service, but it became an unpopular word because of a loophole in the law that allowed anyone who could afford it to pay someone to take his place. When it reappeared again in 1917, the word for it was changed to "draft," which comes from a term used by the British military to describe transferring soldiers from one unit to another. When it was brought back, it was to tap the civilian population to provide troops for the Allied expeditionary force fighting World War I in France. About 4 million men were drafted at that time, and nearly half of them went overseas. As had happened before, the draft was eliminated at the end of the war.

The draft was instituted again in 1940, and before the attack on Pearl Harbor a year later, the Army's ranks had swelled to 1.4 million. By the time the war ended in 1945, the number had reached 8.3 million.

The Army's size shrunk again when peace returned, but in 1950, it grew back to 1.5 million during the Korean War. Ten years later, the Vietnam War brought the number back up to that same level, mostly thanks to the draft, which was still in effect even though World War II had ended. Typically, as the largest of the services, the Army usually gets the lion's share of draftees.

Then, in 1973, the draft was phased out again. Young men between the ages of 18 and 25 are still required to sign up for draft cards, but they aren't subject to any call-up.

Although there is talk every now and then about bringing conscription back, largely on the part of people in government who feel it is more cost-effective than offering recruiting bonuses and other benefits, it would take an act of Congress and the president's approval to make it happen.

> **Tip**
>
> During the 1990s, the military went through what was called a "drawdown." Roughly comparable to corporate downsizing, it resulted in the closing of some bases and early retirement packages for some people with long terms of service. Also like corporate downsizing, it was a way of eliminating some nonproductive personnel. Yes, they existed in the Army, too.
>
> The end result was the creation of the most professional Army that America has ever seen. There are about 484,000 men and women on active duty today. Every one of them is a well-trained specialist.

Not Your Father's Army

Even soldiers who served in Vietnam wouldn't recognize the Army of today. The structure may be about the same, and the tradition hasn't changed, but attitudes and weapons systems have.

Most important, there are more and better opportunities. Today's soldiers aren't very likely to be surprised where they'll wind up after Basic Training. Recruits have a say about how they'll serve out their enlistment. Years ago, you would have been sent wherever there happened to be an opening. Today, the soldier calls the tune.

Different Ways to Be a Soldier

In its advertising, the Army says that there are 212 ways to be a soldier. That's the number of military occupational specialties it offers. They are conveniently arranged under eight general headings:

In Their Footsteps

In a *New York Times* interview, Peter E. Breen, the CEO of an online brokerage firm, said that running a company isn't a whole lot different from his experience running an Army platoon as a first lieutenant. "This city eats people for breakfast," he said of New York. "But I've never felt cowed. In the Army, after soldiers receive a mission, they accomplish that mission come what may."

- **Administrative Services.** Jobs dealing with personnel, administration, legal and information services, and finance. The category includes clerical as well as supervisory jobs.

- **Combat Operations.** Covering reconnaissance, security, and other duties in combat situations. Most, but not all, of these jobs are closed to women.

- **Electronic Maintenance.** Jobs in this classification provide support for the Army's electronics, equipment maintenance, and systems. (Refer to Chapter 21 for more information.)

- **Engineering and Construction.** The category includes technical and structural development and maintenance of buildings, facilities, and combat equipment. The available jobs range from architectural support to plumbing and carpentry.

- **Health Care.** Jobs in the medical and dental field, including veterinarians, some of whom work in clinical settings and others in field situations. (Refer to Chapter 17 for more information.)

- **Intelligence and Electronic Communications.** These jobs deal with participation in the collection and analysis of military intelligence. Some of them involve electronic and psychological warfare.

- **Media, Public, and Civil Affairs.** Jobs that fill the need for communications both within the Army and through civilian media. This classification also includes military musical bands, where there are more openings than you might expect.

- **Transportation and Supply Services.** Jobs that meet the challenge of the movement of personnel, equipment, and supplies everywhere in the world.

Digging Into the Lists

Each of those broad categories has a breakdown of subspecialties within it. In many cases, there are also different available jobs related to those.

For instance, under the administration MOS, the opportunities include legal specialist, administrative specialist, chaplain assistant, finance specialist, accounting specialist, personnel administration specialist, personnel information system management specialist, and personnel services specialist.

In any corporation, any one of those jobs would constitute a career path. The fact is, in some corporations they may be the only jobs available outside the executive suite to keep the company running.

It's pretty easy to figure out for yourself what most of the jobs might be. But there is one that may seem to be unique to the military: chaplain assistant. You're not very likely to find a chaplain on any corporate table of organization, but you'll find several of them on every Army post. But what, exactly, does a chaplain assistant do?

It's one of the most people-oriented jobs the Army has to offer. It is related to some jobs in churches and synagogues in the civilian world, but with some important, and fascinating, differences.

The duties within the specialty listed as MOS-71M are officially described as follows: "… performs and provides specified elements of religious support mission in deployments, combat operations, training, and sustainment."

Yes. Well, what's that supposed to mean?

As is the case with job descriptions anywhere, they are purposely left a bit vague to allow more flexibility and to prevent someone from refusing to do something because "it's not in my job description." Of course, an argument like that would never hold water in the Army, but you ought to find out as much as you can about what any job involves before you sign up for it.

Tip

No organization in the civilian world, from the corner drug store to General Motors can function for long without job descriptions. They are the glue that holds business plans together. Even if you work weekends flipping burgers at McDonald's, chances are that your manager will have a written description of what the job entails, from the frequency of the flips to the size of the burgers. There's a page that describes what the manager should be doing, too. You don't always hear about them until somebody decides you're not doing your job by the book, and tries to throw the book at you.

In the military, though, they are upfront about job descriptions. When you ask a recruiter about a specialty, you'll probably be handed a piece of paper that purports to explain it. But like job descriptions in the civilian world, they aren't always easy to understand when you first read them. They are a good starting point for compiling lists of questions to ask. So always ask to see the job description for any MOS that might interest you. Then read between the lines and start asking questions.

Go Beyond the Job Descriptions

You should always try to read between the lines of MOS job descriptions, even the ones that seem to be obvious. Recruiters have most of them at their fingertips, and many are detailed on the Army's recruiting website: www.GOARMY.com. That same website, by the way, also has a chat room where you can ask questions and get answers in real time.

In the case of that one on MOS-71M, the job of chaplain assistant is far more interesting than its description. The same is true of most of the jobs the Army offers. If you can't figure one out, ask the recruiter. Sometimes they don't know, either. But they do know how to find out.

They will expect you to tell them why you think you are qualified for a job. You have a right to expect them to tell you how a job qualifies for you.

Digging into the duties of a chaplain assistant, to continue our example, will tell you that the essence of the job is coordinating the unit's religious ministry. That ranges from organizing church services to crisis intervention. In combat situations, it ranges from saving lives to improving morale.

The job involves many of the responsibilities that civilian clergy usually reserve for themselves. It generally has more direct people contact than comparable jobs in religious institutions.

Chaplain assistants deal with soldiers' families, too. And civilian visitors to an Army post often meet a chaplain assistant before they talk with anyone else. Except, possibly, the MP at the gate.

In many ways, this is as much a public relations job as almost any listed under the category of media, public, and civil affairs.

Choosing the Right Branch

Many of the specialties the Army offers are duplicated over several different branches, each with its own mission. That gives you a bigger pool to choose from than you might have thought.

Those branches, and the divisions within them are explained in the following sections:

Combat Arms

- ◆ **Airborne.** The guys who jump out of airplanes and into battle. The elite of the infantry, Airborne requires a separate round of Basic Training on top of the one everybody goes through. Not for everyone, but a source of special pride.

- ◆ **Air Defense Artillery.** Including missile defense systems. Special training takes place at Fort Bliss, Texas.

- ◆ **Armor.** Your grandfather called this the Cavalry. But now the horses are under the hoods of sophisticated and powerful tanks and other armored vehicles as well as artillery and even air cavalry. The Army's Armor Center is at Fort Knox, Kentucky.

- ◆ **Aviation.** Including aircraft pilots, mechanics, and air traffic controllers. Many of its missions involve logistics and military intelligence. Its base is Fort Rucker, Alabama.

- ◆ **Corps of Engineers.** Usually, the engineers are the first in and last out in a battle situation. They are as likely to demolish bridges as to build them. They are responsible for establishing minefields and breaching the enemy's. They build fortifications, roads, and airfields. And they get involved in such peacetime activities as building dikes and rebuilding beaches. Its various missions are coordinated from several different bases.

◆ **Field Artillery.**   The Army's fire-support branch, Artillery uses cannons, rockets, and missiles to get the job done. Its base is at Fort Sill, Oklahoma.

◆ **Infantry.**   Still the Army's backbone, the foot soldier has been making a difference since the days of the Roman Legions. The modern infantryman, though, is quite likely to be in contact with the rest of his unit with a handheld computer. The infantry school is at Fort Benning, Georgia.

◆ **Rangers.**   These units date back to colonial times when militiamen fought with guerrilla-style tactics adopted from those used by the Indians. In modern wars, they conduct reconnaissance, lightning raids, and ambushes. To join them, it is necessary to complete Airborne training as well as the special Ranger schools. The Rangers train at various bases.

◆ **Special Forces.**   Wearing the Army's green beret is a sign that you are a very special individual. It isn't easy to get one. In addition to a list of tough mental and physical requirements, you need to volunteer for Airborne training and then go on to the JFK Warfare Center at Fort Bragg, North Carolina. It makes Army Basic seem like a Sunday school picnic. In addition to the tough physical training, the courses there include foreign languages, strategic reconnaissance, direct action, and counterterrorism. The training ranges from jungle to arctic warfare. By the time you put on the green beret, you're ready for anything.

Combat Support

◆ **Chemical Corps.**   This outfit, which is part of the Soldier and Biological Chemical Defense Command at the Aberdeen Proving Grounds in Maryland, is responsible for nuclear, biological, chemical, smoke, and flame operations.

◆ **Signal Corps.**   Communications is at the heart of any military operation, and the Signal Corps uses the most up-to-the-minute electronics to do the job. It operates switching centers and satellite terminals as well as radio relay stations. The Signal Corps is also involved in the development and testing of missile guidance systems, lasers, and computer hardware. Its headquarters is at Fort Gordon, Alabama.

◆ **Military Intelligence Corps.**   This is one of the Army's biggest branches, with 30,000 members serving in all parts of the world. They are involved with such things as radio interception and direction finding, computer analysis, digital imagery, and satellite transmission. The eyes and ears of the Army is headquartered at Fort Huachuca, Arizona.

◆ **Military Police Corps.**   Much more than an ordinary police force, these people can be found behind the lines in every combat operation where they supervise troop movements. In peacetime, they are charged with criminal investigation, crime prevention, and security. They are also in the forefront of counterterrorism. The MP school is at Fort Leonard Wood, Missouri. (Refer to Chapter 19 for more information.)

Bet You Didn't Know _____

During World War II, special forces served in Europe as part of the Office of Strategic Services, the forerunner of the Central Intelligence Agency. Most of them worked in France and Belgium, and began wearing berets like the local members of the Resistance. The color green became standard in the 1950s, following a tradition that had been established by the World War II British Commandos. The black beret, now the standard headgear Army-wide, was first worn in armored divisions.

Because they are brimless, berets are ideal for fire control sights, which allow tankers to aim their cannons from inside the vehicles without running the risk of popping their head out of the tanks and armored vehicles. The color black is perfect because it hides grease stains. Airborne troops wear maroon berets, and Ranger outfits have switched from black to tan.

Combat Service Support

◆ **Adjutant General's Corps.**   This group has responsibility for the Army's personnel management. It works on unit readiness, morale, and career satisfaction for individual soldiers. The AG Corps is involved in every step of a soldier's career from enlistment through retirement. It solves problems, and works to prevent them. The AG school is at Fort Jackson, South Carolina.

◆ **Army Medical Specialist Corps.**   Members of this group are assigned to all of the Army's medical centers and hospitals. They serve as occupational therapists, dietitians, and physical therapists. Their main base is Walter Reed Army Medical Center in Washington, D.C.

◆ **Army Nurse Corps.**   Most members of the Nurse Corps, because of their civilian training, join the Army as officers. They concentrate on actually taking care of patients instead of nonprofessional chores, and the variety of cases is much broader than in civilian hospitals. An Army nurse can serve anywhere in the world, and can change assignments without losing seniority. The Nurse Corps' main facility is the Walter Reed Army Medical Center.

- **Chaplain Corps.**   Army chaplains represent more than 100 different faiths. They minister to both soldiers and their families. After having been endorsed by their denominations, chaplains usually serve with the rank of captain. You'll find at least one chaplain on every Army post.

- **Dental Corps.**   Made up of doctors of dental surgery and doctors of dental medicine, the Dental Corps takes care of all of the Army's preventive and surgical dental needs. Sometimes soldiers fear them, sometimes they love them; it all depends on the toothache. The Dental Corps is based at Fort Sam Houston in Texas.

- **Finance Corps.**   As the name suggests, this division keeps track of payrolls, travel expenses, bonuses, and special allowances. It also oversees payments to civilian suppliers. In combat situations, the Finance Corps makes sure that troops in the field are never short of supplies. The Army's Finance School is at Fort Jackson, South Carolina.

- **Judge Advocate General Corps.**   Providing basic legal services, not just for the Army but for individual soldiers, judge advocates serve both as defense attorneys and prosecutors in military courts. They also practice in state and federal courts on behalf of Army personnel, retirees, and their families.

- **Medical Corps.**   Army physicians handle every facet of medical care. Qualified doctors who join say that they find the work more interesting than private practice. They also like the idea of getting a paid vacation, and most breathe a sigh of relief when they discover that they don't need to pay malpractice insurance premiums, which are going up all the time and already cost many thousands of dollars a year.

- **Medical Service Corps.**   This group, which serves Army personnel, their families, and retirees, is composed of pharmacists, optometrists, and podiatrists. Its ranks also include other medical sciences as well as administration and supply personnel. Its school is at Fort Sam Houston in Texas.

- **Ordnance Corps.**   These are the people who develop and purchase the Army's weapons systems, from ammunition to missiles, to every conceivable type of vehicle, from humvees to half-tracks. Ordnance is so large, it is divided into several units: Tank/Automotive, Missile/Electronic, Munitions Management, and Explosive Disposal. Its headquarters are at the Aberdeen Proving Grounds in Maryland.

- **Quartermaster Corps.**   Everybody knows that an Army travels on its stomach, and buying food is one of the main jobs of the Quartermaster Corps. It is also responsible for buying all of the petroleum products the Army needs, as well as spare parts and weapons systems. The Quartermaster School is at Fort Lee, Virginia.

- **Transportation Corps.**   Delivering the goods is the basic mission of the Transportation Corps. And there is no limit to the ways they do it. They use trucks, ships, planes, and trains. During the war in Afghanistan, they also used mules, just as their predecessors did generations ago. The Army's Transportation School is at Fort Eustis, Virginia.

◆ **Veterinary Corps.** In an Army that concentrates on electronics, heavy-duty equipment, and aircraft, there wouldn't seem to be much of a future for a horse doctor. But there is. There are laboratory animals to care for, and the dogs who serve the K-9 corps need attention, too. More important, vets serve as food inspectors and nutritionists, as well. And they are in the forefront of preventative medicine. They are also on call for the benefit of the pets that Army families love.

In Their Footsteps

At the height of the Meuse-Argonne campaign during World War I, the First and Second Battalions of the 308th Infantry, along with two companies of the 306th Machine Gun Battalion and a company of the 307th Infantry, were ordered into the forest where the First Army was pinned down. They went down in Army history as the "Lost Battalion." The force was much larger than a battalion but, then again, they weren't "lost" either. Their buddies knew exactly where they were. The problem was that nobody could get to them.

Within an hour or two of their assault, the three-pronged attack fell apart and the flanking units fell behind. That left the men in the middle trapped in a ravine with no support and enemy troops on every side. They dug in for a long siege, even though they were only armed with light weapons that would have been appropriate for their planned mission. They had only one-day's rations, and they didn't have any warm clothing either. The nearest water was a half-mile away, on the other side of German-held territory.

Planes that went out to help were shot down. Food that was dropped fell into the enemy's hands. Casualties were high, but there were no medics to help. The Germans called for their surrender early on the fifth day, but the commander, Major Charles Whittlesey, ignored them. His men also ignored the heavy bombardment that followed. Their agony ended that same day when an American patrol made its way into the ravine.

Of the 600 men who had taken cover there, 170 were dead and another 200 wounded. But the rest survived, and that was the important thing. Major Whittlesey and Captain George McMurtry were both awarded Medals of Honor for the leadership that prevented the total loss of the Lost Battalion.

Dividing It Up

You're part of a team in the Army, and the team is divided into a bunch of components:

◆ A *squad* is usually made up of 10 enlisted personnel under a staff sergeant.

◆ A *platoon* consists of four squads under a lieutenant.

◆ A *company* is four platoons with a headquarters section headed by a captain.

◆ In armored units, a company is called a troop, and in the artillery, a *battery*.

- The *headquarters* section is the administrative arm of the unit, usually connected to anything above the level of a company.

- A *battalion* is four or more companies, with a headquarters section, commanded by a lieutenant colonel.

- In armored units, a battalion is referred to as a *squadron*.

- Three or more battalions form a *brigade*, under a colonel.

- Three brigades, along with various support units, headed by a major general, are a *division*.

- Two or more divisions, with corps support forms an *army corps*, led by a lieutenant general.

- A *field army* is composed of two or more corps, and is commanded by a general.

The Pecking Order

The first thing you'll learn in the Army is to salute everybody. As time goes by, and you advance through the ranks, it will only be necessary to salute people who outrank you.

This list of ranks, from top to bottom, also includes the rating system that goes with them, expressed as sequences of letters and numbers after each one. That tells you how much everybody gets paid. For the actual pay scale, which varies according to length of service, log on to www.defenselink.mil/specials/militarypay2002.

Commissioned Officers

- General (O-10)
- Lieutenant General (O-9)
- Major General (O-8)
- Brigadier General (O-7)
- Colonel (O-6)
- Lieutenant Colonel (O-5)
- Major (O-4)
- Captain (O-3)
- First Lieutenant (O-2)
- Second Lieutenant (O-1)

Enlisted

- ◆ Sergeant Major (E-9)
- ◆ Master Sergeant (Command E-8)
- ◆ First Sergeant (E-8)
- ◆ Sergeant First Class (E-7)
- ◆ Staff Sergeant (Command E-6)
- ◆ Specialist Sixth Class (E-6)
- ◆ Sergeant (Command E-5)
- ◆ Specialist Fifth Class (E-5)
- ◆ Corporal (Command E-4)
- ◆ Specialist Fourth Class (E-4)
- ◆ Private First Class (E-3)
- ◆ Private (E-2)
- ◆ Private (E-1)

Warrant Officer

- ◆ Chief Warrant Officer (WO-5)
- ◆ Chief Warrant Officer Four (WO-4)
- ◆ Chief Warrant Officer Three (WO-3)
- ◆ Chief Warrant Officer Two (WO-2)
- ◆ Warrant Officer (WO-1)

Special Specialties—Warrant Officers

The designation of warrant officer has existed in the military since the Napoleonic wars. The American Army didn't institute the rank until the 1980s.

Warrant officers are technical experts who manage complex battle systems and special training. They have the status of commissioned officers, but they don't usually get involved in command and staff positions.

Warrant officers concentrate on specific career fields. They may be involved as trainers or they may manage technical systems. But whatever their specialty, they stick with it, and advance within it for their entire military career.

A career like this begins with graduation from a warrant officer candidate school at Fort Rucker, Alabama. In order to qualify in the first place, a candidate needs to demonstrate a level of competence, through experience and education. It is the military's version of professional graduate school.

Up to Your Neck in Sergeants

When you report for duty in the Army, a sergeant will take control of your life. And it doesn't end when Basic Training does. As long as you are an enlisted soldier, there will be a sergeant watching over you.

What may surprise you, though, is that not all sergeants are equal. It takes all kinds to run an army:

- *Command sergeant majors* are at the top of the list. They are responsible for making sure that everybody is singing from the same songbook. They keep an eye on performance standards, training, appearance, and conduct of all enlisted personnel. That includes other sergeants, too. Sergeant majors generally operate without any direct supervision. They make their own decisions—but they are expected to make only right ones.

- *First sergeants* take charge of individual units. They direct formations, supervise platoon sergeants, assist in training on every level, and directly advise the commander. The title of address for these people, by the way, is not "sergeant," but "*first* sergeant." Unless you love doing push-ups, you'd better get that straight right away.

- *Master sergeants* are the first-line high-level noncommissioned officers. Leadership goes with the job, but they don't have as many direct supervisory responsibilities as first sergeants do.

- *Sergeant first class* is the rank assigned to platoon sergeants. They may have several staff sergeants working under them. They serve as assistants and advisers to platoon leaders. Sometimes they may even assume command themselves. This is the first level where the term "senior NCO" applies. Generally, people holding the rank have 15 or more years of Army experience behind them.

- *Staff sergeants* are responsible for the performance of sergeants under them, as well as for the large number of soldiers and equipment that those sergeants are charged with.

- *Sergeants* are responsible for making sure that every member of their unit is properly trained for the MOS they signed up for. They are also responsible for all property issued to soldiers in their unit. They are expected to know where every member of their unit is and what they are doing, 24 hours a day, seven days a week.

◆ *Corporal* is the NCO level below sergeant, a rank that has existed in the Army since George Washington was in command. Corporals usually serve as team leaders; you might call them assistant sergeants. In spite of its long history, the rank of corporal seems to be disappearing. During the Vietnam Era, the Army established the NCO Candidate Course, whose graduates are promoted directly to sergeant or staff sergeant.

Starting at the Bottom

Unless you go into the Army as a commissioned officer with a college degree or through an ROTC program, you'll be a buck private for a while. But that's just an entry-level designation.

After you graduate from the nine weeks of Army Basic Training, you'll go right on to Advanced Individual Training (AIT) and your life will start to seem normal again. AIT is where you will acquire the skills in the MOS you chose when you signed up. Most programs last eight or nine weeks, but some can take as long as a year.

During that time, you'll be a student and your life won't be much different than it was at any other school you've been to. Classes are smaller, and you'll get more one-on-one attention, but the big difference will be in the teaching methods. Unlike many of the schools you've attended, the military's teachers know what they know from personal experience and not things they have learned from books. The teaching aids, including multimedia tools, are much better than anything you've probably seen before. It makes learning easier. The equipment you'll use is up-to-the-minute, too. Much of the work involves hands-on training.

Your Contract

You can call them enlistment papers if you want to, but the Army calls the piece of paper you sign at the recruiting office a contract. It is a legal document that generally obligates the Army to all the things it said it would do in terms of your MOS, your rating, your pay, and any cash bonuses that were promised up front.

There is wiggle room in there for the Army, though if conditions change, it has the right to change its mind. But it doesn't happen very often.

You, on the other hand, are bound to every word of the contract, so carefully read it from start to finish before you sign it. You won't get a chance to change your mind. If fact, you can go to prison if you violate the length of service terms.

Your New Life

If your vision of Army life is all rigid regimentation, get over it. You can expect some regimentation, to be sure. The military invented the word, after all. You'll have to account for where you've been and where you're going on any given day. And some days, you're going to be told where to go.

Day-to-day life in the Army may be a bit more formal than where you grew up. Officers expect to be saluted. They expect to be called "sir" or "ma'am," too. You're expected to be respectful, not just to your superiors, but to everyone else as well. You can expect respect in return.

The Army frowns on sudden impulses to go hang out at the mall or to go fishing on the first nice day of spring. But it doesn't keep its soldiers in cages either.

You will get time off. Lots of it. You're entitled to a month's vacation right away. That's something unheard of in a regular job. You'll get holidays and weekends to yourself, too. Naturally, the Army itself runs 24 hours a day, 7 days a week. But if you work on a weekend or a holiday, you'll get time off for it. Sound too good to be true? Well it is. The work schedule is just one of the pleasant surprises you're going to find in Army life.

In most civilian jobs, you're expected to be on hand from nine in the morning until five in the afternoon. But they don't tell you about overtime. Some companies will pay you for it, some won't, but most expect it of you. And it often comes along when you least expect it. Some bosses seem to think it's fun to ask you to come in early or stay late when they know you've made other plans.

An Organized Life

That's the good part about Army regimentation. You know when your day will begin, and you know when it will end. You know exactly how much spare time you'll have at the end of the day to take a college course or just take a break.

In nearly every Army job, you'll work five eight-hour days a week. A small percentage of jobs might require you to work weekends or nights, but even those don't demand more than 40 hours a week. The rest of the time is your own.

Come as You Are

You'll have to wear a uniform while you're on duty. But you'll probably look good in it, anyway. And it's given to you free.

You can wear civilian clothes during your off-duty time. And you're going to be pleasantly surprised at the discounts you'll get when you buy them at the PX.

Not every Army base has a barracks complex like this one at Fort Lewis, Washington, but most have upgraded their facilities, and more are in the planning stage.

The Army does expect you to be well dressed and well groomed all the time. If your idea of that is cut-offs and sweatshirts, you'd better start reading some fashion magazines. Casual is fine, extremes are not.

You can have your own car in the Army, too. Parking is free. And it's secure. A bunch of tough MPs will keep an eye on it for you.

Until you get a permanent assignment, there isn't any need to change you car's registration from your home address. Obviously, though, you will need to be careful to obey the local and vehicle and traffic laws wherever you are. If your driving gets you in trouble, you aren't just going to deal with the local police, but the military police as well. And violations will appear on your military record as well as on your drivers' license. That can come back to haunt you when you go for a promotion or a transfer.

A Place to Live

Everyone in the Army gets free housing. Single soldiers with a rank above sergeant first class can live off-post and get a housing allowance to make it possible.

If you are married, you can live in special on-post furnished housing. Under a new program that was begun in 2000, new houses are being built by the hundreds on Army bases all over the country. Old houses are being renovated under the same program. All these new homes are built to commercial standards with such features as double sinks in the bathrooms and fully equipped laundry rooms.

The neighborhoods behind the main gate often include green space, playgrounds, running and biking trails, and even an occasional fountain. Rent comes under the basic allowance for housing (BAH), which also includes money to pay for utilities.

When government housing isn't available, the BAH covers the cost of housing off-post. The actual amount depends on a soldier's pay grade and housing costs in the area.

In Their Footsteps
The children of soldiers who are raised on Army posts are usually called "Army brats." Many of them join up when they're old enough, and live their entire lives as part of the Army. Corporal Frank Anders was one of those. He grew up at Fort Abraham Lincoln in the Dakota Territory during the Indian Wars. After joining the North Dakota National Guard, he was shipped to the Philippines in 1898. The Army was putting down an insurrection there.
During an offensive on the city of San Isidro, Anders was chosen as a sharpshooter in a scouting expedition that turned into an all-out assault. Along with four of his buddies, he advanced in short rushes, firing all the while. By the time they reached the outskirts of the city, none of the defenders was left alive. But when they entered San Isidro itself, the enemy counterattacked. The Americans took refuge in a church and held them at bay for four long hours before the main body of friendly troops relieved them. All five of the men, including Corporal Anders, received Medals of Honor for saving the day.

Barracks Life

Most soldiers live on post, with the quality of their digs directly reflecting their rank. It's pretty basic during Basic Training, but it gets better right away.

Enlisted personnel usually live in barracks that more closely resemble college dormitories than drill halls filled with bunk beds. You can expect to live two-to-a-room with communal shower facilities. There is always room for recreation and, more important, study with computer access handy.

Army Chow

No one would ever confuse an Army chow hall with a gourmet restaurant, but the food is, believe it or not, quite good.

Married personnel get $220 or more a month for separate rations, depending on their rank. Their spouses and children are eligible for more. Single soldiers can get meal cards that allow them to forage for their own food elsewhere if they're picky eaters.

If you'd rather live on Pepsi-Cola and cupcakes, they are available on post, too, as are other snacks. But that's one of the bad habits that the Army gives you a chance to break.

Where Will You Go?

There are Army posts in nearly every state in the Union. Which one you will be sent to depends on your MOS and the branch you are assigned to. The Army has installations all over the world, too, and an overseas posting isn't out of the question.

A fairly sure thing is that you will be moved from one place to another a couple of times, even in the shortest enlistment period. Stateside, about a third of all military personnel are based in California, Texas, North Carolina, or Virginia. Overseas, the biggest concentration is in Germany, although there are bases in other European countries. The Army also has a strong presence in the western Pacific area.

Job Security

Army jobs, like those in the other uniformed services, give you more job security than any you will fill in the civilian world. You can stop reading the business pages—there is no such thing as an economic downturn in the Army.

There have been occasional "drawdowns," such as the one that reduced the overall size of the military, and eliminated some bases in the 1990s. But such things are rare, and chances are good we won't see another one in our lifetime. On the other hand, the overall economy is cyclical, and whenever the stock market drops, you can expect to see companies dropping personnel as well. Even people with strong union contracts can be affected. But the Army, and the rest of the military, is typically immune to outside economic forces, and its personnel have the most secure jobs of anyone in the country.

The Least You Need to Know

- The Army won't bait and switch you on your choice. There are rare occasions when its needs may change and you get reassigned, but its goal is to fill its needs with people who *want* to be doing specific jobs.

- Almost any civilian job has a direct counterpart in an Army job. Some Army MOSs are specific to military needs, but the majority of jobs available to you in the Army match up with what you have done, or want to do, in civilian life.

- The Army, and life in it, is different than it ever has been. The living conditions are better and training is state-of-the-art.

- The Army has evolved from an infantry-based fighting machine into a technology-oriented organization. That adds up to more opportunities to find a job that you'll like and to get the best possible training to make you good at what you do.

- Army life is more like civilian life than you might imagine. In many ways, it is better. You get more vacation time and never work more than 40 hours a week. You can even dress like a civilian in your off-hours.

Chapter 13

Anchors Aweigh with the Navy

In This Chapter

- The traditions of the Navy
- Getting to know the fleets
- Career choices in the Navy
- Life and work on the high seas
- How the Navy is structured
- From Seabees to SEALs

When the Revolutionary War ended in 1781 after the British surrender at Yorktown, Virginia, General Washington knew that credit for the victory belonged as much to naval forces as to his army. But it wasn't an American navy that had made the difference.

After the main British force established its base at Yorktown, Washington knew that as long as the Royal Navy could keep it supplied, the British could hold out there for years if they felt like it. The only way to prevent that from happening was to blockade the fleet. But Washington didn't have any ships at his command, so he did the next best thing. He asked the French navy to do the job.

Their ships were already in the Caribbean, and 28 of them sailed north to the mouth of the Chesapeake Bay. They had time to land their marines, who joined with the Americans to keep the British army pinned down. Then the English ships arrived. And more French ships came into sight at about the same time. The battle had all the earmarks of a standoff. After three of their vessels were disabled, the British gave up the fight and sailed off in the general direction of New York. That left their army high and dry, and the minutemen moved in to finish them off.

New Beginnings

The American colonists knew it wasn't going to be easy when they decided to fight the British for their independence. The Royal Navy was the most powerful in the world, as it had been for more than 200 years.

Even though they were concentrated along the Atlantic coast, most Americans were farmers. The seafarers among them depended on England's navy to protect their businesses, and they weren't too eager to bite the hand that fed them.

They weren't opposed to a little piracy, though. After General Washington chartered a fishing schooner to raid British supply ships, 10 more fishermen signed up to help. In less than six months, Washington's little 11-ship navy captured more than 55 of the enemy's ships. All of the supplies on board went to the Continental Army.

"I have not yet begun to fight!"

The enemy called these early American raiders "pirates," but they called themselves privateers. The most successful of them was Captain John Paul Jones.

In 1778, Captain Jones began attacking the west coast of England itself. When he went to France for a bigger ship so that he could do more damage, the American ambassador, Benjamin Franklin, made it possible. In gratitude, Jones renamed the ship *Bonhomme Richard* in honor of Franklin, the author of *Poor Richard's Almanac*.

She gave a good account of herself off Britain's Flamborough Head in 1779. Jones attacked the Royal Navy frigate *Serapis* at long range with an 18-pound cannon. But when one his guns burst, he moved in for a closer engagement.

He lashed his ship to the enemy's and the battle that followed lasted all night long. At dawn, the British captain called for his surrender, but Jones defiantly called back, "I have not yet begun to fight!"

Meanwhile, a fire had broken out aboard the *Serapis*. As flames raced toward her powder magazine, her captain struck his colors. *Bonhomme Richard* had been literally reduced to splinters by then, and the Americans transferred over to the captured ship.

A few days later, they sailed into a Dutch harbor with the American flag fluttering from the top mast above the Royal Navy ensign.

Although John Paul Jones was first to carry the American flag into a foreign port aboard a captured enemy ship, he wasn't the founder of the U.S. Navy. That institution had already existed for four years by then.

The Navy's Birthday

On October 13, 1775, in the early months of the Revolution, the Continental Congress authorized the building of two sailing vessels that could be used to intercept British transport ships.

Before the war came to an end, the Navy had grown to include 40 ships. They not only captured transports on the way to America, but took the war to England itself. They captured more than 200 vessels belonging to the mightiest navy the world had ever seen.

The original congressional declaration was made at Philadelphia. That was also where the Navy's first four ships were built. But there are several other places that call themselves "the birthplace of the Navy."

Machais, Maine, is one. It was where colonists seized a British schooner in 1775. Whitehall, New York, claims the honor as the base of a small fleet that was deployed on Lake Champlain early in the war. Both Marblehead and Beverly, Massachusetts, point with pride to the fact that they provided the boats that George Washington used to capture enemy supply ships. And Providence, Rhode Island, claims that it deserves credit as the Navy's birthplace because its citizens were the first to suggest such a thing.

Tip

The fact that so many places are still slugging it out for credit as the birthplace of the Navy is a good sign of how Americans feel about their Navy. But where the Navy was born isn't as important as what it has done over the last two centuries. Nor what it is doing right now.

Navy Strength

Wherever it actually began, the U.S. Navy has grown into the most formidable naval force in the world. There are about 382,000 people on active duty in the Navy today. Close to 54,000 are officers, 322,850 are enlisted personnel, and 4,200 are midshipmen, studying full-time for naval careers. The Navy's Ready Reserve Force includes more than 166,400 trained people. The Navy also has 183,425 civilians on its payroll.

A proud tradition.

The Navy has well over 4,000 operational aircraft as well. But it is ships you think of first when you think about the Navy's strength. There are close to 320 of those.

At any given time, 120 ships are away from their homeports, about 38 percent of the total. Eighty-five are likely to be on deployment, following a specific mission beyond training exercises. Eight of those will be submarines.

The Navy's Fleets

The modern Navy is divided into five numbered fleets (although the numbers aren't consecutive). The Second Fleet, based at Norfolk, Virginia, serves in the Atlantic sector. Its flagship is the USS *Mount Whitney* (LCC20). The Sixth Fleet, headquartered on the command ship USS *LaSalle* (AGF-3), patrols the Mediterranean.

The Fifth Fleet, whose headquarters are in Manama, Bahrain, serves in the Persian Gulf and the Middle East. It was originally formed during World War II, and then deactivated in the 1980s to cover operations in the Middle East. It operates under the authority of Naval Forces Central Command (NAVCENT), and its forces are deployed from either the Atlantic or Pacific Fleets.

The Third Fleet, operating from San Diego, California, covers the eastern and northern Pacific Ocean. Its flagship is USS *Coronado* (AGF-11). The Seventh Fleet, whose command ship is USS *Blue Ridge* (LCC19) has bases in Japan, Guam, and other places throughout the western Pacific and the Indian Ocean. It is the largest naval command in the world.

Bet You Didn't Know

The concept of dividing the Navy into separate fleets came about after the end of the Spanish-American War. The war had given the United States new bases in the Pacific and in the Caribbean, but there wasn't any organizational structure in place to protect them. President Theodore Roosevelt ordered the establishment of the Atlantic Fleet in 1906. Not long afterward, separate Asiatic and Pacific squadrons were put in place. But President Roosevelt combined them as the Pacific Fleet in 1907.

During his first administration (1901-1905) he obtained congressional authorization to build 10 new battleships, 4 armored cruisers, and 10 smaller ships. The battleships were assigned to the Atlantic Fleet and all the others added to the strength of the Pacific Fleet. In 1922, the fleets were combined into one, called the United States Battle Fleet, with its main concentration of ships in the Pacific and those in the Atlantic charged with scouting duties.

The fleets were reorganized again in 1941, when American naval power was divided among the Asiatic, Pacific, and Atlantic areas so that forces could be developed independently of each other according to strategic requirements.

Ghost Fleets

Some of the Navy's fleets that don't actually exist right now, are sometimes referred to as "ghost fleets": First, Fourth, Eighth, Tenth, and Twelfth.

The First Fleet, actually refers to the Coast Guard, although that isn't an official designation. It dates back to the 1790s, when there wasn't any navy and the cutters that eventually became the Coast Guard were the only waterborne defense America had.

The Fourth Fleet was established during World War II to track blockade-runners and enemy submarines in the southern Atlantic. It eventually became Fleet Air Wing 16, and its base was moved to Natal, Brazil.

The Eighth Fleet, which has become part of the Second, was originally formed to assist in amphibious landings in North Africa and Europe during World War II.

Among the other fleets that no longer exist, except in naval history, is the Tenth, which was established as a special antisubmarine unit. Its job was mostly coordination, and in the two years it existed, from 1943 to 1945, it never had more than 50 people assigned to it. It didn't have any ships, either. But although it was a fleet that never went to sea, the Tenth got the job done by sending others in the right direction to do theirs.

There is also a special place in naval history for the Twelfth Fleet. It was organized in 1943 to control training and operations for landing craft and other aspects of the cross-channel invasion of France that finally took place on June 6, 1944. Without the Navy, D-Day couldn't have happened.

In Their Footsteps

Of all the actions that earned the Navy's Medal of Honor, the most unusual was by a guy named Edouard Izak. He was a gunnery officer aboard the troopship USS *President Lincoln*. On her way home after delivering 5,000 troops to France during World War I, she was hit squarely in the middle by torpedoes fired from the crack German raider *U-90*. Izak was thrown into the water and soon taken prisoner aboard the submarine. His dog tag identified him as a lieutenant, and the German captain had orders to capture any officers he found.

Apart from explaining that he wasn't the captain of his sunken ship, Izak kept his mouth shut and bided his time. Pretending to be in a crazed state of shock, he wandered aimlessly around the U-boat. Nobody challenged him, since they thought he was crazy. Besides, how could anybody escape from a submarine? But it was all an act. Izak was fluent in German, although he never let them know it; in his wanderings he made mental notes about everything he saw and heard. He memorized charts and schedules, and paid close attention to the ship's layout. When the sub reached port, he was transferred to a land-based prison. His mind was filled with information, and at the top of it was figuring out how to escape so that he could get to where the information would do the most good.

His first attempt failed, but with the help of dozens of other prisoners he was able to stage a break. They split into twos and threes and headed toward neutral Switzerland. The Germans were on their trail with bloodhounds, but Izak had bought large quantities of red pepper through the prison black market and they used it to disable the dogs, who couldn't smell a thing after inhaling red pepper. It took Izak nine days to get across the mountains and to the U.S. embassy in Berne. He was transferred right away to Washington for a debriefing, and his information was vital to Allied intelligence.

Ironically, before the report could be circulated, the Allies had captured the U-boats themselves. While Lieutenant Izak was dictating his information, the Germans surrendered and World War I was over. Before that day, the information he had was priceless, but the armistice had rendered it worthless.

The Pacific Fleet

When the Pacific Fleet was established in 1821 as the Pacific Squadron to defend America's interests in the waters beyond the West Coast, America didn't have a West Coast to defend. California wasn't admitted to the Union until almost 30 years later.

The territory it defends today, known in the Navy as "Westpac," runs along the International Dateline, west of Hawaii, to the Indian Ocean. From north to south, it runs from pole to pole. It is the largest naval command in the world, extending over two oceans, touching on six continents, and covering more than half of the earth's surface.

If you choose duty with the Seventh Fleet, Westpac's core, you'll be part of the Navy's most active fleet. Its ships are 17 days closer to Asia than if they were based on the American mainland. The fleet handles a responsibility that would otherwise require five times their number of ships and personnel. If its base were in the United States, it would need to have more ships constantly patrolling out to the outer limits of its territory. Some days it seems as though they're doing the job of hundreds. There is never a dull moment out there.

Carriers at sea always have plenty of company. But it isn't every day that an Air Force B-1 bomber buzzes the flight deck.

Seagoing Jobs

More than 50 ships are assigned to the Pacific Fleet, but 19 of them form its permanently forward deployed force, that is, ships that are operating from bases away for the United States. You can request an opportunity to sail on any one of them. Or you might prefer to serve with Carrier Wing FIVE at the Naval Air Facility in Atsugi, Japan. Either way, if there are openings available, you will get your wish.

The fleet's command ship is the USS *Blue Ridge* (LCC19). It is based at Yokosuka, Japan, along with the carrier *Kitty Hawk* (CV-63) and her battle group. These two ships alone have a complement of nearly 4,000 personnel, and the carrier's air crew adds 2,000 more.

Fleet Activities Sasebo, also based in Japan, and named for the town where its ships are berthed, is an amphibious ready group. Its basic function is to transport Marines from their base on the island of Okinawa to anyplace they are needed.

The biggest of Sasebo's ships is the USS *Essex* (LHD2), an amphibious assault ship. Others are the USS *Juneau* (LPD10), an amphibious dock landing ship, USS *Germantown* (LSD42), and USS *Fort McHenry* (LSD43), also dock-landing ships. Together these vessels have crews adding up to more than 1,900, and they can transport 2,600 troops into battle.

Sasebo is also the homeport of the mine countermeasure ships USS *Guardian* (MCM5) and USS *Patriot* (MCM7). They are constructed of oak, Douglas fir, and cedar with a fiberglass skin to bring a nonmagnetic property to minesweeping operations. Each of them is operated by 81 officers and enlisted personnel.

Repair and logistics services for the fleet's ships and aircraft are coordinated from a base in Guam's Apra Harbor. Other Pacific Fleet installations are located in the Republic of Korea and Singapore.

In Their Footsteps

On February 20, 1942, a formation of enemy-heavy bombers was sighted headed directly for the carrier USS *Lexington*. Its fighter planes scrambled, but two of them were stranded on the flight deck with mechanical problems. That left Lieutenant Edward H. "Butch" O'Hare out there alone between his ship and nine twin-engine bombers. He attacked them at close range and made every bullet count. He shot down five of them and crippled a sixth. The action only lasted about four minutes, but it was time enough for other planes to get into the air to finish off the rest of the attackers.

O'Hare had single-handedly saved the *Lexington* and all the men aboard. Five planes shot down in combat is the requirement to be qualified as an ace, and O'Hare was the first in the Navy's history to earn the title. He was one of only two carrier-based pilots to win a Medal of Honor during the war. If the name is familiar, it's probably because the international airport in Chicago was named for him.

Living Conditions

When your ship is at sea, you live on board, obviously. But when she's tied up, you live ashore, either on base housing or in rental units nearby.

Many of the people stationed at foreign ports are encouraged to live in the surrounding area. One of the Navy's missions is to interact with the people who live in the areas it serves, and its personnel often do double duty as ambassadors.

The Navy maintains housing on its bases both overseas and stateside for its people and their families. In fact, it manages about 71,000 units of its own around the world.

It also has a large inventory of what it calls "substandard" housing, which usually is best translated as "small." People assigned to such units pay either a fair market rent or 75 percent of their Basic Housing Allowance, whichever is less. These quarters are most often used by personnel assigned to ships that are being overhauled or repaired away from their homeports. As "transients," they can still collect an allowance to maintain housing at their regular homeport.

Commuting to the Job

A larger number of Navy families take advantage of the local housing market, though. It is the Navy's policy to encourage that, and it regularly scouts for available apartments near its installations. But availability is only part of what it looks for.

Among its considerations is travel time. The Navy won't recommend any housing that is more than an hour's commute from the base. It also requires that the rent shouldn't be higher than the basic allowance it provides for housing. Sometimes a landlord might ask for more, but the Navy has a formula for what it considers affordable "out-of-pocket" costs for rent and utilities, and it won't reimburse for anything higher.

All things considered, Navy personnel and their families can, and usually do, live virtually rent-free in civilian housing. Living aboard ship is another matter.

A Sailor's Life

Back when ships were made of wood and their crews were called iron men, most of the seamen slept in hammocks. It was a practical matter. The hammocks could be stowed when they weren't being used for sleeping, and space was at a premium.

These days, even though aircraft carriers in the Nimitz class, the biggest ships afloat, are more than 1,000 feet long and 250 feet wide, space is still a rarity at sea. There is much less room aboard smaller carriers and other ships; available space is downright miniscule on submarines. Enlisted personnel on all the Navy's ships sleep in "racks," sets of berths with a little bit of space nearby for their personal gear.

One veteran sailor compared the living arrangements aboard ship to sleeping inside a dumpster. He recommended that if you want to duplicate the experience, you should first line the inside of it with a random assortment of pipes and wires and that you should paint it gray. You should also, he added, repaint it every couple of weeks whether you think it needs it or not.

He was only partly right. Shipboard life isn't the Ritz, but it isn't uncomfortable, either, once you get used to the lack of space. It beats climbing in and out of a swinging hammock every night.

Ships' officers generally get better living arrangements. Most have staterooms. But remember, the Navy isn't operating luxury cruises. Even on the largest ships, junior officers can expect to share a stateroom with as many as five bunkmates. Even lieutenant commanders and above double up.

Getting Hungry?

Officers take their meals in wardrooms. Aboard smaller ships that have just one, they dine with the commanding officer. Their meals are usually more formal than you might expect in the military, with tablecloths, cloth napkins, and even waiter service. Diners are expected to dress for the occasion in the uniform of the day.

Among the formalities, anyone joining the mess is required to address the senior officer present and ask for permission to sit down at the table. When the meal is over, custom demands that you carefully fold your napkin and ask for permission to be excused.

On larger ships, there is usually more than one wardroom. On aircraft carriers, one will be designated the "dirty-shirt" wardroom. This is where the aircrews take their meals, and they show up in their working uniforms. The service is cafeteria-style, and the atmosphere informal.

The wardrooms on bigger ships are also sometimes used for "midrats"—midnight rations—for people on the night shift or those who are too hungry to wait for breakfast.

The enlisted mess is always cafeteria-style aboard ship. It is open four times a day, for a total of about 10 hours. It is a simple matter of grabbing a tray and some silver, and finding a seat. If you don't mind standing in long lines, you can go back for seconds. You'll probably want to.

There is also often a special area set aside on mess decks for first class petty officers. The best food of all can be found in the chief's mess, which has its own galley and gets its groceries outside the regular supply system. The master chief petty officer pretty much runs things, even though rated as a noncommissioned officer when there are higher ranking officers aboard. Rank has its privileges, but it should be noted that even the captain of the ship doesn't usually eat as well as the chief and his staff.

Couch Potatoes

Life aboard ship isn't all work and no play. If your idea of play is sitting around watching television, you won't have a problem in the Navy. But you will have to watch what's on at the moment.

All but the smallest ships have television systems. Recreational spaces and some workspaces have monitors plugged into them. Usually those in recreation areas have the largest possible screens.

There are three available channels, each of which offers programming on 12-hour cycles. The first shows recently released feature films; the second, network programming like series and situation comedies; and the third streams special training films for the ship's personnel.

Officers have access to television in the wardrooms, where they also have VCRs and libraries of videotapes.

Most ships also have recreation areas where you can curl up with a good book, play cards, keep up with your schooling, or just stare off into space. Most also have exercise facilities. Quite well equipped ones on larger ships, in fact.

On-Board Amenities

When your ship visits a port, you can usually count on some shore leave to have a look around. If you plan to buy souvenirs, most ships have ATMs that will dispense the cash you need.

After you come back aboard, you'll probably want to share the adventure with the folks back home, or even send them the pictures you took. That's made easy by the miracle of e-mail.

All the Navy's ships are connected to each other and to land-based installations by a secure military network, and all of them also have access to the Internet. Most crew members can access the World Wide Web through readily available PCs. Many use them for the college courses they are taking, but many are finding it a neat way to keep in touch without waiting for mail call. The Navy is working at assigning an individual e-mail address to every sailor, and the goal is in sight.

In terms of a naval career, shipboard LANs (local area networks) use off-the-shelf hardware and software. That means that whatever you learn about working with computers in the Navy will have a direct link to the skills you'll want for civilian life.

Taking a Grand Tour

The Navy has always promoted itself as the perfect way to see the world, and it is as true today as it ever was.

Typical of ordinary sea duty was a six-month cruise by the Nimitz-class nuclear-powered aircraft carrier, USS *Eisenhower* (CVN-69) when she was put to sea again after a three-year overhaul. There were 5,680 people aboard, and the itinerary would have made any cruise-ship line green with envy. Her ports of call were Naples, Italy; Cannes, France; Antalya, Turkey; Corfu, Greece; Cartegena, Spain; Marseilles, France; Rhodes, Greece; and Dubai, United Arab Emirates.

Sailing in Good Company

The *Ike*'s crew members were able to go ashore at all of those places. They sampled the local cultures, soaked up the history, and relaxed on some of the world's best beaches. They also saw a lot of other Americans doing the same thing. A carrier rarely travels alone.

There are 11 carrier groups in the Navy. They usually include two cruisers, three destroyers, three frigates, one submarine, and one auxiliary ship. It is often called a carrier task force, but not a fleet, and each of the escorting ships extends the carrier's mission and protects it. There is, after all, safety in numbers.

Among the ships in a typical carrier group:

◆ Cruisers are air-warcraft ships carrying surface-to-air missiles, surface-to-surface missiles, antisubmarine rockets, 5-inch deck guns, and a LAMPS-III helicopter. Their crews are usually comprised of 24 officers and 340 enlisted.

◆ Destroyers, whose crews usually include 23 officers and 300 enlisted, carry surface-to-air missiles. Destroyers are also equipped to fuel and rearm helicopters. California-class destroyers are nuclear-powered.

◆ Frigates carry a LAMPS-III helicopter and provide secondary missile support. Of the 40 frigates in service, one quarter are assigned to the Navy Reserve. Their crews include 13 officers and 287 enlisted.

◆ Submarines assigned to carrier groups are the "Fast Attack" type. They are powered by nuclear reactors. They carry attack and antiship missiles and 14 torpedoes. They are also capable of deploying mines. Their crews consist of 13 officers and 116 enlisted.

◆ Auxiliary ships are used by the battle group to replenish supplies of fuel, munitions, supplies, and freight while underway. They carry two Sea Knight helicopters to transfer heavy loads, and they have long fuel lines to transfer petroleum. They can carry 177,000 barrels of fuel as well as 2,150 tons of munitions. And they can supply 250 tons of refrigerated food. Their crews are usually 600, including 33 officers.

Inside the control room of a nuclear-powered submarine.

Air Wings

The planes on a carrier have a variety of jobs to do. Some provide fleet defense, with attack and strike missions. Some provide airborne warning and electronic warfare. Others take care of day-to-day logistics.

Air wings are self-contained units operating under their own commanding officer with large support staffs. The number can vary, but a typical air wing (CVW) consists of:

- ◆ F/A-18 Hornet: three squadrons of 12 planes each.
- ◆ F-14 Tomcat: two squadrons of 14 planes each.
- ◆ E-2C Hawkeye surveillance: one squadron of four planes.
- ◆ S-3 A/B Viking attack: one squadron of eight planes.
- ◆ ES-3B Viking surveillance: one detachment of two planes.
- ◆ EA-6B Prowler electronic warfare: one squadron of four planes.
- ◆ SH-60 Sea Hawk helicopter: one squadron of six planes.
- ◆ C-2 Cod cargo/transport: one detachment of two planes.

Carrier groups respond quickly to localized flash points where a sudden enemy threat is perceived. They are highly self-sustained and can stay in areas that other forces can't reach for long periods of time.

Their manpower needs are enormous, and the range of skills needed to serve them is almost endless. All of that adds up to making carrier task-force duty one of the best, and most varied, that any branch of the service offers.

It takes a lot of manpower to clear an F-14 from a carrier's flight deck.

Ranks and Rates

Enlisted Navy personnel don't have "ranks," they have "rates." The rating badges they wear at the top of their sleeves consist of chevrons that indicate their rate, or pay grade, with a device above them just below the eagle that tells you their rating, or occupational specialty. That little symbol is called a crow, by the way.

Officers, who do have ranks, wear identifying devices in various ways, depending on the uniform of the day. With the working uniform, khakis, they are in the form of collar pins. Officers wearing whites will be identified by striped shoulder boards. When the dress is blues, the stripes are sewn on the bottom of the sleeve.

Bet You Didn't Know _____

Uniforms identify members of every service, and the differences among ranks in each of them. But the uniforms aren't always the same. Most of the time, when their is work to be done, naval personnel wear khaki uniforms that aren't a lot different from what you would expect to see being worn by a soldier or a Marine. When a ship is about to enter a port, everyone aboard switches to more formal uniforms, usually white if it is in a warm climate, and blue for colder spots. Among the general orders issued by the Captain every morning, the appropriate "uniform of the day" will be announced.

The following list of the Navy's pecking order also includes the pay designations, expressed as letter/number combinations. Pay varies according to length of service and is always subject to change as across-the-board raises come along. For the latest pay scales, log on to www.defenselink.mil/specials/militarypay2002.

Commissioned Officers

- Admiral (O-10)
- Vice Admiral (O-9)
- Rear Admiral (upper half) (O-8)
- Rear Admiral (lower half—formerly Commodore) (O-7)
- Captain (O-5)
- Commander (O-5)
- Lieutenant Commander (O-4)
- Lieutenant (O-3)
- Lieutenant Jr. Grade (O-2)
- Ensign (O-1)

Enlisted

- ◆ Master Chief Petty Officer (E-9)
- ◆ Senior Chief Petty Officer (E-8)
- ◆ Chief Petty Officer (E-7)
- ◆ Petty Officer First Class (E-6)
- ◆ Petty Officer Second Class (E-5)
- ◆ Petty Officer Third Class (E-4)
- ◆ Seaman (E-3)
- ◆ Seaman Recruit (E-1)

Warrant Officer

- ◆ Chief Warrant Officer (WO-4)
- ◆ Chief Warrant Officer Three (WO-3)
- ◆ Chief Warrant Officer Two (WO-2)
- ◆ Warrant Officer (WO-1)

In order to qualify as a naval officer, you will have to be a college student or, better still, a college graduate. You can earn higher rank through a naval ROTC program or by attending the U.S. Naval Academy at Annapolis. Before moving up, you will be enrolled at the Officers' Candidate School at Pensacola, Florida, for a special 13-week course. Professionals such as doctors, lawyers, and clergymen are automatically appointed to officer ranks.

Tip

The standard work schedule in all of the services is a 40-hour week with weekends and holidays off, plus a month's vacation each year. But that isn't always practical in the Navy, where you could be at sea for months at a time. The eight-hour work day still applies, although sometimes it might be a work *night*, but the time off will accumulate until it is more convenient for you to take the time off. Most of the time you can count on shore leave when your ship calls at a foreign port. And when you get back to your home port, you will probably have a lot of leave time accumulated.

Determining the Job You Want

The Navy offers hundreds of career paths. But to make it easier for you decide which one is right for you, it has devised a simple questionnaire called the Life Accelerator.

It gives you a chance to spell out what you like and what you don't like, what interests you, and what skills you have.

It is like an aptitude test, but with more emphasis on your personality than on basic aptitudes. It shouldn't be confused with the Armed Services Vocational Aptitude Battery. It isn't intended to tell the Navy what you can do, it is meant to tell *you* what you might be most comfortable with.

The profile it creates will narrow your options down into six likely areas. But you don't have to stop there. You can start over again. You can take the Life Accelerator test as many times as you want, which is sometimes a good idea if you don't recognize yourself in the choices it indicated. Because it is a personal measure, the results aren't saved. But you can have them placed in your "locker" at the Navy's recruiting website: www.navyjobs.com.

The six interest areas your profile produces is really just the tip of the iceberg. They are drawn from lists of available Navy jobs grouped into 29 different types of careers. Every one of them has dozens of subcategories.

General Enlisted Career Fields

After you take the Navy's Life Accelerator test, you will get a recommendation of six different career areas that you appear to be best-suited for, based on your general interests and your personality. They will come from these general enlisted career fields that are available in the Navy:

- Arts and Photography
- Aviation
- Business Management
- Computers
- Construction and Building
- Education
- Electronics
- Emergency, Fire and Rescue
- Energy and Power
- Engineering
- Finance and Accounting

- Food, Restaurant, and Lodging
- Human Resources
- Information Technology
- Intelligence and Communications
- Law Enforcement and Security
- Legal
- Mechanical and Industrial
- Medical and Dental
- Music
- News and Media
- Office and Administrative Support
- Purchasing and Supply
- Religion
- Science
- Special Operations
- Telecommunications
- Transportation and Logistics
- World Languages

Keep in mind that these are *general* categories, and that there is a wide range of choices within each of them. Keep in mind, too, that nearly all of these career categories apply to all of the services. It might be a good idea to take the Navy's Life Accelerator test even if your leaning toward actually choosing a different branch. It may help you discover a career path you hadn't considered. If you see yourself in one of them that the profiler seemed to have overlooked, go for it.

What's in a Name

Sometimes, just looking over a list of occupational opportunities within a broader classification might lead you astray unless you dig a little deeper.

Under the broad category of Administration/Deck/Weapons, (which is one of the sub-categories under "Office and Administrative Support") for instance, you might see a job called ship's serviceman. What do you suppose that means? First of all, it doesn't mean it's a category closed to women. It doesn't mean repairing ships, either. This rating includes barbers, tailors, dry cleaners, and shoemakers, among other things. They also work as clerks in exchanges, gas stations, and commissaries. Some servicemen even manage Navy clubs for officers and enlisted personnel.

Electronic technicians do more than just poke around the insides of high-tech machines. There's paperwork, too. Lots of it.

You might also think that signing up as a signalman will get you involved in electronics. Wrong again. You'll find those jobs in such other categories as Electronics and Communications. A signalman (or woman) deals with visual communications: semaphore flags, flashing lights, and things like that. They also often serve as navigators.

Don't know what a yeoman does? You may have already put in some time working as one. It's how the Navy categorizes people who do clerical or secretarial work.

Navy-Specific Jargon

The Navy has a language all its own. The secretary of the Navy is always called SECNAV, for instance; the Pacific Fleet is WESTPAC; the executive officer on a ship is known as an XO; and an organization that everybody gets involved with is the Bureau of Naval Personnel, a.k.a. BUPERS. Beyond those, and hundreds more like them, there are some other terms you might find helpful:

- **Ahoy!** You already knew that one, didn't you? But did you know it was a word the Vikings used as a battle cry?

- **Bow.** The front end of a ship (or an aircraft), it comes down to us from the Vikings who put boughs of tree branches at the front of their vessels to make the sighting of distant objects easier.

- **Eight Bells.** Bells are rung every half hour during a four-hour watch. Eight bells means it's quitting time. (A "watch" is one of the oldest of all naval traditions. It refers to the time on duty aboard a ship. Officers and seamen take turns keeping an eye on things four hours at a time.)

- **Fathom.** Just when you thought you knew the difference between a foot and a meter, along comes the Navy with its fathoms. A measure of depth, it represents six feet. The word comes from Old English, which means "to embrace." The measure is based on the distance, from fingertip to fingertip, of a man about to hug his girlfriend.

- **High Seas.** By international law, the high seas, which don't belong to any nation, begin 12 miles out from shore.

- **Log Book.** In today's Navy, the ship's log, a record of every hour of every day, is kept in a computer. In the days of sailing ships, though, they were written on strips of wood cut from logs.

- **Pea Coat.** On a cold night on deck, you'll be glad you have one of these. Its name comes from the heavy twilled cloth it is made from. It was developed for ship's pilots, and was known as P-cloth. They have been standard Navy issue since 1723. Nobody has since figured out how to make a warmer coat.

- **Scuttlebutt.** The word is often used in the Navy to describe a drinking fountain. It also means "rumor," usually spread at those drinking fountains. It comes from two words: "scuttle," a hole in the hull big enough to make a ship sink, and "butt," a cask of drinking water where the crew gathered to socialize. You're going to hear plenty of scuttlebutt in the Navy. Just don't believe most of it.

- **Starboard.** The earliest sailors called the sides of their ships "boards." The oar used for steering, known as the star, was placed on the right side. Their ships were tied to their docks on the opposite, or left, side so that the oar could stay in place. The left side was called "larboard" because it was the loading side. But sometimes it's hard to hear the difference between the two in a pounding sea, and so the left side's name was changed to "port," the side where you tie up when you're in port.

- **Stern.** The rear of a boat. The term comes from the Viking word *stjoñrn*, which means "steering," because they placed their steering oars in the rear of the boat, and ships' rudders are still located at the stern.

The more you get involved with the military—and the Navy is no exception—the more you'll understand that there are some language differences between the service and civilian life.

You'll get used to them. But when you go job hunting at a recruiting office, be very careful to ask for definitions. You probably aren't aware that an aerographer's mate in the Navy is a weather forecaster. Who knew?

Don't leave any stones unturned when you pick your Navy career. You're going to have to live with that job for a couple of years. You might as well choose something you'll enjoy.

How Tough Are You?

Every branch of the service has an elite fighting unit, and each of them claims that theirs is the toughest combat force in the world. Fortunately, they've never had a tournament to prove who's right. But as far as the Navy is concerned, the SEALs (Sea, Air, Land) could win it during their lunch hour.

In Their Footsteps

The Navy's construction battalions, called "Seabees," usually describe themselves a "part sailor, part Marine." What some of their officers have called them may be unprintable. After the outbreak of World War II, using civilians for construction jobs was out of the question, because under international law they would have been classified as guerrillas and subject to execution. The next best thing was to make them part of the military, and the Navy was the first to make it happen.

Guys who had built highways, dams, skyscrapers, and airports jumped at the chance to serve. The Navy wasn't interested in their physical condition, just their construction experience. In order to get men with the most experience, they winked at age requirements, too, and some of the first Seabees were over 60. Their average age was 37. They had to go through the Navy's boot camp, but it was a quick three-week tour. Then they got to work.

There was nothing they couldn't accomplish, from building bases to carving highways and creating airfields. Any enemy who tried to get in their way wound up wishing he hadn't tried. A bunch of roughnecks with almost no training in military discipline, the Seabees did it their way. It turned out to be the right way. But try telling that to their officers who had to look the other way while their men were getting the job done in untraditional ways.

One of the few all-male outfits in the Navy, the Sea, Air, Land teams were originally made up of volunteers selected from the naval construction battalions (Seabees) during World War II. Organized into what were called Navy combat demolition units, their assignment was to clear beach obstacles in advance of troops going ashore in amphibious landings. They eventually became known as combat swimmer reconnaissance units, or "frogmen."

During the 1960s each branch of the armed forces established its own counterinsurgency units, and the Navy's frogmen were turned into SEALs. Their mission was to conduct unconventional warfare, counter-guerrilla actions, and clandestine operations in watery environments. Today, it also includes underwater demolition and hydrographic reconnaissance.

SEALs are trained at the Naval Amphibious Base in Coronado, California, which claims to have the toughest military training in the world. Nobody is giving them an argument.

Man-overboard drills are routine in SEAL training. They always get their man.

If you think you'd like to try it out, and feel the pride that goes with being a SEAL, you need to start out as an active duty or active reservist member of one of the armed forces. You don't necessarily have to be a Navy man.

You'll have to be an American citizen, too, because candidates need to have a secret-level security clearance. Beyond that, you only need to be smarter than the average guy, and a whole lot tougher.

The Least You Need to Know

- ◆ The Navy really is the best way to see the world. Its ships call at ports on every continent, and their crews usually get time off for some sightseeing.

- ◆ Many of the Navy's larger ships, as well as submarines, are nuclear-powered, and the people who maintain the reactors learn a unique skill, not generally available in the other services.

- ◆ Planes and helicopters are as much a part of the Navy as its ships. If aviation interests you, you'll find a surprising number of aviation careers in the Navy.

- ◆ Life at sea is cramped but generally comfortable, and rarely boring. Even the smallest ships have recreation rooms with television, and every crew member has access to the Internet, often with their own e-mail address.

- ◆ Many Navy personnel are posted on dry land, too, and almost never step aboard a ship. The crews of ships also have quarters on land that they use when their ship isn't at sea.

Chapter 14

The Wild Blue Air Force

In This Chapter

- ◆ The origins of the modern Air Force
- ◆ Rising through the ranks
- ◆ Making a connection with NASA
- ◆ Technology opportunities
- ◆ The planes the Air Force flies

In 1909, six years after Wilbur and Orville Wright flew the first airplane, they sold an improved version of their invention to the U.S. Army, which named it *Signal Corps No. 1.*

It was based at Fort Sam Houston in San Antonio, Texas, where the first crew was assembled. It included a noncommissioned officer in charge, whose job it was to maintain day-to-day records. Under him were an oiler, responsible for the motor compartment; a wiper, who took care of fueling the craft and lubricating the engine; two assistant cleaners, whose jobs were keeping the flying machine clean inside and out; and a supernumerary, who filled in for all the others and was in charge of securing supplies, like spare parts and gas and oil.

There was also a pilot, of course. That was Lt. Benjamin Foulois. He had some experience flying a Signal Corps dirigible (a lighter-than-air craft) over the Philippines, but he had only logged 54 minutes in a heavier-than-air craft, with Orville Wright at his side. Then he was ordered to deliver *Signal Corps No. 1* to San Antonio. Part of his orders were to "teach yourself to fly it."

It wasn't easy. For one thing, the airplane didn't have any wheels. It was catapulted from a one-rail track by a heavy weight dropped from a tower at the back end with a force that propelled the plane forward with a lurch. If the wind shifted, the track and the tower had to be moved.

Constant moving of the catapult was part of the pilot's job, and so was supervising maintenance, which, as it turned out, took up almost all his time. The plane was as fragile as it was temperamental, and every minute in the air led to at least an hour in the shop.

Although today's airplanes aren't anything at all like that Wright Type A flying machine, the basic makeup of the crews that keep them flying is still pretty much the same as it was back in 1909. One big difference is that it takes more of them to keep a plane in the air.

Among the other differences is how they live with the job. Those guys had to build their own hanger in a far-off corner of Fort Sam's drill field. Then they found themselves billeted in it. They had to walk more than a mile to the mess hall until they were finally given 75 cents a day to pay for meals at local homes.

By 1911, a second plane was delivered to San Antonio, along with three pilots who had been trained by pioneer Glenn Curtis. After one of them, Lt. George Kelly (the namesake of Kelly Air Force Base in San Antonio), became the first Army pilot killed in a crash, the base commander banned takeoffs from his drill field. The two-plane Air Corps was moved to College Park, Maryland. Its most experienced pilot, Benny Foulois, was given a desk job in Washington.

The story of the Army Air Corps was onward and upward after that. Planes got more sophisticated, and safer. And the romance of flight became an important part of the American Dream.

America Goes to War in the Air

When war came to Europe in 1914, America's president, Woodrow Wilson, decided to sit it out. Germany, England, and others, meanwhile, were taking the idea of fighting the war in the air very seriously. A lot of young Americans were, too.

Since their own country didn't seem interested in giving them a taste of this new kind of action, they joined the French air force as a unit they called the Escadrille Américane. It later became the Lafayette Escadrille, also known as the 94th Aero Squadron, the first squadron of the U.S. Air Service.

The 94th was an elitist outfit. All of its original pilots were recent Ivy League graduates looking for adventure, and maybe a bit of glory on the side. Then along came Eddie Rickenbacker.

The early fliers would be amazed at the aircraft America has today. The F-117 Nighthawk fighter is among the most amazing.

Rickenbacker had never been to college. He went to work as an automobile mechanic when he was 12 years old. And by the time he reached college age, he opted for a correspondence course in mechanics. He landed a job test-driving new cars, and at the age of 19, he was making $40,000 a year as a racecar driver.

When America finally did get involved in the war, Rickenbacker proposed forming a flying squadron of racecar drivers like himself who understood machines, and could handle them under pressure. The Army thought that was a terrible idea. But, as a sort of consolation prize, it gave him a job as personal driver for Gen. John J. Pershing, the commander of the Allied Expeditionary Force. Pershing listened to Rickenbacker's ideas, but he pooh-poohed them. In his opinion, flying was a young man's game and his driver was already 27 years old.

Fate stepped in when Col. Billy Mitchell, the head of the Air Service, offered Rickenbacker a job as chief mechanic in his squadron. It represented a chance to learn to fly. Within two months, Rickenbacker became the squadron's oldest pilot. Within two more months, he had shot down five enemy planes, the number that qualifies a pilot as an "ace," a flyer's highest honor, short of the Medal of Honor. Rickenbacker earned one of those on his second day in combat.

In Their Footsteps

During World War I, German artillery observers directed fire from posts suspended under huge gas bags. They looked like easy targets, but shooting one down involved hitting a small area near the top where a concentration of hydrogen kept them aloft. To make it tougher, they were ringed on the ground by antiaircraft guns, and pursuit planes kept their engines running so they could attack any pilot foolhardy enough to get anywhere near one of the balloons.

Frank Luke loved the challenge. After he shot down his first balloon, he bagged another a day later. His Spad was put out of action after he downed two more, and he found himself grounded for a couple of days. That was when he came up with a plan. He decided to attack only at sunset when his plane would be virtually invisible. The landing field would be invisible, too, by the time he got back. But Frank Luke wasn't the kind of guy who sweated little details like that. On his first night out, he bagged three balloons, then two more the next night. In all, he had 11 of them to his credit. He also shot down five enemy planes in a 10-minute dog fight during another mission.

An Idea Whose Time Had Come

After the experience of the First World War, Air Service people began lobbying for a separate air arm, independent of the Army or the Navy. They were convinced that it should carry out strategic operations against an enemy's industrial heart rather than just supporting troops on the front lines.

The biggest booster was Billy Mitchell. He ruffled some feathers among the Navy brass by suggesting that airpower could do a better job of protecting the seacoasts than any fleet of ships.

To prove his point, he had his bombers sink three captured German warships off the coast of Virginia. A couple of months later, they sunk the decommissioned battleship USS *Alabama*, and made it look easy.

The Navy said it wasn't impressed, but nonetheless began building its first aircraft carrier before the year ended. The Army general staff, Mitchell's bosses, brushed him aside. Then when he began taking his ideas directly to the public, they suspended him from the service.

Fortunately, the idea didn't die there, although the Air Corps stayed under the Army's control. The Navy, meanwhile, established an air arm of its own.

Mitchell's theories were proven right during World War II, of course. And in 1947, after the war had ended, the Army Air Corps became the U.S. Air Force. It already had a solid tradition by then, as well as a glorious history. But that was like nothing at all compared to what the future would bring.

Bet You Didn't Know

The plane that proved Billy Mitchell's theories about what an air force could be was the Boeing B-17, also known as the Flying Fortress, which was produced in 1935, the year before Mitchell died. It served in every combat zone during World War II, but it is most famous as the workhorse of daylight bombing raids over Germany by the Eighth Air Force from their bases in Britain. The plane, powered by four 1,200 hp engines, had 13 .50-caliber machine guns, and carried a three-ton bomb load. Its 10-man crew included two pilots, a navigator, a bombardier, and a radio operator. The top-turret gunner doubled as the flight engineer. There were also gunners spotted along each side of the fuselage, in blisters under the nose and the tail, and in a ball turret under the ship's belly.

The last Queen of the Sky was built in May of 1945. By then, more than 12,725 had been flown into service. Their range was 1,850 miles, and that made delivering them to England as dicey as flying them over Germany. Although they started the trips in Newfoundland with full fuel tanks, they ran a strong risk of running out of gas before they reached Britain. A stronger-than-average headwind made it nearly certain.

The Air Force Structure

The Air Force is divided into nine major commands and 35 field operating agencies. It also includes the Air Force Reserve, a major command unit, and the Air National Guard.

The basic unit for combat capability is the *wing*. Many wings operate more than one type of aircraft, but most that fly single aircraft types stand ready to go anywhere they are needed. There is a host of support personnel attached to each wing, including intelligence and testing, training, and logistics.

Air Force Units

You're part of a team in the Air Force, too, and the team is divided into a bunch of components:

♦ The lowest subdivision of the Air Force is a *flight*. It is usually used for small mission elements incorporated into a larger unit.

♦ The combined mission units under an operational command is called a *squadron*.

♦ Two or more squadrons, operational, support, or administrative, are designated a *group*.

♦ A *wing* has two or more assigned mission squadrons in an area such as combat, flight training, or airlift.

◆ *Numbered air forces* are operational designations controlling two or more wings with the same mission or the same geographical location.

◆ *Major commands* are Air Force subdivisions assigned to major segments of its mission.

The major commands are ...

◆ Air Combat Command, Langley AFB, Virginia.

◆ Air Education and Training Command, Randolph AFB, Texas.

◆ Air Force Materiel Command, Wright-Patterson AFB, Ohio.

◆ Air Force Reserve Command, Robins AFB, Georgia.

◆ Air Force Space Command, Peterson AFB, Colorado.

◆ Air Force Special Operations Command, Hurlburt Field, Florida.

◆ Air Mobility Command, Scott AFB, Illinois.

◆ Pacific Air Forces, Hickam AFB, Hawaii.

◆ U.S. Air Forces in Europe, Ramstein AFB, Germany.

Space Operations

After the end of World War II, America began building on the success of German scientists who developed the first cruise missile, the V-1, and the first ballistic missile, the V-2.

Tip

Germany's V-1 missile, which Londoners at the receiving end during World War II called "buzz bombs," was essentially a pilotless aircraft. It was set to detonate as a bomb when its propellers had turned a predetermined number of times calculated according to the length of time it took it to get from launch to target. It led to today's family of cruise missiles, which are electronically guided and usually detonated by sensors detecting the heat of a target, often an aircraft engine.

The German V-2 rocket, which was the prototype for the rockets that send satellites into space, was fired straight up with a pre-planned trajectory that would bring it back to Earth at a specific time and place. During the London Blitz in World War II, people were terrified by the roar of the V-2's engine as it homed in on them. But even more so when the engine stopped and they knew it would fall from the sky a few long seconds later. The technology evolved into more sophisticated long-range (usually intercontinental) ballistic missiles that are armed with nuclear warheads.

By 1958, when the National Aeronautics and Space Administration (NASA) was formed, the Air Force was already at work developing a space tracking network through a division called the Air Research and Development Command.

A year later, it coined the word "aerospace" for its new mission. The Air Force has been a key player in NASA's mission ever since. It has been responsible for the development and deployment of weather satellites and the hugely successful NAVSTAR global positioning system, among other systems. It is also at the cutting edge of satellite tracking and telemetry.

It is Air Force personnel who are in charge of the launch commands at the Cape Canaveral Air Station in Florida and Vandenberg AFB in California where space shuttle missions usually end. Many of the astronauts who fly into space on those big birds are former Air Force officers.

All of America's missile warning, space surveillance, and satellite control are organized within the 14th Air Force. The 14th, which was famous in the Pacific Theater during World War II as the "Flying Tigers," is divided into two launch wings: the 30th Space Wing at Vandenberg and 45th Space Wing at Cape Canaveral.

Technology Rules

Of all the uniformed services, the Air Force is the most technological. It not only uses sophisticated weapons and equipment, but Air Force people are often the ones who develop it.

Right now, teams of airmen are working on the problems of laser technology. They still have a way to go, but in the meantime, the research is providing some of the most fascinating jobs available anywhere in the world.

And that is just one example. All kinds of things we take for granted today, from digital communications to rockets to the moon, were developed and tested on Air Force bases.

Career Paths

There are close to 352,000 men and women on active duty in today's Air Force. There are about 160 career fields open to the officers among them, and 185 available for enlisted personnel.

All pilots are officers, of course, but they represent only 17 percent of the total of all Air Force officers. As part of the new way of doing things, pilots are being rotated from one type of aircraft to another. It makes their experience more valuable to the Air Force and to themselves.

When it was split off from the Army, the Air Force decided not to place its specialties into the traditional system of corps, but instead placed them in units where they would all be able to work together. The result was a division into highly specialized units. But the system is being changed, and that's good news for future Air Force officers. The new approach, called the Developing Aerospace Leaders Program, is intended to broaden career opportunities and develop a more well-rounded officer corps.

How Officers Are Developed

Men and women who go into the Air Force as second lieutenants, whether through an ROTC program, graduation from the Air Force Academy, or some other academic or skill qualification, are assigned and trained in specific specialties. These junior officers are selected for promotion into the middle grades and eventually into senior grades.

Under the new program, officers are assigned to their specialties for the first six years of their ten years of service. After that, they are trained to become aerospace specialists by learning new skills. In that way, they become generalists and more likely to reach the very top. The result is that no Air Force officer is likely to be in a dead-end job.

Career Choices

Air Force personnel are involved in more different kinds of jobs than you might imagine. They maintain and control aircraft and spacecraft, to be sure, but they also build and repair roads, tend to the sick, cook meals, ship supplies around the world, and even, every now and then, pull guard duty.

Yes, the food is good in the Air Force, and the people who keep it that way are very carefully trained.

The list of Air Force jobs under the heading Base Operations alone includes more than 50 specific jobs, from airfield management to vehicle control and analysis, to heating and air-conditioning specialists, to environmental control specialists (they're known as exterminators in the civilian world).

If it's a career in flight you are looking for, consider becoming a pilot or a navigator. Why not? The jobs are open. They're practically yours for the asking.

There are nearly 40 other kinds of jobs related to flying. You might consider aerospace propulsion, where you will install and maintain engines. Or you might find a career in airport operations. Airmen in a specialty called tactical control make sure that smart bombs have their heads on straight.

The Personnel Department

Every large organization has people who keep track of the other people on the payroll. If you're scoping out possible enlisted career paths in the Air Force and passed over a job called personnel apprentice, go back and take another look. The Air Force is no ordinary organization. You didn't think that its personnel center would be ordinary, did you? It is just one more example of military job classifications that aren't quite the same as their civilian counterparts.

One of the basic jobs of the Air Force personnel center is knowing where everybody is. Air Force people are almost constantly on the move. They are taking leave, going to school, transferring to new bases, or serving on temporary duty somewhere. Personnel people keep tabs on them.

The ones with the toughest, but most interesting, job are the staff at the Personnel Readiness Center at Randolph Air Force Base in Texas. After the attacks on the Pentagon and the World Trade Center, it was their job to account for all Air Force personnel who might have been affected. That included active duty, guard and reserve, and civilian employees.

On top of that, the twin disasters brought a flood of requests from former airmen to get back to active duty, and they had to deal with that, too.

When U.S. forces were sent to Afghanistan, the personnel people had another job to do. In previous conflicts, personnel officers airlifted vans loaded with computer systems into remote areas to supply basic services. These days, they use laptops and a secure Internet connection. All they need where they are going is a telephone line ... and there are other airmen at work putting them in place.

These people don't just follow the troops, they're usually there on the first flight. The basic personnel complement is two members for every 150 airmen. The teams in the field start with two and then grow from there, two at a time.

Their job is to keep records up to the minute—for schooling, for promotions, for future retirement, and to make sure everybody gets paid. They also make sure that personal requirements, like paying bills, are handled while an airman is far from home. And they establish communications lines with the families of those people sent to help fight a war.

Special Tactics Groups

The Air Force's Special Operations wings are comparable to the Army's Green Berets and the Navy's SEALs. Their motto, which they live up to every day of the week, is "Anytime, Anyplace."

These wings were originally formed as air commandos when the Air Corps was part of the Army. The guys who served in Europe during World War II called themselves "carpet-baggers." Among their exploits was dropping agents and supplies behind enemy lines. More often than not, the spies stretched out on a plane's bomb bay doors, which were opened to dump them out when the plane was over the target. On one mission into Norway, they heisted a German V-2 rocket and flew it back in a stripped-down C-47.

During the Vietnam War, they were the first to use helicopters to rescue troops stranded behind enemy lines. They were also the ones who turned helicopters into deadly gunships.

Today's Special Operations airmen serve as pararescue teams. They also conduct intelligence operations, and many of them are dropped into combat situations to act as air controllers. They are also key players in the war against narco-terrorists in Latin America.

Pulling Rank

Air Force insignia for officers are identical to the Army's. Enlisted personnel insignia consists of a star above an appropriate number of chevrons. They are worn on both sleeves. The following list of Air Force ranks also includes the pay scales, expressed as combinations of letters and numbers that go with them. The actual amount varies by length of service, and rates are always subject to change. For the latest pay scales, log on to www.defenselink.mil/specials/militarypay2002.

Commissioned Officers

- General (O-10)
- Lieutenant General (O-9)
- Major General (O-8)
- Brigadier General (O-7)
- Colonel (O-6)

- Lieutenant Colonel (O-5)
- Major (O-4)
- Captain (O-3)
- First Lieutenant (O-2)
- Second Lieutenant (O-1)

Enlisted

- Chief Master Sergeant (E-9)
- Senior Master Sergeant (E-8)
- Master Sergeant (E-6)
- Staff Sergeant (E-5)
- Sergeant Senior Airman (E-4)
- Airman First Class (E-3)
- Airman (E-2)
- Airman Basic (E-1)

Bet You Didn't Know _____

When the Air Force was split off from the Army, it brought along its old symbol, a circle inside a star. Not long afterward, a pair of eagle's wings, called Hap Arnold Wings, sprouted above the circle. (Arnold was the Air Corps commander during World War II.) Then, in 2000, everything changed.

The new symbol, created at a cost of more then $800,000 (including lengthy opinion surveys), combines the elements of the old one, but it may take a bit of imagination to figure out how.

The wings have become highly stylized and represent the men and women of the Air Force, "the stripes of our strength." The modernization, which uses strong angularity, is said to evoke swiftness and power.

The wings are divided into six sections, representing aerospace superiority, global attack, rapid mobility, precision engagement, information superiority, and agile combat support.

The lower half contains a sphere representing the Air Force's global reach. The area around it is in the shape of a star. Its five points refer to the Air Force family: active duty, civilian, guard, reserve, and retirees. The star includes three diamonds that symbolize the Air Force's core values: integrity, service, and excellence.

The overall impression is of an eagle, the symbol of the nation. It has also been interpreted as resembling a medal. You might see a stealth bomber in there somewhere.

Warrant Officers

- ◆ Chief Warrant Officer (WO-5)
- ◆ Chief Warrant Officer Four (WO-4)
- ◆ Chief Warrant Officer Three (WO-3)
- ◆ Chief Warrant Officer Two (WO-2)
- ◆ Warrant Officer (WO-1)

The Force Behind the Force

The Air Force flies dozens of different types of aircraft. Each of them has its own job to do, but combat aircraft are usually considered more glamorous than others. Among those are bombers and fighters, as well as noncombat aircraft.

Bombers

The designation of these aircraft "Bomber," also indicates their use. Each carries a different size load of bombs.

B-1B Lancer

The backbone of the long-range bomber force, the B1-B, with its tight wing/body configuration, is capable of flying almost anywhere in the world at supersonic speeds. In 1995, it set an aviation record with simulated bombings on three continents in a single mission. It is 146 feet long with a wingspan of 137 feet, which can be swept back to 74 feet. It can fly at more than 900 MPH (Mach 1.2) at a ceiling of over 30,000 feet. It carries a crew of four:

- ◆ Aircraft commander
- ◆ Co-pilot
- ◆ Offensive systems officer
- ◆ Defensive systems officer

The active duty Air Force flies 72 of these heavy bombers; 18 are assigned to the Air National Guard.

B-2 Spirit

This airplane is the next best thing to being invisible. It's "stealth" characteristics make it capable of penetrating the most sophisticated defenses. Even the best radar can't see it coming. Special coatings that resist infrared, acoustic, and electromagnetic defensive systems enhance its profile. Because it is so hard to spot, the B-2 has complete freedom of action at altitudes as high as 50,000 feet. That increases its range and gives a wider field of view for its sophisticated sensors. It can fly 6,000 nautical miles without refueling. And it has the capability of delivering nuclear weapons. It is 69 feet long with a wingspan of 172 feet. Its speed is described as "high subsonic." The Air Force has 21 B-2s in the air, each with a crew of two pilots.

Tip

In the measure of distance that we use in the United States, one mile is exactly 5,280 feet, or 1.609 kilometers. A nautical mile, which measures distances at sea or in the air, is equal to 1.150 land miles, or 1.852 kilometers.

It's a bird! It's a plane! When a B-2 stealth bomber flies into their sectors, radar operators are the last to know.

B-52 Stratofortress

This long-range heavy bomber has been delivering the goods since 1954, before the people who fly them today were born. Engineering experts are convinced that they'll still be flying 40 years from now. There isn't a job they can't perform in a conventional conflict. They are used for strategic attack, for air interdiction, and for offensive counterair operations.

During Operation Desert Storm, B-52s delivered 40 percent of all the weapons dropped over Iraq. Also during the Gulf War, B-52s accomplished the longest strike mission in history. They took off from Barksdale Air Force Base in Louisiana, launched cruise missiles over Iraq, and then flew back to Barksdale. It was a nonstop, 35-hour mission. The

B-52 can carry nuclear weapons or guided conventional bombs and missiles. Its low-level flight capability is enhanced by infrared and high-resolution television sensors for targeting and battle assessments, and its pilots wear night-vision goggles for attacks in complete darkness.

With aerial refueling, the B-52 can stay aloft almost indefinitely. Without refueling, it has a range of more than 8,800 nautical miles (about the same as from Washington, D.C., to Bangkok, Thailand, and well over twice the distance from New York to Paris). The plane is about 160 feet long, with a wingspan of 185 feet. It is powered by eight turbofan engines, and can carry 70,000 pounds of bombs, mines, and missiles. The B-52 has a crew of five:

◆ Aircraft commander

◆ Pilot

◆ Radar navigator

◆ Navigator

◆ Electronic warfare officer

The active duty Air Force flies 85 B-52s and the reserves fly nine.

The B-52's flight crew is only part of the team that keeps these big birds flying.

Fighters

These planes are direct descendants of the biplanes that engaged one another in World War I dogfights. There may not have much of a family resemblance, but their mission is the same. Many of these aircraft also include bombs and missiles in their armament.

F-111

Luke Skywalker would be right at home in an F-111 airplane. It has an automatic terrain-following radar system that flies it at a constant altitude following the contours of the earth. It flies through valleys and over mountains regardless of weather conditions, day or night. Its two crew members, a pilot and a weapons systems operator, sit side by side in a cockpit module. In an emergency, the module becomes an escape vehicle that floats to the earth beneath a parachute. Airbags under it soften the impact, and also serve for flotation if it is ejected over water. The module can be ejected at any speed and even underwater.

The F-111 flies at twice the speed of sound at high altitudes, which can be as high as 60,000 feet. But its variable-sweep wings allow it to land in short spaces without a drag chute or reverse engine thrust. It is powered by two turbofan engines. The F-111 is a tactical fighter-bomber. It is 75 feet long, with a wingspan variable from 32 to 63 feet (either by pulling the wings back closer to the fuselage to reduce wind drag in flight, or extending them outward to increase it for landing when slower speeds are needed). It has a range of 3,565 miles (about the distance from New York to London) with external fuel tanks, and it carries a load of 25,000 pounds of bombs, rockets, and missiles. It is also capable of delivering four nuclear bombs. There are 225 of them in the Air Force's arsenal.

Tip

The prefix "Mach" used with airspeeds indicates supersonic speed. It comes from the name of Ernst Mach (1838–1916) a physicist who pioneered the study of the speed of sound. That measure has been established as 1,088 feet per second at sea level at 32°F, and varies at other temperatures, increasing as the temperature drops. Sound waves travel faster through water, and faster still in iron. In air, it takes about five seconds for sound to travel a mile. When a plane moves at the speed of sound, it is called Mach 1. Twice the speed of sound is Mach 2. When the sound barrier is broken, it produces a sound like a thunderclap, called a sonic boom. It can be heard on the ground, but not by the pilot of the plane.

F-117A Nighthawk

This is the first aircraft designed with stealth technology. It has electronic fly-by-wire flight controls, and an automated mission control system. With air refueling, its range is unlimited and it can fly at high subsonic speeds. It is 63 feet long, with a wingspan of 43 feet. It has digital avionics for navigation and attack that make it highly effective in combat. The F-117A, which has a crew of one, is powered by two turbofan engines. The Air Force is currently flying 54 of them.

F-15 Eagle

She can fly in any kind of weather, and the F-15 can outperform and outfight any aircraft that any potential enemy is flying today. It has a display system on the windscreen that gives the pilot all the information needed to track and destroy targets without looking down at the instruments. Some of that information comes from a Doppler radar system that can track targets both above and below. The electronic warfare system also provides automatic countermeasures against potential threats.

The Eagle can be armed with a variety of different air-to-air weapons. It is a two-seat tactical fighter, with CRT displays in the rear cockpit for systems and weapons management. The F-15 is 63 feet long with a wingspan of 43 feet. It can fly at 1,875 MPH (Mach 2.5) at an altitude of 65,000 feet. It is powered by two turbofan engines. The Air Force has 396 Eagles, and the Air National Guard flies 126 of them.

F-16 Fighting Falcon

The bubble canopy over the cockpit gives an F-16 pilot unlimited forward and upward vision, which makes it a formidable weapon in a dogfight. But there are other ways of seeing, and its radar systems can single out any target under any conditions. In air-to-surface combat, the F-16 can fly more than 500 miles, deliver its weapons while defending itself at the same time, and then fly back to its base. Its range is more than 2,000 miles.

The F-16 is 50 feet long, with a wingspan of 32 feet. It can fly at an altitude of 50,000 feet with a top speed of 1,500 MPH (Mach 2). It is powered by a single jet engine, and can carry a crew of two. The plane was developed for use by NATO countries as well as the U.S. Air Force, and four of them have made it the centerpiece of their air defenses.

A-10/OA-10 Thunderbolt II

The first Air Force jet aircraft designed for close air support of ground forces, the Thunderbolt is used against all kinds of ground targets, like tanks and armored units. Their pilots use night-vision goggles and their radar systems make it impossible to hide from its seven-barrel gatling gun that fires 3,900 rounds a minute. The Thunderbolt also carries eight tons of ordnance, including cluster bombs, laser-guided "smart" bombs, and Sidewinder missiles.

It is 53 feet long, with a wingspan of 57 feet, and is powered by two turbofan engines. It can fly at 420 MPH at an altitude of 45,000 feet. Its range is 800 miles, but it was designed to fly in and out of small airfields close to the battle zone. The Air Force flies 213 of them, the Air Force Reserve flies 52, and the Air National Guard has 102.

Noncombat Aircraft

Of course, we cannot forget the noncombat planes that have become legends of their own in the Air Force.

KC-135 Stratotanker

Most warplanes would have a problem reaching their targets without refueling along the way. That is the job of the KC-135. It does the job so well, in fact, that it is used by Navy and Marine Corps as well as by most allied nations. Four turbofan engines mounted under the wings can lift the Stratotanker with a load of some 322,500 pounds.

All the fuel loaded inside can be pumped out through a flying boom. A special valve at the end is attached to probes on another aircraft. It isn't as easy as filling you car's gas tank, but after years of experience, the Air Force manages to make it look like it is. The job gets done by a crew of four:

- ◆ Pilot
- ◆ Co-pilot
- ◆ Navigator
- ◆ Boom operator

The aircraft, which also carries cargo and up to 37 passengers, is 136 feet long and its wingspan is 130 feet. It has a range of 1,500 miles at 50,000 feet, and it can fly 530 MPH. The Air Force currently has 253 Stratotankers on duty, the Air National Guard flies 222 of them, and the Air Force Reserve has 70.

E-3 Sentry (AWACS)

The letters stand for Airborne Warning and Control System, and that sums up the E-3's mission. It is basically a Boeing 707/320 with a 30-foot rotating radar dome mounted 14 feet above the fuselage. The sophisticated radar inside has a range of 250 miles, and even further when the job is to track aerospace vehicles at high altitudes.

The E-3 was originally developed in the 1970s as a mobile warning system that would be better able to survive than ground-based radar stations in battle situations. It also added the element of mobility. The Sentry can fly 360 MPH at an altitude of 29,000 feet. It can stay in the air for eight hours without refueling. When in-flight refueling is necessary to extend a mission, there is a rest area on board for the crew.

The basic size of the flight crew is four, but the mission crew can range from 13 to 19. These people are usually computer and radar operators and analysts. Sometimes the mission crew might include customs agents on the trail of smugglers. The Air Force has 33 AWACS planes on duty.

C-130 Hercules

This giant can take off from almost anywhere, from a dirt strip to a developed airfield. It is generally used to air-drop troops and supplies into remote areas. It can drop 22,000 tons during a single trip. It can easily accommodate 128 combat troops or 92 paratroopers. The cargo can range from helicopters to armored vehicles to ordinary supplies. It is often used in weather reconnaissance, for the resupply of bases on the Antarctic ice, and for aerial spraying missions and fighting forest fires, as well as disaster relief operations. It is 112 feet long and 38 feet high with a wingspan of 132 feet. Its cargo compartment is 55 feet long and 9 feet high. It is powered by four turboprop engines rated at 4,200 horsepower each, and can fly 1,968 miles with a 35,000-pound payload.

Hercules has a crew of five:

- ◆ Two pilots
- ◆ Navigator
- ◆ Flight engineer
- ◆ Loadmaster

For medical evacuation missions, one flight nurse and two medical technicians are added to the crew. The Air Force has 186 of these aircraft, 217 are assigned to the Air National Guard, and 107 to the Air Force Reserve.

Getting In on the Action

Not everybody qualifies as a pilot or for the equally crucial job of navigator. It all starts with an early interest in math and science. A lot depends on the state of your health, and a lot more on your character. But if you have what it takes, you can earn your wings. Thousands before you have done it.

And don't forget, the first pilot the Air Corps had to teach himself how to fly. It isn't that easy. It all has to do with your desire and your self-discipline. If you see yourself in the pilot's seat, the Air Force will bend over backwards to help you get there.

On the other hand, there are more than three dozen other important jobs right behind every one of those seats. Without people to fill them, those planes aren't going anywhere.

Making sure that the tail gun on a B-52 is going to work when it's needed is all in a day's work for some airmen.

The Least You Need to Know

◆ The Air Force has more technology-related jobs than any of the other services. Its aircraft, missiles, radar, and surveillance systems all include state-of-the-art electronics.

◆ Airmen are at the cutting-edge of new developments. They test and refine electronics systems, engines, and missiles as well as the aircraft that is at the heart of the Air Force mission.

◆ The Air Force mission extends all the way to outer space. Airmen are an important part of every space probe, from launching to recovery, and they also launch and track satellites.

◆ Promotions tend to come faster in Air Force careers, thanks to a unique program that encourages officers to move into different specialties as they move up.

◆ For every pilot, there are dozens of people making the job possible. While the Air Force couldn't exist without pilots and navigators, it is the people on the ground who keep them flying.

Chapter **15**

The Few, the Proud, the Marines

In This Chapter

- ◆ The tradition of the Marine Corps
- ◆ Training after Boot Camp
- ◆ Life at sea on the way into battle
- ◆ Opportunities for fast advancement
- ◆ Changing your life forever

The Continental Congress passed a resolution creating the Marine Corps on November 10, 1775. Eighteen days later, Samuel Nichols was commissioned as a captain in the Continental Marines, and was senior officer for the duration of the Revolutionary War. He is remembered as the Corps' first commandant.

Another officer who was appointed at the same time was Robert Mullen, whose civilian job was running the Tun Tavern in Philadelphia. His responsibility was finding a few good men, and he found most of them on the opposite side of his bar. It became the Marine Corps' first recruiting station.

The congressional naval committee met to create this new fighting force in an upstairs room at the Tun Tavern. But then, as now, it was the men who responded who made all the difference.

Marines on the Move

During the War of 1812, Marines were on hand to slow down their British counterparts bent on burning down Washington, D.C. Not long afterward, they fought beside Gen. Stonewall Jackson to victory in the Battle of New Orleans.

In the years that followed, Marines turned up in the Caribbean, in the Falkland Islands, in Sumatra, and in West Africa.

In the mid-1840s, Marines made a difference during the Mexican War with landings on both the Gulf and Pacific coasts. Inland, they fought their way all the way to Mexico City and the Halls of Montezuma.

During the Civil War, Marines took part in blockading actions around several southern ports, and a Marine battalion saw action during the first Battle of Bull Run.

The Few. The Proud.

Bet You Didn't Know _____

The Marines made their first battle landings in raids on the beaches of the British-held Bahamas in 1776. But when the war ended seven years later, the Navy sold its ships and went out of business. Its partner, the Marines, shut down, too.

The Corps was reactivated in 1798 to help stop French raids on U.S. merchant ships. Three years later, its men were dispatched to the shores of Tripoli in a war to stop Barbary pirates who were looting American ships in the Mediterranean.

In those days, the Marine uniform included a high leather collar that protected their necks from the scimitars wielded by the Arab enemy. This is how they came to be known as "Leathernecks."

The World Wars

During World War I, when Marines first began flying into battle, more than 30,000 of them slugged their way across France. They were so good at it that the enemy began calling them "Devil Dogs," something they've been calling themselves ever since.

The U.S. Marines captured the world's imagination during World War II. Their amphibious landings made such obscure Pacific islands as Okinawa, Iwo Jima, Tinian, Saipan, Kwajalein, and Tarawa as famous as Washington or Tokyo. By the time the war ended in 1945, the Corps had grown to six divisions and five air wings. Its strength grew to more than 485,000. Unfortunately, more than 87,000 of them didn't get to go home.

The Marine Corps Memorial at Arlington, Virginia, is a tribute to the Leathernecks who went ashore at Iwo Jima in World War II.

Glory on Top of Glory

In the years since, the Marines have made a difference in the landings at Inchon and the Battle of Chosin Reservoir during the Korean War. They landed at Da Nang in Vietnam in 1965, and during that war, about 85,000 Marines were in the thick of it. At the end, it was the Marines who evacuated the embassy staff and American citizens after the fall of Saigon.

During the Gulf War, it was Marines who drove Iraqi forces back from the coast of Kuwait.

When America took the war on terrorism to Afghanistan, Marine units were at the leading edge, doing what they always do best: fighting a tough enemy in strange territory and making it look like a job they were born to do.

In Their Footsteps

Pappy Boyington, a.k.a. Maj. Gregory Boyington, USMC, shot down 26 enemy planes in the Pacific during World War II. He had six kills to his credit, and qualified as an ace before the war came to America with the attack on Pearl Harbor. Pappy became a Marine pilot in 1935, but he resigned his commission six years later and became a soldier of fortune with Claire Lee Chenault's Flying Tigers in China. When the Marines went to war, he offered to rejoin them. But the top brass had had enough of this hard-drinking brawler and they turned him down.

The Army Air Force wanted him, but he didn't want any part of them. He took his case directly to the secretary of the Navy, who agreed to bury the hatchet, and Pappy became a Marine again. He brought along a few well-chosen antiestablishment flyers with him and formed them into a squadron he called, appropriately, the Black Sheep. Before long, just the sight of their corsairs, the fast fighter planes they flew, sent the enemy running.

Boyington and his men liked nothing better than running after them. He won the Medal of Honor in 1944 when he led a mission of 24 fighters supporting a bombing raid over the Solomon Islands. As the bombers dropped their load, the Black Sheep circled the enemy airfield, daring the Japanese fighters to do something about it. Not one left the ground. The next day, the Black Sheep flew back, this time without any bombers. To make the enemy believe they were being attacked again, Pappy kept up a steady stream of radio chatter. They took the bait. The Black Sheep shot down 20 fighters without losing a single plane of their own.

Making a Difference

But Marines do much more than fight their country's battles, as the song says, in the air, on land, and sea.

Throughout all the years of its history, the Marine Corps has always been the outfit of choice to evacuate American citizens from hot spots around the world. They fight wild fires, clean up after floods and hurricanes, and are on the front lines in the war on drugs.

There doesn't seem to be anything the Marines can't do. And, thanks to Corps tradition, they always do it better.

As President Ronald Reagan put it: "Some people live an entire lifetime and wonder if they have ever made a difference in the world, but Marines don't have that problem."

Number One

There are 170,600 Marines on active duty today. Except for the Coast Guard, it is the smallest of the services, a tight little outfit.

It is also the only service that routinely, year after year, goes over the top in its recruiting goals. And it seems to be able to do the job with the least effort. The Corps offers the same educational benefits as the other services, and it has a bonus program, too. But they never make a big deal out of it.

"What we're offering," says a recruiter, "is a chance to be a Marine."

As if to prove that's a pretty great thing to be, the Marine Corps has the highest retention rate of all the services. Two thirds of all enlistees reenlist when their first tour is over. The pattern has been steady for more than 10 years.

Higher Standards

The Department of Defense has set a policy of requiring 90 percent of recruits among all the services to have a high school diploma. The Marines insist on no less than 95 percent, and consistently recruits higher percentages than that.

The DOD also has a goal that 60 percent of enlistees score in the top half of the mental ability section of the Armed Forces Vocational Aptitude Battery. The Marines make that 63 percent. And they actually recruit higher percentages there, too.

Why the Marines?

Some people who have made a study of Marine Corps success are convinced that it is because the Corps is well known as the toughest of all the services. Strange as that may seem, they have surveys to back up their theory.

According to statistics gathered in Department of Defense surveys, people in the 17–24 age group seem to have risen above the materialistic attitudes of their parents. To them, the studies say, making a difference is much more important than making big bucks.

They want to be leaders, they tell the questioners, but they also feel a need to be led. They are looking for a moral alternative.

Right now, you're probably saying, "I'm in that age group, and that isn't what I'm thinking."

Maybe not, but even if you're more interested in being a corporate executive than a military officer, consider the advice printed in the business magazine *Inc.*, which called the Marine Corps "the best management-training program in America."

A Marine officer quoted in the *Washington Times* said that he believes young people are becoming Marines because of the personal development it offers. "The Marine Corps is the Cadillac of the military service. We require more of them," he said.

A Special Specialty

Every Marine has a Military Occupational Specialty, some of which cover high-tech jobs. Marines fly airplanes and conduct sophisticated intelligence operations, and many are even assigned to guard American embassies around the world. That job involves participating in balls, parties, and other social functions that are part of embassy life. Nothing says "class" in quite the same way as a Marine in dress blues.

But the biggest MOS in the Corps is the one designated 0300: infantry. Like every other specialty, training for it begins right away after you graduate from boot camp. But infantry training is what boot camp is all about, right? Not quite.

The basic mission of the fighting Marine is to kill the enemy and keep himself and his buddies alive at the same time. That is where special infantry training comes in. You might call it the school of hard knocks.

The Marines maintain two schools of infantry. SOI West is at the San Onofre section of Camp Pendleton in California. SOI East is at Camp Lejeune, North Carolina. The routine is the same at both of them. Their mission is the same, too: turning out educated "grunts."

Right after you graduate from one of the Marine boot camps, you'll be given a 10-day leave. If you have an infantry MOS, you'll report directly to one of the infantry training battalions after that.

Toughening Up

The school of infantry also includes marine combat training, which is required of every Marine in every MOS category. It is boot camp plus one.

Before you begin schooling to learn your trade, you'll go through 15 days of learning leadership skills that could save your life some day, not to mention the lives of a lot of people around you. During those 15 days, you'll get three days off … if you're lucky.

Grinding Out Grunts

The three-week infantry training program ranges from overland navigation to street fighting. Students get Sundays off, but they have almost no other time to themselves. On paper, they get an hour or two of free time in the evenings. But usually there isn't any time left over for that.

There is more training required after those first three weeks. Expect another four weeks of specialized training in handling the weapon you chose earlier as the one you will use as a Marine. There are several of them, as you'll see in the section that follows.

Marine Corps Weapons

A well-trained Marine is the deadliest weapon in America's arsenal. But the weapons they work with make them even more formidable.

Every Marine is an expert with the M16A2 rifle. They don't leave home without it. In its semiautomatic mode, it can fire single shots or a three-round burst. It fires a .223-caliber cartridge. The M16A2 uses 30-round magazines, but it can also accept 40 rounds. Its range is about 800 yards. An M203 grenade launcher can also be fitted onto it. Other weapons are as follows:

 ◆ The M2249 is a light machine gun that fires the same ammunition as the M16A2. It fires 725 rounds a minute. Its range is about a thousand yards. One man in every four-man fire team is equipped with this automatic weapon.

 ◆ The M9 pistol, carried by officers and staff NCOs, as well as special-duty enlisted Marines, fires a standard 9mm round from 15-round clips. It replaced the Colt 45mm as standard for all the military services because it is less prone to going off by accident. The smaller round also allows a Marine to carry more ammo.

 ◆ The M240 is a medium machine gun that has replaced the M60. It fires .30-caliber rounds in three adjustable rates from 650 to 900 rounds a minute. It has a range of more than a mile.

 ◆ The automatic grenade launcher MK19 fires 40mm grenades at the rate of 40 rounds a minute, although that can be increased to 375. Its range is $1^1/_3$ miles. The weapon weighs 72 pounds and is usually handled by teams of four Marines.

 ◆ The M2.50 a 50-caliber machine gun is often mounted on vehicles, but it can also be used in stationary positions handled by teams of two or three Marines. It is one of the Corps' most lethal weapons.

◆ The AT-4 antitank rocket is fired by two-man teams, usually serving in the heavy weapons platoon of a rifle company.

These are the average Marine's choice of weapons. After Boot Camp, where you'll get some exposure to all of them, you'll eventually settle down and become an expert with one of them.

Bet You Didn't Know

Marine Infantry Training begins with a hike. A long one. No one in the military anywhere takes more long hikes than these guys. Almost all the training takes place in the field. Although there is some classroom time involved, just about everything taught at these schools is hands-on.

Hikes (which the Marines call "humps") in an infantry training battalion program often mean covering 25 miles with a full pack. (Tough as Basic Training may be, recruits sometimes get to ride from one area to another in buses. There is no such thing out in that remote corner of Camp Pendleton.) The Marine Corps' School of Infantry West is located in the midst of a mountain ridge, with some fairly steep hills to add to the fun.

A Lot to Learn

As if hiking isn't enough, physical training is routine in the infantry training battalions. It takes place whenever there is an odd moment to spare. As a student, you will also spend hours patrolling and encountering sudden combat action drills.

Through it all, you'll get lots of practice with your M16A2 rifle. You'll also learn the basics of the M249 automatic weapon and the M2203 grenade launcher. These three are the basic working tools of every rifle squad.

One thing you won't find at infantry school is the time-honored military punishments for guys who screw up. Nobody is going to ask you to drop for a round of push-ups. You won't have to run around with a rifle high over your head, either.

Problems are handled by base administrators. Because that means your problem is more likely to show up on your record rather than in your calf muscles, you learn quickly not to make mistakes.

Training Women

For a dozen years after 1980, women were assigned to all-female platoons because what the top brass called "physiological differences."

You don't have to tell a Marine anything about the differences between men and women. But since 1992, when the Department of Defense mandated sexual equality across the board, men and women have been drawing assignments based on little more than the first letter of their last name. Men and women have been going through the same training ever since.

It is done separately, with minor adjustments for those physiological differences. But female Marines aren't coddled. Like the guys, they are brought up to their maximum potential. There aren't any shortcuts in the Marines. The pattern was set in 1985 when Basic Training for female recruits was extended from 8 to 11 weeks—the same as their male counterparts.

Women go through their own training program under the eyes of female drill instructors. But it is no less demanding. Women are trained in day and night tactics and rappelling. They go through the confidence course and defensive field training. They run in boots with backpacks and rifles. And they are tested in close-order drill with rifles. They also experience the 54-hour Crucible before they graduate (see Chapter 4).

The Best MOS in the Corps

Are you a pretty good piccolo player? The Marine Corps has a job for you. Somebody has to add sparkle to "The Stars and Stripes Forever," and nobody does it like the Marine Band. It has been "the President's own" since the days when John Philip Sousa waved the baton. It might easily be called the most elite of the elite.

The Marine Band doesn't only play for White House ceremonies. In 1991, it led Desert Storm veterans up Broadway in a New York–style ticker-tape parade.

There are hundreds of military bands you can join, not just in the Marine Corps, but in all of the services. But none of them holds a candle to the Marine Band. If you're good enough, joining is easier than you might have thought.

First of all, you have to wait for an opening. They are announced through music teachers and college band directors. The next step is an audition at the Marine Barracks in Washington.

Most band members have musical degrees, but that isn't a requirement. You will be required to be a U.S. citizen, and to get top secret security clearance for White House access. You will also have to fit the Corps' physical requirements plus a special height/weight standard.

But here is the best part: As a member of the Marine Band, you are considered an active-duty Marine. But you won't have to go through recruit training.

You will have to sign up for a four-year hitch, beginning with the rank of staff sergeant. And you will be entitled to all the pay and other benefits that go with it. You and your dependents get free medical and dental care. You can take advantage of the discounts at military commissaries, too.

Band members also qualify for tuition assistance as well as the benefits of the Montgomery GI Bill. Simply put, they are Marines just like any other. The difference is that they get to serenade the president on a regular basis.

Does the New York Philharmonic or the Boston Symphony offer perks like that?

Another advantage: You will spend your entire tour based in Washington, D.C., and you can't be transferred into any other unit.

Now, aren't you glad your mother made you practice the piccolo?

Dress Blues

One of the most striking things about members of the Marine Band, or those standing at attention outside the offices of ambassadors, is their uniforms.

The style of the so-called dress blues has hardly changed since 1912. And even before that, Marines on parade and in public ceremonies have always worn blue uniforms. But today's model doesn't show its age. It has become the most recognized, and admired, military uniform in the world.

At one time only officers wore coats with pockets, but now enlisted Marines have pockets, too. It eliminated the only difference there was. Apart from their rank insignia, the only way to tell an officer from an enlisted man is that officers' coats are slightly darker, their belts are blue, and the uniform has a bit less red trim. NCOs wear swords at their side. All leather items are black.

Women Marines have a version of dress blues, too. About the only difference, except that they usually wear shirts with the blue jackets, is that they wear a necktab rather than a tie.

The Marine Emblem

As world famous as the Marine Corps dress uniform, the globe and anchor is a symbol that commands respect everywhere. Permission to wear it is the number one goal of every recruit in boot camp.

When the Corps was established in 1775, its identifying symbol was a "foul anchor," that is, a representation of an anchor with a turn of a chain around it. Over the years, the badge of honor changed a lot, but the anchor stayed. It symbolizes the amphibious mission of the Marines.

The current design was made official in 1868. A globe was added to symbolize worldwide service. The eagle spreading its wings above it is another reference to worldwide readiness. It is not a bald eagle, the symbol of the United States, but a crested eagle, which is found in just about every part of the world.

Above it all is a ribbon that contains the Marine Corps' Latin motto: *Semper Fidelis*, "Always Faithful." The device isn't used on representations of the emblem on uniforms. Marines carry that in their hearts and don't need to display it on their caps and lapels.

Tip

Whenever ex-Marines get together, in person, in Internet chat rooms, or in letters to one another, they always sign off with an enthusiastic "Semper Fi!" It's their equivalent of "Have a nice day." But it is much more than that. It's a reminder of the Corps' motto: *Semper Fidelis*, which means "Always Faithful." It's a reminder, too, that once a Marine, you're always a Marine, and always faithful to the Corps. No fraternity in the world has as many fiercely loyal—and proud—members.

Through the Ranks

The Marine Corps emblem sets Marines a cut above members of the other services. It is a visible symbol that you have become the best of the best. Enlisted insignia is basically the same as the Army's, but features crossed rifles directly under the chevrons. The following list of Marine Corps ranks also include the pay scales that go with them. The actual amount varies by length of service, and rates are always subject to change. For the latest pay scales, log on to www.defenselink.mil/specials/militarypay2002.

Commissioned Officers

♦ General (O-10)

♦ Lieutenant General (O-9)

   ◆ Major General (O-8)

   ◆ Brigadier General (O-7)

   ◆ Colonel (O-6)

   ◆ Lieutenant Colonel (O-5)

   ◆ Major (O-4)

   ◆ Captain (O-3)

   ◆ First Lieutenant (O-2)

   ◆ Second Lieutenant (O-1)

Enlisted

   ◆ Sergeant Major (E-9)

   ◆ Master Gunnery Sergeant (E-9)

   ◆ First Sergeant (E-8)

   ◆ Master Sergeant (Master Chief) (E-8)

   ◆ Gunnery Sergeant (E-7)

   ◆ Staff Sergeant (E-6)

   ◆ Sergeant (E-5)

   ◆ Corporal (E-4)

   ◆ Lance Corporal (E-3)

   ◆ Private First Class (E-2)

   ◆ Private (E-1)

There are no Warrant Officers because the Marine schools, which are where Warrant Officers would serve, are usually run by the Navy.

Moving Up

Although every Marine career begins with Boot Camp, officers are often graduated from it as second lieutenants. They are recruited from the Naval Reserve Officers Training Course, which you can access with paid scholarships; from the Officer Candidate Class Program, a 10-week course open to college seniors and graduates; or by graduating from the U.S. Naval Academy.

The Corps also offers a platoon leaders class for college undergraduates who train during the summer. In addition, it has programs for enlisted personnel to earn commissions.

In Their Footsteps

Back in 1918, young Lewis B. Puller, a freshman at Virginia Military Institute, quit school and joined the Marines. He said he wanted to go where the action was. He was given a commission as reserve second lieutenant a year later, and then he was sent home. He joined up again as an enlisted man and cut his battle teeth during five years of service in Haiti. Later on, he fought rebels in Nicaragua, where he earned his first Navy Cross, the highest honor for battlefield gallantry short of the Medal of Honor, and the nickname Tiger of the Mountains. He was also known as Chesty to his men because of his barrel chest. Many of them said it was made of iron, and perhaps they were right given all the medals he could have worn on his chest.

Before his career ended, as a lieutenant general, Chesty Puller had won the Navy Cross five times. During his 37 years as a Marine, he became the most decorated Marine in history. He earned his reputation in actions from the landings at Guadalcanal and Peleliu in World War II, to the invasion of Inchon and the battle at Chosin Reservoir in the Korean War. He once told his troops: "The Marine Corps will live forever ... and that means *you* will live forever."

Training Officers

All newly commissioned Marine officers are sent to Quantico, Virginia, for a 23-week course that covers leadership and esprit de corps, among other things. At the end of the program, these new officers are given a choice of three occupational specialties and their first duty station.

The most senior officer training school is the Command and Staff College. The nine-month course prepares majors and lieutenant colonels for command at higher levels.

Colonels and higher rank can go on to top-level schools, with a long list of options, from the Naval War College through the NATO Defense College.

Most Marine officers are assigned to unit leadership positions as soon as they complete the basic program at Quantico. Infantry officers lead platoons of 42 men; tank officers lead 16-man platoons with four tanks; assault amphibian vehicle officers lead platoons of 34 men with 10 assault amphibian vehicles.

Bet You Didn't Know

Esprit de Corps, which literally means the "Spirit of the Corps," is the most important lesson a Marine learns. It is a concept based on tradition that every Marine believes is what makes them different from, and better than, any fighting force the world has ever know. It is largely an attitude, and when Marines get together, the conversation will probably turn to a discussion of "Esprit," as they call it.

Going Up Fast

Marine officers usually work their way into command positions earlier than their counterparts in the other services. The Corps' table of organization requires that only captains with 5 to 10 years of service can be promoted to commanding officers of companies and batteries. But that's about the only Marine Corps rule that ever gets broken. It isn't at all that unusual for an officer to move up to CO duty with just three or four years of experience.

Such a thing would never happen in any of the other services. But then, the other services aren't the Marines. They start out with the best and then build from there.

Instant Response

Right at this moment, around the world, large contingents of Marines are aboard ships ready for orders to go ashore and possibly into battle.

They are assigned to seven standing expeditionary units that are deployed for six months at a time to make sure that the Marines are able to respond to any crisis, anywhere, any time.

Their mission isn't always to go into battle, although it sometimes is. These troops are also on call to rescue American citizens in harm's way abroad or to provide disaster relief.

Gator Ships

Back in World War II, and in the years before, Marines were moved from place to place in lumbering, uncomfortable troop ships (packed like sardines into flat-bottomed landing craft on their way to hit the beach). They are still prepared to storm ashore in battle landings, but compared to the old days, today's Leathernecks might seem to be living the good life.

Not only that, but the new breed of craft in what Marines call the Gator Navy are faster and more flexible than ships that were in service as recently as the 1960s. They're more stable, too, so seasickness has become virtually a thing of the past in the Corps. They are run by U.S. Navy crews, but their purpose is to get Marines where the action is. Marines can be rightly considered the Navy's land force.

The Marine expeditionary units, about 2,300 men each, are deployed among fleets of three or four gator ships. The craft and the Navy people who run them are called Amphibious Ready Groups (ARGs).

On the East Coast, squadrons of ARGs are based near Hampton Roads, Virginia. They are deployed in the Mediterranean region. West Coast squadrons, based at San Diego,

California, range as far as the Indian Ocean and even into the Persian Gulf. There are also forward bases in Japan and on the island of Okinawa. There are always several at sea at any given time.

Landings Made Easy

The innovation that makes all the difference between today's amphibious ships and the ones Marines used to use is the submersible well deck.

The well deck is a big open space inside the ship. It has a tailgate at the stern end that serves as a ramp for loading—and deploying—tanks, trucks, and other vehicles. But the aft end of an amphibious ship can be lowered 30 feet. When the well fills up with water, loaded landing craft can be floated aboard. The stern gate closes when the water is pumped out, and everything is tied down. When it's time to go into action, Marines board the vehicles in the well deck and drive off.

Not only is it faster that way, but there is no more climbing over the side of the ship on rope nets and ladders. There isn't as much need to wade ashore anymore, either.

Helicopters have also dramatically changed the logistics of amphibious landings. They are making it possible for a Marine to storm a beachhead without getting his feet wet.

Amphibious Transport Docks

The earliest class of Gator Navy ships with a helicopter landing deck is the Austin class of amphibious transport docks LPD (Landing Pad Dock), introduced in the 1960s. Its landing deck, taking up close to half the ship's aft end, can land two giant cargo helicopters.

An LPD is capable of carrying more than 900 Marines, plus 2,500 tons of the supplies they'll need to carry out their mission. The draft (the shallowest water it can operate in) of the 570-foot ship is just 23 feet, which makes it possible to get close in to shore.

The well deck of an LPD can hold two fully loaded landing craft and dozens of smaller boats as well. Almost any World War II vet would be awe-stricken by what these vessels can do. But there are other amphibious ships that can do the job even better.

Landing Ship, Docks

The Landing Ship, Dock (LSD), introduced in the 1980s, is almost 40 feet longer than an LPD. It has the latest in electronics aboard, too. But for all that, it can't carry as many Marines. That's good news for the Marines, though, because the available space is used to make their lives more comfortable.

The well deck of an LSD has more than three times the available space of any ship that came before it. That makes it possible to deploy the new M1A1 Abrams tank and other armored vehicle along with the first wave ashore. Its flight deck is also equipped to handle the MV-22 Osprey.

Amphibious Assault Ships

The new workhorses of the Gator Navy, amphibious assault ships LPH (Landing Pad Helicopters) can handle more helicopters and deliver more Marines than an LPD or LSD.

They can deploy nine helicopters from the flight deck and store 42 more. They also serve as bases for AV-8 Harrier jets that can take off without a runway. And they can carry more than 2,000 battle-ready Marines.

Bet You Didn't Know

Marines have been storming beaches all over the world since the beginning of their existence. One of their bloodiest victories was the taking of Iwo Jima in early 1945. It was one of several Japanese-held islands that were like stepping stones to Japan itself, and were considered key spots for airbases that would make it possible to steadily bomb the homeland. Iwo Jima is a tiny island, about eight square miles of volcanic rock and thick jungle. By the time the Marines landed, the Japanese had spent two years building defenses that included 800 pillboxes, three miles of underground tunnels, and even deeper concrete bunkers. Every inch of the beach was covered by guns, and there was heavy artillery back in the jungle. Also hidden back there were 20,000 fanatical troops armed with rifles and machine guns.

Before the invasion, Navy ships bombarded the rock for three days, but the defenders waited it out below ground. When the Marines went ashore, the Japanese were at full force. Intelligence had underestimated their strength by a long shot and hadn't taken the enemy's mood into account. Their homeland was being threatened, and they were determined to die honorably, which to them meant taking as many Americans as possible along with them. They killed nearly 6,000 American Marines, and left another 17,000 wounded. The battle lasted 26 long days.

The Future

The next step forward for the Gator fleet is the USS *San Antonio*, the first of 12 ships in her class. She is everything her predecessors are, and a whole lot more.

For the average Marine, it represents heaven on earth (or water). The innovations start with chow lines ... there may not be any. More than 180 sailors and Marines can find a seat on the mess deck at any one time. The space around the sleeping racks, have been increased by more than 40 percent, too, so there won't be as many problems storing personal and battle gear.

Marines on board will have their own showers and head facilities. In the old days, they had to share them with the Navy crew. It's a good deal for the sailors, too, who will also have their own facilities. And as an improvement over just about every other ship in the Navy, the sleeping racks are arranged so that an average-sized person can actually sit up in them without bumping his head. Nothing is too good for a Marine!

Want more? These ships will also have a central mall where Marines can relax and enjoy the boat ride. It has a post office, a barber shop, a ship's store, and a bulkhead lined with vending machines.

Life at Sea

These San Antonio class ships are still in the future, although it is the *near* future. But in the meantime, life at sea for a Marine looking for a fight isn't nearly as bad as it was back in the good old days.

Not too many years ago, a Marine assigned to an expeditionary unit found his living space comparable to a phone booth. He slept on webbed folding racks stretched out along super-heated passageways. There wasn't any room for simple socializing and the head facilities sometimes required hikes that were long even by Corps standards.

But those days are gone forever. Aboard most Gator ships even now, the sleeping racks are equipped with mattresses. They are fixed in place in special compartments, and there is room under them to stow gear.

The sleeping areas are curtained off, and there are reading lights and air-conditioning vents in there. There is only about two feet of space above the mattress, so it isn't possible to sit up in bed as it will be in the future.

There isn't any need for "Navy showers" with salt water anymore, either. And Gator ships also carry washers and dryers so that Marines can count on wading into battle with clean utilities, as their combat uniforms are called. Most of the ships also have workout rooms, too, and the flight decks are great for morning runs.

Navy chow is the best there is, and nobody knows that better than Marines on expeditionary unit duty. If there is a downside, it is that there isn't a heck of a lot for a Marine to do on one of these six-month cruises. They use the time for weapons maintenance and brush-up training. Many use the time to catch up on their college work. There are evening movies, too, and endless card games.

The Least You Need to Know

- The Marine Corps is a tough outfit, with good reason. It has a tough job to do, and pride in its glorious past keeps its men and women at the top of their form.

- The majority of Marines are infantry, and proud of it. They consider themselves a crack fighting force, and every Marine believes they have to prove that whenever the occasion demands it.

- The route to a Marine commission is often faster than other services. Officers are routinely moved up to higher ranks after just a couple of years.

- Women get special, but equally tough, training. The Marine Corps is the only branch of the service that trains women separately. But the results are the same.

- Amphibious landings have been made easier, and more effective. Marine units are constantly at sea and ready for battle. But new types of ships are making the waiting experience more comfortable.

- Once you become a Marine, you're always a Marine, no matter what else you do with the rest of your life, the pride never goes away.

Chapter 16

Patrolling the Shores with the Coast Guard

In This Chapter

◆ At the cutting edge of homeland security

◆ The Coast Guard's multiple missions

◆ The Coast Guard's wartime role

◆ The Coast Guard fleet

◆ Available jobs

◆ Civilians in Coast Guard service

After the terrorist attacks on the Pentagon and the World Trade Center, America mobilized a massive effort for homeland security. Few people realize that it's a job the Coast Guard has been handling on its own for more than 200 years.

After September 11, the Coast Guard stepped up its readiness role almost overnight. Coast Guard craft were on the job in New York Harbor, in fact, at the same time the city's police and firefighters arrived on the scene.

In the days right afterward, the Coast Guard went into high alert at more than 360 American ports. It established 124 tight security zones. When prisoners began arriving from Afghanistan, it built up port security at Guantanamo Bay in Cuba. It started escorting cruise ships in and out of ports from Miami to

Honolulu, with Coast Guard security people assigned to the bridges and engine rooms. Its special agents began serving as air marshals aboard commercial airliners—the only military personnel authorized for this service.

In the meantime, the Coast Guard has been doing all the things it has always done, only more so. *Every month* since the terrorist attacks, it has, on average …

- Conducted 6,000 port security patrols.
- Flown 600 air patrols.
- Boarded 350 vessels.
- Escorted 1,000 ships in and out of port.
- Handled 1,250 search and rescue operations.
- Assisted 2,000 mariners in distress.
- Saved 135 lives.
- Stopped 125 illegal migrants.
- Responded to 20 pollution emergencies.
- Assigned sea marshals to escort 200 vessels.
- Seized more than five tons of cocaine and marijuana.

The Coast Guard called up 2,000 of its reserves to handle the added load. Its normal complement is about 7,000 officers and 28,000 enlisted personnel.

Compared to the Army's strength of 471,600, and even the Marine Corps' 170,600 active-duty personnel, the Coast Guard may seem tiny. But its role is anything but puny.

Coast Guard cutters and HH-65A helicopters are Johnny-on-the-spot whenever there is an emergency on the water.

The guard patrols some 95,000 miles of America's coastline. But that is only part of what it is asked to do. In fact, the Coast Guard has five basic missions:

- **Security at sea.** Coast Guard people provide America's frontline defense against the flow of illegal drugs, aliens, and contraband over maritime routes. They stop illegal fishing, and they take actions against waterborne violators of federal laws.

- **Water safety.** When you have an emergency aboard a boat, you can't dial 911 for a tow truck or an ambulance. Instead, you holler "Mayday" into the radio, and the Coast Guard will be there before you know it. The Coast Guard is the first to respond to distress calls from ships and boats of every size. In this phase of its mission, its job is not just to save lives—which it does virtually every day—but to cut down on property damage. They routinely inspect vessels, from oil tankers to weekend boaters' craft, to fishing boats and cruise ships. It's their job to make sure there aren't any mechanical problems that are accidents waiting to happen.

- **National security.** As one of the five American armed forces, the Coast Guard is on call in any national emergency. Its participation in stepped-up homeland security is just part of the story. It has served in foreign wars throughout its history, too.

- **Ensuring mobility.** As an arm of the U.S. Department of Transportation, the Coast Guard is responsible for making sure that commercial ships are able to get where they're going without any delays. The responsibility also extends to recreational boating. It includes manning icebreakers on the Great Lakes and in the far north, and keeping channels open along rivers and harbor entrances. The Coast Guard is also responsible for maintaining aids to navigation from buoys to light stations and electronic beacons. It prepares navigational charts, too, so that anybody piloting a boat of any kind knows what's down there under their keel.

- **Protecting natural resources.** It is the Coast Guard that shows up first when there is an oil spill. Coast Guard people are also first on the job when tropical storms rearrange the coastline. They are also constantly watching for subtle natural changes along the shore and under the water.

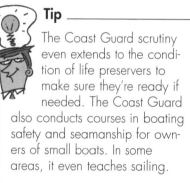

Tip

The Coast Guard scrutiny even extends to the condition of life preservers to make sure they're ready if needed. The Coast Guard also conducts courses in boating safety and seamanship for owners of small boats. In some areas, it even teaches sailing.

Tip

The average Coastie is a combination of military expert, humanitarian, and law enforcement officer. Some days his or her duty might involve all three skills. There isn't any such thing as an average day on the job. That's summed up in the Coast Guard motto: *Semper Paratus*. It means "Always Ready," and that means ready for anything.

The Coast Guard's ice-breaker USS Polar Sea *keeps sea lanes open for the research station in Antarctica, among other duties.*

In the Beginning

The Coast Guard is America's oldest maritime service. Its history officially began in 1789 when Congress established the Lighthouse Service.

Nothing fires the imagination quite like a lighthouse. At some point in everybody's life, they have dreamed of getting away from it all and becoming a lighthouse keeper. But that's one of those jobs that technology has eliminated.

Today's lighthouse operations are all automated. But it is the Coast Guard that keeps the lights burning. The maintenance work ranges from polishing the lenses to keeping the structure sound, just as a lighthouse keeper has always done. The difference is that nobody lives there anymore.

The Lighthouse Service

Until the federal government took over, lighthouses and beacons were built and maintained by individual states. For the first 50 years, maintenance went along just as it always had. Each structure had a keeper and his family, and they rarely saw anybody except for the crew of an occasional supply ship.

They didn't even always know who was in charge. The service began as an arm of the Treasury Department. Then it was attached to the Commerce Department. Lighthouses didn't become the Coast Guard's responsibility until 1939.

Today, the Coast Guard maintains more than a thousand lighthouses around the country. They guide ships into harbors not just in coastal waters, but along the Great Lakes and the inland river system.

The Lighthouse Service was also responsible for more than 120 lightships as well. They were, in effect, floating lighthouses, permanently anchored at potential trouble spots like the mouths of harbors—where land to build an actual lighthouse might be miles away. Like lighthouse keepers, they have become a thing of the past. Many have been replaced by large buoys, and some, like the one at the entrance to New York Harbor, are now mounted on huge platforms like the ones used for offshore oil drilling rigs. (Incidentally, protecting those rigs is another one of the Coast Guard's jobs.)

Seagoing Revenuers

In the early days of the American republic, taxes collected on import and export cargoes accounted for the lion's share of the money it took to run the country.

To make sure nobody beat the system, Alexander Hamilton's Treasury Department outfitted 10 small cutters to keep an eye on things. That branch, called the Revenue Cutter Service, was another of the Coast Guard's ancestors.

Responsibility for the government's finances was only one of the things Hamilton demanded of the fleet. He made sure they understood that the Revenue Cutter Service were the people's servants. "Their countrymen are Freemen," he wrote, "and as such are impatient of everything that bears that least mark of a domineering spirit."

In the 1820s, revenue cutters protected commercial vessels against pirates. In one sweep of the Caribbean, they put five pirate ships out of action. They also confiscated the contraband aboard, a job that has become routine in the modern Coast Guard.

One responsibility that hasn't been passed down to today's service is intercepting slave ships from Africa. But as early as 1794, it was part of their standing orders. After importing of slaves was outlawed in 1808, that part of the job intensified, as revenue cutters were sent out to stop slavers from delivering their human cargo to American ports. The ships they stopped were generally turned around and sent back to Africa. But it was a nearly impossible job. Enough slipped through the net that in the first 50 years the law was in effect, more than a quarter of a million black Africans were illegally imported into America as slaves.

Chasing Rumrunners

In the 1920s, when alcoholic beverages became illegal, gangsters cashed in by "importing" booze aboard fast boats of every description. Of course, it was the Coast Guard's job to stop them. But that was easier said than done.

The bootleggers souped up the engines of the boats they called "rumrunners." They had money enough to hire the craftiest pilots for them, too. On top of that, the Coast Guard didn't have any jurisdiction beyond coastal waters, which extended 12 miles out. But a boat-load of whiskey was worthless out at sea. It added up to a cat-and-mouse game that lasted as long as Prohibition did.

Gunrunners and Drug Busts

When Prohibition was repealed in 1933, many of the old rumrunners were pressed into service smuggling guns into Central America. It was the Coast Guard's job to stop them. Stopping them on the way back for more guns was even more important, because they were always carrying drugs. Although at that time, unlike today, the flow of drugs from Central America was a comparative drop in the bucket, there was enough traffic to keep the Coast Guard busy.

In the 1930s, most of the drugs coming into the United States came aboard ships sailing from the Far East. The packages containing opium and other narcotics were generally dropped over the side in international waters before the ships ever reached port. The buyers would pick up the packages in their own small boats, and the smugglers were able to clear U.S. Customs with only legitimate cargoes.

Coast Guard cutters usually followed the incoming ships for miles out at sea so that they could observe the drops and be able to retrieve the waterproof packages before their buyers did. Although they had the authority to board freighters within the country's territorial waters, they couldn't do it in international waters, which was where the drops were made.

During the 1970s alone, Coasties confiscated more than $4 billion in drugs, mostly marijuana and cocaine. They seized more than 300 hundred vessels, and made almost 2,000 arrests.

Boarding ships and confiscating contraband is one of the Coast Guard's most important assignments.

Going to War

Although its basic mission is protecting America's shores, the Coast Guard has hit the high seas in just about every war the country has fought.

It was the only maritime service there was after the Continental Navy was eliminated in 1790. When the U.S. Navy was established eight years later, the revenue cutters were required to serve in its fleet whenever needed, and they were needed during the War of 1812 when the Navy found itself short of shallow-draft vessels. In fact, it was a cutter that made the first capture of the war.

During the Mexican War, it was revenue cutters that towed Marine landing craft ashore on their way to the Halls of Montezuma. In the Civil War, the cutters served on both sides. (Some were confiscated in southern ports when the war broke out.) Serving the Confederate Navy, they concentrated on raiding commercial ships, whose cargoes were captured for the southern cause. On the other side, they tracked raiders and provided fire support for troops on shore. It was a revenue cutter that fired the first shot in the war.

Tip

When applied to ships and boats, the term "draft" describes how far a vessel extends down below the waterline when afloat. Coast Guard cutters are often shallow-draft, which allows them to maneuver close to shore or in rivers. Even the smallest Navy ships can expect to get stuck in the mud at the bottom of a body of water that is less than about 30 feet deep.

During the Spanish-American War, cutters blockaded the port of Havana. Others were sent to the Philippines. During that time, the Navy was stretched thin, and gave the job of watching the coast to the Life-Saving Service—another of the Coast Guard's ancestors that had been formed to stand watch along stretches of the shore where shipwrecks were common, and pull survivors out of the water.

Full-Time War Footing

The modern Coast Guard was created in 1915 by combining the Life-Saving Service and the Revenue Service. While its predecessors had served the Navy in previous wars, the newly created service became its full partner in 1917 at the start of World War I.

Six Coast Guard cutters served throughout the war in Gibraltar, where they escorted ships sailing to Britain. They also took on patrol and escort duty all over the Mediterranean.

When war broke out in Europe again in 1939, the Coast Guard went back into action, defending American neutrality abroad. A year later, its mission was expanded with the power to seize ships carrying explosives. Even though America was still technically neutral, the Coast Guard stopped 65 ships from carrying weapons and ammunition into

European ports. After war was finally declared, the Coast Guard officially became part of the Navy.

During the course of the war, its ships sank 11 German U-boats, and its aircraft sank another for good measure. Coasties landed Army troops and Marine forces in every major amphibious landing in North Africa, Italy, and France, including D-Day, as well as in the island-hopping invasions in the Pacific.

Back stateside, armed Coast Guardsmen patrolled docks and beaches. Cutters patrolled the offshore waters and rescued more than 1,500 survivors of attacks by German submarines along America's east coast. Coasties operated 802 cutters during the war, but they also handled 351 Navy and 288 Army vessels.

In Their Footsteps

About 2,000 Coast Guardsmen who served abroad during World War II were decorated for bravery. Six earned the Navy Cross and one the Distinguished Service Cross. Signalman First Class Douglas Munro was awarded the Medal of Honor. Serving as a petty officer in charge of 24 Higgins boats, he was charged with evacuating a Marine battalion pinned down at Point Cruz on the island of Guadalcanal in August, 1842. Although they were faced with intense crossfire from machine guns on the island, Munro carefully maneuvered five of his craft toward the shore. When he reached the beach, he signaled the others to land as well, and then he placed his own craft as a shield between the other boats and the shore. When the evacuation of the 500 Marines was nearly finished, Doug Munro was killed by enemy fire. But his crew followed his plan and held their position until the last boat was loaded and clear.

Korea and Vietnam

The Coast Guard went abroad again during the Korean War. This time, though, Coasties served in communications and weather services. They took care of port security, too, and trained people in the care and handling of live ammunition.

The Coast Guard's expertise was brought into play again in Vietnam. Its men were involved in river patrols, and they handled port security in Saigon. While they were there, Coasties developed an inland navigation system throughout Vietnam, and established a Loran navigational network of radio beacons that pinpoint the latitude and longitude of ships and airplanes for all of Southeast Asia.

Alaska and the Gulf of Mexico

When Alaska became a U.S. possession in 1867, the Revenue Service had a brand-new job. Not only did it add 40,000 miles of shoreline to keep an eye on, but it presented them with a whole new environmental challenge.

There weren't too many people up there in those days, but those who were seemed determined to make seals an extinct species. More than a million were killed in less than four years before Congress passed a law to limit the slaughter.

But the only law in Alaska was the Revenue Service. It turned out to be enough. The service was put in charge of the enforcement of all of Alaska's game laws.

At about the same time the future Coast Guard was camping out on the Alaskan shore watching over herds of seals, their counterparts in the Gulf of Mexico were baby-sitting for some endangered fish and sponges.

The Coast Guard is still on the job in the Gulf, in Alaska, and everywhere else there is an endangered marine species, from sea otters to sand sharks, in need of its help.

The National Strike Force

Back in 1973, the Coast Guard formed what it calls the National Strike Force (NSF) to deal with water pollution, and especially oil spills. It is divided into three highly professional teams, covering the Atlantic and Pacific Oceans and the Gulf of Mexico, with advanced equipment to respond to oil and other pollution incidents.

Their training and equipment is mainly geared to cleaning up waterways, but it was a Coast Guard strike force that ran the first air quality tests on the ground after the World Trade Center disaster.

They are on hand right away after an airplane crashes in the ocean, and they participate in the cleanup after floods (like the floods that struck the middle of the country in the 1990s).

Tip

Oil spills are a recurring nightmare for the Coast Guard whose job it is to clean up the mess and keep it from spreading. The biggest challenge came in 1989, when the tanker *Exxon Valdes* went aground in Alaska's Prince William Sound and dumped more than 10 million gallons of the gooey stuff into the water. Another oil tanker, *Argo Merchant*, went aground off Nantucket, Massachusetts, in 1976 and spilled 7.7 million gallons into the Atlantic. But there are other kinds of oil spills to deal with as well.

A coastal storage tank at Sewaren, New Jersey, dumped 8.4 million gallons into the water in 1969, and two years earlier a dragging anchor beneath a ship jabbed a hole into an oil pipeline under the Gulf of Mexico off Louisiana, and 6.7 million gallons of oil bubbled up to the surface. There have been blowouts and fires aboard offshore oil rigs around the world, too. There hasn't been a major event like that in U.S. Coastal waters, but it is the Coast Guard's job to routinely inspect them so that there won't be.

NSF people also train other Coast Guard personnel to handle the job of dealing with waterborne pollution. And they prevent problems from happening by enforcing pollution laws.

Tools of the Trade

The Coast Guard is in the process of modernizing its fleet. But until the new ships begin pulling up to its piers, it is doing quite nicely with an inventory of 90 large cutters and 90 special-purpose vessels like buoy tenders and floating cranes. Its fleet also includes about 300 small ships and boats and some 200 aircraft, including helicopters. The following sections describe some of the "tools" in their arsenal.

High-Endurance Cutters

Powered by diesel engines and gas turbines, these big 378-foot ships can go just about anywhere and do just about anything. They have a helicopter flight deck and a retractable hangar.

There are 12 of these giants serving the Coast Guard today. Two are based at Charleston, South Carolina, two at Honolulu, Hawaii, two at Seattle, Washington, and two at San Diego, California; four are based at Alameda, California.

A "cutter" is a Coast Guard vessel longer than 65 feet. They always have enough space for their crews to live aboard. They usually have a motor-surf boat aboard, as well as a rigid-hull inflatable boat. Included in the cutter class are such specialized ships as buoy tenders, patrol boats, and construction tenders.

Polar Class Icebreakers

The largest ships in the Coast Guard fleet, these 399-foot powerhouses not only carve sea lanes through the Arctic icepack, but they conduct scientific research and meteorological services. They also serve as supply ships for remote stations in the far north.

These are often the ships that are used to track the courses of icebergs. If they had been available in 1912, maybe the *Titanic* would still be sailing. Thanks to the Coast Guard, there are a lot of ships at sea today that might otherwise be down at the ocean floor.

The Coast Guard operates two of these big icebreakers, the *Polar Sea* and *Polar Star*. Each has a reinforced hull and a system that can shift the ballast to concentrate weight up forward to the business end. The ballast is the material that is placed below a ship's waterline so that its weight is concentrated downward to keep it from tipping over. In the case of these giants, that weight can be shifted to the front when there is thick ice to be broken, and the icebreaker's bow drops deeper into the water so that it can plow into the ice like a charging bull.

The Coast Guard also has smaller 290-foot inland icebreakers that do the job on lakes and rivers.

Boats

One of the first things you learn if you join the Navy is that its fleet is composed of *ships*, never *boats*. The Coast Guard, on the other hand, has lots of boats, somewhere around 1,400 of them. By their definition, it means a craft less than 65 feet long. They usually operate close to shore or on inland waterways.

They range from 52-foot motor lifeboats to rigid-hull inflatables. In between are utility boats, pursuit boats, aids to navigation boats, and transportable security boats. They range from 21 to 47 feet long.

Aircraft

The Coast Guard flies some 211 aircraft. They are used for search and rescue, law enforcement, environmental response, ice operations, and air protection. Fixed-wing aircraft, such as C-130 turboprops and HU-25 Falcon jets, operate from coastal air stations. Rotary-wing aircraft, like the HH-65 Dolphin and HH-60 Jayhawk helicopters, also operate from larger cutters.

A Trophy Ship

The pride of the Coast Guard fleet, and of all America for that matter, is the tall ship *Eagle*, whose homeport is the Coast Guard Academy at New London, Connecticut.

A four-masted square-rigged sailing barque, her highest mast is 147 feet tall. Her overall length is 295 feet. *Eagle* was built in 1936 at Hamburg, Germany, as a sail training ship commissioned as *Horst Wessel*, honoring the first Nazi soldier killed in battle. She saw service as a fighting ship during World War II, with two downed Allied planes to her credit.

When the war ended, the United States took the tall ship as a war prize, and in 1946, a Coast Guard crew sailed her across the Atlantic to her new home, where she was rechristened *Eagle*. A distinctive red slash, the identifying mark of all Coast Guard vessels, was painted on her bow.

The ship serves as a seagoing classroom for future Coast Guard officers. More than 150 Coast Guard Academy cadets or officer candidates are taking cruises aboard the tall ship at any given time. They learn seamanship from her five officers and crew of 30.

Eagle has become as much a symbol of America as the Statue of Liberty, which is appropriate because, like most Americans, the ship and the statue have roots on foreign shores.

They also learn plenty from the ship itself. They learn about leadership and respect for the sea. And they get lessons in endurance, working aloft handling 22,000 square feet of canvas and 5 miles of rigging. It is seamanship training done the old-fashioned way—which is still, many believe, the best way.

Although *Eagle* may look like something out of an Erroll Flynn movie and recalls the days of wooden ships and iron men, her hull is actually made of steel. Even the weather decks, though covered with teak, are steel plate. *Eagle* may not look the part, but she is every inch a modern ship, taking advantage of everything shipbuilders have learned over the centuries.

Hidden away down there under those decks are marine engines. But *Eagle* can go half again as fast under full sail. And there isn't a sight like it anywhere in America's fleet.

In Their Footsteps

All the European explorers who mapped the eastern side of North America were looking for just one thing: a northwest passage connecting the Atlantic and Pacific Oceans that would shorten the trip to gather the riches of the Orient. None of them found it. Over the centuries, modern explorers with stronger ships tried to sail across the top of the continent, but they all failed, too.

Then, in 1957, the U.S. Coast Guard cutters *Storis*, *Spar*, and *Bramble* finally did it. They sailed from Seattle up through the Bering Strait, and then into the Arctic Ocean. Their route took them through a twisting series of bays, gulfs, and straits, some of them uncharted. Although the voyage took place through July and August, the Canadian Navy's icebreaker *Labrador* opened a path for them through Bafin Bay and onto the Atlantic. The trip to New York, their destination, was a piece of cake from there on.

Wide-Open Opportunities

Like all of the services, there aren't any racial or ethnic barriers to Coast Guard service. But the Coast Guard goes the rest of them one better. There isn't any job in its rate list that is closed to women.

Generally, the military rules out women when it comes to filling jobs that might lead to combat. But unless there is an all-out war, the Coast Guard doesn't send people into combat.

The only qualifications you'll find are that you need to be a U.S. citizen or resident alien; you need to be between the ages of 17 (with parental consent) and 24; and you need to be a high school graduate with less than two dependents. You will also need to take the Armed Services Vocational Aptitude Battery and pass a physical examination.

It would also be helpful if you enjoy being around the water. But you don't necessarily have to know how to swim. They'll teach you.

Coast Guard Ranks

Even though they try to deny it, the Coast Guard generally follows Navy tradition in its insignia. The Coast Guard shield is worn on both sleeves by officers and on the right sleeve by enlisted personnel. The following list of Coast Guard ranks also includes the pay categories that go with them. The actual amount varies by length of service and rates that are always subject to change. For the latest pay scales, log on to www.defenselink. mil.specials.militarypay2002.

Commissioned Officers

- Admiral (O-10)
- Vice Admiral (O-9)
- Rear Admiral (upper) (O-8)
- Rear Admiral (formerly Commodore) (O-7)
- Captain (O-6)
- Commander (O-5)
- Lieutenant Commander (O-4)
- Lieutenant (O-3)
- Lieutenant Junior Grade (O-2)
- Ensign (O-1)

Enlisted

- Master Chief Petty Officer (E-9)
- Senior Chief Petty Officer (E-8)
- Chief Petty Officer (E-7)
- Petty Officer First Class (E-6)
- Petty Officer Second Class (E-5)
- Petty Officer Third Class (E-4)
- Seaman (E-3)
- Seaman Apprentice (E-2)
- Seaman Recruit (E-1)

Warrant Officer

- Chief Warrant Officer Four (WO-4)
- Chief Warrant Officer Three (WO-3)
- Chief Warrant Officer Two (WO-2)
- Warrant Officer (WO-1)

Picking a Rating

Following naval tradition, the Coast Guard calls its job specialties "ratings." As a new recruit, you'll start out without one, but right after Basic Training at Cape May, New Jersey, you'll go on to an "A" school for classroom training or for "Strikes," which is on-the-job training at a Coast Guard base or station.

As a relatively small organization, the Coast Guard doesn't offer as many specialties as, say, the Army. But there are more then 30 to choose from, ranging from quartermasters to helicopter pilots to electronics technicians.

As often happens when studying lists of career opportunities in the military, you'll find that the title doesn't always describe the job.

Among Coast Guard rates, one of those is boatswain's mate. It's a big job. Once you've gone through the on-the-job training required, you'll be able to handle any job on the deck of any ship. You'll know all there is to know about hoists and winches, navigation, and piloting small boats. You'll be able to take command of any deck crew, too.

Boatswain's mates often serve as officers in charge aboard patrol boats, tugs, and shore units. In that capacity, you will also serve as a federal law enforcement officer.

Plans are already well along to merge the similar quartermaster rate with boatswain's mate. The idea is to open new opportunities for advancement. It will become possible quite soon for boatswain's mates to operate any kind of vessel in the Coast Guard's fleet, and to compete for command of them.

Quartermasters in the present system usually serve as navigators. They plan voyages, maintain charts, and care for navigation equipment—including Global Positioning Satellite systems and radar.

Senior quartermasters are in charge of boarding teams when ships are stopped for searches and inspections.

Marine Science

The Coast Guard offers some jobs you won't find in the other services, like marine science technician, a fascinating specialty that involves analyzing pollution incidents and serving on the National Strike Force. The rating can also involve weather forecasting and working in research laboratories. It requires some background in math, and begins with eight weeks of training at the "A" school in Yorktown, Virginia.

Dive Schools

Possibly the toughest ratings you can qualify for is diving officer and its close cousin, aviation survival technician. It begins with a five-week scuba course that teaches the physics of diving as well as the basics of using scuba equipment. It also includes training in ordnance disposal and treatment of diving casualties.

Coast Guard divers get involved in servicing aids to navigation, hull inspections and cleanings, as well as salvage operations and research projects. They are usually assigned to the larger cutters and specialized ships, and dive teams nearly always include medical personnel who themselves qualify as divers.

Many aviation technicians serve as helicopter rescue swimmers. They perform rescues in the midst of hurricanes, on the face of cliffs and glaciers, and from ships at sea. Others with the same rating inspect and maintain aircraft safety systems, ranging from oxygen systems to wing rafts. But they, too, qualify as rescue swimmers.

Coast Guard Life

If you were to plan a vacation at a beach resort in Florida or California, you would expect to spend hundreds or even thousands of dollars for the fun of it. But when you look out of your hotel room window, there is a pretty good chance that you'll see a Coast Guard station just down the beach. The men and women who work there live there, too. And they have a better water view than you probably do.

When the Coast Guard was based on Governor's Island in New York, the Coasties assigned to it had straight-on views of the Statue of Liberty on one side and the Manhattan skyline on the other. Not only that, but the whole island, a hundred yards or so from the tip of Manhattan, was off-limits to civilians.

Coast Guard personnel and their families are usually assigned housing right where they work. As in the other services, you can get a basic allowance for housing to live off base. But the general rule is not to make it available unless Coast Guard housing is full.

One reason is that Coast Guard facilities are often located in port cities or in resort areas where housing is expensive. But as Coast Guard personnel, you get to live in those places free.

The Coast Guard Auxiliary

Like the other services, the Coast Guard offers opportunities to serve as a reservist. Unlike the others, its reserves report for actual duty at Coast Guard stations on weekends and during their two-week annual tours. But it also has a civilian arm, called the Coast Guard Auxiliary, which allows you to serve its mission without a military obligation.

The physical requirements are next to nonexistent. The age limit extends all the way up to 64. Members go though special training courses in seamanship and boat handling. And, oh yes, it helps if you have a boat.

The auxiliary was formed during World War II when regular Coasties were sent abroad. Civilians filled the gap. They went out into coastal waters in their own boats, in what was called the "Put-Put Navy," looking for possible foreign invaders. (They found some, too.)

Those who didn't have boats signed up for port security. About 20,000 civilians patrolled piers and warehouses to keep an eye out for saboteurs and spies, as well as suspicious fires. Some of them patrolled beaches on horseback. Others who were interested in radio maintained communications stations that were not only valuable to other military branches who needed to know what was going on, but to direct others in the auxiliary as well.

Still others who owned small airplanes volunteered to fly over coastal water, lakes, and rivers, with much the same mission.

Bet You Didn't Know

In spite of its name, the Coast Guard's mission extends through every one of the 50 states. Pleasure boating is one of the things that keeps it the busiest. There are some 20 million craft in that category, from fishing boats to the ones that tow water skis, with boats of every size and shape in between. It's up to the Coast Guard to make sure that the 27 million people who have fun with them don't run into problems. The Coast Guard Auxiliary helps them do that.

When tall ships paraded into American harbors in the 1980s and 1990s, thousands of small boats crowded around them. During the Statue of Liberty's Centennial in 1986, more than 30,000 pleasure boats showed up. Keeping all of them from bumping into each other turned out to be the biggest peacetime operation in Coast Guard history. They are on hand in the Atlantic off Florida for every NASA launch, and they keep order during America's Cup races, too. In fact, every time someone boards a boat anywhere in the country, the Coast Guard is on hand to make sure they get the day of fun that they bargained for.

By the mid-1950s, the auxiliary's mission expanded to include training in safe boating. To this day they conduct free classes for boat owners, their families, and their guests. They've gotten so good at it that insurance companies offer discounts in premiums for boats whose owners have taken the courses.

The auxiliary still helps the regular Coast Guard in search-and-rescue missions and harbor patrols. They check and recheck nautical charts for accuracy, too. And they monitor and respond to distress calls.

Uniforms

What the well-dressed Coast Guardsman wears has changed almost constantly over the years, more often than not to distinguish him or her from Navy people. Finally, in 1941, when they were in fact an arm of the Navy, the dress-code rivalry seemed to die forever. But don't count on it. The rivalry is still very strong.

As in the Navy, Coast Guard officers wear "combination caps," peaked hats whose covers are interchangeable to match khaki, white, or dark winter uniforms. The difference is in the device above the visor. In the Coast Guard, it is a spread eagle with an anchor in its talons above a shield. In the Navy, the eagle is smaller and appears over crossed anchors. The Navy eagle is silver, the Coast Guard's is gold.

Unlike the Navy, Coast Guard uniforms have a shield above the sleeve rank stripes. The buttons are different, too, but at first glance, Navy and Coast Guard personnel are practically identical twins.

Bet You Didn't Know

From the earliest days of maritime service, sailors have worn trousers that flare out at the bottom. It isn't a fashion statement. Back when a big part of the job was scrubbing the decks, the design made it easier to roll them up. Bell-bottoms also made it easier to pull them off if you happened to fall overboard. The tops are as tight as they can be, and the jackets that go with them are short and tight. That was so a sailor could climb the lines up the masts of sailing ships without his clothes getting in the way. The standard issue always came in the darkest blue possible because the rigging on sailing ships was always coated with tar for weather protection. The blue pants and jackets didn't show the stains. Modern Coasties don't scrub decks, and they don't climb masts, either. But they still dress like they do. Call it tradition.

The Least You Need to Know

- The Coast Guard is more than just a military career. They are involved in policing America's waterways, and the job never stops.
- You can be involved in saving the environment. The Coast Guard protects coastal and marine wildlife as well as people. It also supervises cleanups after oil spills.
- You may serve as a federal law enforcement officer. The Coast Guard intercepts illegal drug shipments, as well as other smuggled goods, and the officers and crews of its cutters can stop any ship for boarding.
- The Coast Guard is responsible for the safety of all of the country's pleasure boats as well as commercial ships. They conduct routine inspections and are responsible for rescue operations.
- There are no Coast Guard jobs closed to women.

Part 5

Special Cases

Would you rather skip the idea of serving in uniform? Find out how you can still serve your country and get many of the benefits the military offers as a civilian employee. Maybe you think your future is in working with computers. Those devices were created for the military, and it is still on the cutting edge of the latest and best in computer technology. There is no better place to keep ahead of the curve.

On the other hand, you might have scored high in the mechanical section of the Armed Services Vocational Aptitude Battery (ASVAB). If that points to a career as a mechanic, you're going to find more opportunities in the military than anywhere else. It offers a greater variety of jobs, and it gives you good reasons to be proud of your choice. Better still, the experience can lead to an amazing number of good-paying civilian jobs.

Chapter 17

A Dream Realized

In This Chapter

◆ How to get an M.D. degree free
◆ How the military's medical training works
◆ What the military expects in return
◆ The steps you need to take

For more than 20 years now, the Harris Poll has been asking Americans what they think is the county's most prestigious profession. The results vary a little from year to year. Military officers ranked pretty far down in the list of the top 15 when the polling began, for instance, but now they're among the top five. They rank well above engineers, lawyers, and architects, in fact. Even athletes seem to have less prestige among their fellow Americans.

But there is one profession that has never budged from the number one spot since the annual lists were first published: doctors.

The Cost of a Medical Degree

At one time or another, you may have thought you'd like to become one. But it's not only a long row to hoe, it's almost impossibly expensive.

At the end of 1998, the *Journal of The American Medical Association* (JAMA) reported that new doctors were almost invariably deep in debt when they hung out their shingles. It estimated that, at best, most wouldn't be debt-free for at least a decade, maybe longer. This means that by the time the debt is paid off, a doctor will most likely wind up paying back $3 for every $1 that was borrowed.

That was a few years ago, of course. Educational costs have been rising in the years since at a much faster rate than virtually anything else in the average family's budget. According to the U.S. Department of Education, tuition costs at four-year private universities averaged $13,973; and by 2001, the number had jumped to $15,532. Medical school fees have been going up just as dramatically, and it is reasonable to assume that today's new doctors are going to start out even deeper in the hole. Medical school can add as much as $30,000 with another $15,000 a year tacked on for expenses such as room and board.

According to JAMA, more than half of recent medical school graduates borrowed at least $75,000 to finance their education. A third of them were in hock for more than $100,000. Other studies say that a large percentage of medical school graduates probably start out owing $150,000 just for that portion of their education, without even taking their undergraduate schooling into account.

If prestige was all that was at stake, numbers like that wouldn't make any sense. But, of course, it's the least of the reasons why anybody would want to become a doctor. Still, those numbers often stand in the way of people who have everything it takes to become a good physician ... except the money to pay for the schooling.

This doesn't always have to be the case. For premed students who qualify, medical school can be free. Not only that, they can actually be *paid* for the experience. And the payback time isn't even close to the time it would take to pay off those onerous student loans.

How to Get a Free M.D. Degree

The better way to become a doctor, a dentist, or an ophthalmologist is called the Health Professions Scholarship Program. The Army, Navy, and Air Force, all of which offer it, call it HPSP. If you are planning to become a doctor, you'll call it a godsend.

Each branch has slight variations on the program, but the idea works just the same in all three, and the one you choose won't affect its value.

Simply put, the military will pay for your medical education. It covers every dime of tuition—in civilian schools. It pays for all the books you need. It pays for your lab fees. It gives you a generous monthly allowance. This is just too good a deal to ignore.

Why is the military being so generous? Because the armed forces need doctors. It's as simple as that. But it's a fact of life that most practicing physicians would rather stay in civilian life, where they can make more money and control where and when they work.

They don't usually consider such benefits as avoiding malpractice insurance premiums, chasing after deadbeat patients, buying expensive equipment, or catering to the whims of a health maintenance organization.

Be all that as it may, the military realizes that its best option is to draw on a pool of new doctors. And it is willing to go to the expense of keeping the pool filled.

How Does a Premed Student Qualify?

First of all, you need to be a *good* student. In order to qualify for an HPSP scholarship, you'll have to have a 3.5 GPA with a 19 on your MCAT (Medical College Admission Test) or 19 on your DAT (Dental Admission Test). You are going to need to submit the following:

♦ An application form, similar to a medical school application

♦ Originals of your undergraduate or graduate transcripts

♦ A minimum of three letters of recommendation from professionals or professors

♦ School entrance exam scores: MCAT, DAT, OAT (Optometry Admission Test), or GRE (Graduate Record Examination)

♦ A letter of acceptance from a civilian professional school

Although you are required to be accepted at a school before you apply for the scholarship, you can transfer to another before you even start. The HPSP is transferable.

What Happens Next?

Your application will be considered, along with all the others submitted, by a special board of professionals from various fields. When their decisions are made, your name will fall in one of three categories:

♦ **Selected.**   You're on your way.

♦ **Alternate.**   You haven't been selected, but you are first in line if other applicants change their mind.

♦ **Nonselected.**   If your application is declined, you can resubmit it after waiting for one year.

If you make the selected list, you'll be notified within three weeks. You don't have to accept the scholarship on the spot, but if you want it, you should accept it as soon as you can. You need to get commissioned as soon as possible. Plus, if you don't really want the spot, it is best to open one up for an alternate.

Tip

If the military seems to have raised the bar a bit high in screening applicants for its medical school program, keep in mind that most medical schools themselves have similar requirements.

Tip

Although most recruiters are aware of the benefits of the Health Professions Scholarship Program, you'll get faster and better-informed answers from the specialists among them. Give them a call first. Army: 1-877-MED-ARMY; Navy: 301-319-4546; Air Force: 1-800-531-5800; AFHP Scholarships: 1-800-443-4690.

Before You Leave for School

Although the school you're going to is a civilian institution, you're going as a military person. And that means you start with a physical examination.

In your case, though, the exam is going to be a bit different than for the run-of-the-mill recruit. You are being commissioned as an officer, and you are going to get the red carpet treatment. Just be careful to get it scheduled for a day when the red carpet isn't rolled up in the corner. Your recruiter can guide you.

What's It Worth?

If you apply, and are accepted, for the Army's version of the HPSP, you will automatically get …

- ◆ Professional school tuition. This covers 100 percent of the tuition at any accredited professional school you choose in the U.S. or Puerto Rico.

- ◆ Books, equipment, and most academic fees. You will be reimbursed for these items after you turn in your receipts. They won't be paid in advance for you.

- ◆ A monthly stipend for $10^1/_2$ months of each school year. At the moment, the monthly amount is $1,058, which translates to $11,109 for the school year. This amount is taxable.

- ◆ Army officer's pay—active duty second lieutenant's pay for the remaining $1^1/_2$ months. At the current rate, this is $1,997.70 per month, for a yearly total of $2,996.66, for the short time each year that you are serving in the military. This amount is also taxable.

- ◆ If you are married, there is no additional benefit for your dependents until after you graduate from medical school and start serving in the military full-time.

- ◆ Basic allowance for housing (BAH) during active duty. At current rates, this will be $639.45 for the month and a half you'll be out of school. It is tax-free.

- ◆ Basic allowance for subsistence (BAS), a nontaxable total of $227.25.

- ◆ Total active duty pay: $3,863.25 per year for just six weeks of actual service.

Now, isn't that better than going into debt while you're going to medical school?

The Fine Print

You've probably already guessed that you're not going to get all this without giving something back. You guessed right. But the payback is a lot less than you might have guessed.

All they ask is that you put in one year of active duty for every year you spent at school with the military picking up the bill. You will also have to serve an equal length of time in the inactive reserves.

Generally speaking, that means the military has your services as a full-fledged, licensed doctor for four years. Residency requirements vary for different types of practice—three years for family practice, and five for general surgery, for instance—but longer residency requirements won't necessarily add years to your obligation.

You should be careful, though, where you spend your residency, the mandatory part of medical school training that takes place in hospitals or medical centers. Residency time isn't generally counted as part of your obligation, but if you extend the time, it will count as time spent getting your medical degree and will add to the number of years you will be required to serve as a military doctor. For example, the Air Force adds a year of active duty for every year over five in extended residencies at its own hospitals. Yet, if you spend that time in civilian hospitals, it won't count against you.

Serving While Learning

The Air Force will divide your active duty commitment into four parts. It begins right away with commissioned officer training.

The contract you'll sign says that this is a 45-day program, but in practice, it lasts just 30 days. During the other 15 days, you're pretty much free to do anything you want. You can't travel anywhere without permission, though, so most people just go home and relax.

This training isn't anything at all like boot camp, although there is some physical training involved. In general, you may have to run a mile and a half, and be able to do a couple of push-ups. Nothing strenuous, though. Although the program is always being fine-tuned, in recent years physical training has been held just on alternate days.

The main business of commissioned officer training is academic. It includes leadership, rules and responsibilities, and things like that. It ends with a multiple-choice test that 90 percent pass with flying colors. In the rare event that someone doesn't, they go back to square one, and pay for their own medical schooling.

The second active duty tour, again lasting 30 days out of a 45-day activation, takes place after your first year of medical school. This is where you will get a taste of how medicine is practiced in the military.

The experience is repeated during your third and fourth years. During these short tours, you'll do clinical tours in military hospitals. It's no different from similar rotations all medical students experience in civilian hospitals. But in this case, you'll be collecting active duty officer's pay for the experience.

Tip

Some people prefer civilian residencies, often for no better reason than they'd like to be closer to home. But in some cases, a medical student looking for the best experience in a chosen field might feel that the civilian side offers them better options.

Residencies

At the end of your third year, you'll be offered a choice of a residency in a military hospital or a deferment to spend the time in a civilian facility. They don't have to grant the deferment that will allow you to apply for a civilian residency, but they usually do. The consideration is based on the service's need for specific specialties. About 98 percent of those in the HPSP program get their first or second choice.

Active Duty

The moment of truth comes when you've finished your residency, and see the letters M.D. after your name. In the Army and the Air Force, you'll see "Captain" in front of it, and in the Navy, it will be "Lieutenant."

You'll have to pay the military back at the rate of one year of service for each year it took you to get your degree. In most cases, that means four years of active duty and another four in the reserves. If your schooling takes longer, your obligation may increase.

You can expect to move up through higher ranks after the end of your first tour. And if you stick with the military, you'll make retirement, not 20 years from when you went on active duty, but 20 years from the date you started medical school. That's one reason why you shouldn't waste any time getting commissioned after you've been accepted.

Where Will You Go?

One thing the military never offers is iron-clad guarantees. And that applies to where you will serve more than almost anything else. In most cases, people who go to medical school on an HPSP scholarship can expect to be stationed at a military hospital in the United States. You will be given a chance to pick your location, but whether you get it or not is another story.

Then, in most cases, a three-month "window" opens up about every 15 months. During that time, you might be sent just about anywhere in the world, although you'll still retain your home base and will go back to it at the end of the three months. It's intended to broaden your horizons, and is not a permanent transfer.

It adds to your experience, to be sure, but it can also work a hardship on your family, who can't move with you because the military doesn't cover the cost of relocation. They may not want to pack up and go for such a short time, anyway.

There are also opportunities for permanent overseas duty, but you need to request it.

Try It, You'll Like It

Once your initial commitment is taken care of, you are free to get on with your life. You can start a private practice, form a partnership, join a hospital, or you can stay put.

A surprising number do sign up for more tours of duty. The military is interested in providing the best medical care for its personnel and their families. That interest is reflected in policies without any of the restrictions doctors face in the civilian world. There is only one consideration: If it is the best thing to do, do it. And it is generally conceded in the medical world that America's military hospitals are the best in the business, hands down. They all have the most up-to-date equipment—for one thing— sometimes long before civilian medical centers do.

There is another advantage for these doctors-in-service. They are also entitled to postgraduate specialty training while they are serving. A military doctor can become a surgeon by training at government expense, for instance. There is no limit to what you can do, except for the limitations of having to pay for it.

Bet You Didn't Know

Although the military's willingness to foot the bill for an expensive M.D. degree is at the heart of the HPSP program, it is intended to help all health-care professionals and not just physicians.

There are similar scholarships available for dental students, too, and for optometrists, veterinarians, and nurses, as well as nearly every other career in medical services. The benefits and the obligations are roughly the same in all of them.

An Alternative Route

With the Health Professions Scholarship Program, medical students have a relatively short commitment. Although they get credit for full-time active duty, they only serve in that capacity for six weeks a year. The rest of the time, they are just students.

But there is another category where they possibly could make two or three times as much money for going to school, because they are serving on active duty even though they are full time students. They not only collect base pay full-time, but are also eligible for other money benefits such as the Basic Housing Allowance. All this is available for students attending the military's own medical school: the Uniformed Services University of the Health Sciences (USUHS) at the Bethesda Naval Medical Center near Washington, D.C.

You need to apply and to qualify, of course, just as you would with any other medical school. And if you are already enrolled in a civilian medical school, you can transfer to Bethesda.

Don't let the name fool you. Although the students are uniformed, the staff includes many civilian professors. The medical center itself also serves civilian patients. It is where the president and members of Congress usually get their hospital services.

A Few Basic Differences

USUHS students are more visibly a part of the military. They are commissioned as second lieutenants or ensigns and collect the same full year-round pay as other officers in the O-1 category. They are given their textbooks free, their lab fees are paid, and they collect a housing allowance for a place to live and a subsistence allowance for their food. Third- and fourth-year rotations for internships take place at military hospitals, and students are more often than not given a choice. They are also given first choice over HPSP students for available internships.

They wear uniforms to school, but their daily routine is exactly the same as for any civilian medical student.

USUHS internships and residencies take place in military hospitals, and the options can take you just about anywhere in the world you think you might want to experience. The military pays for all moves.

As a USUHS graduate you will owe seven more years of military service. But you'll start out, along with your medical degree, with a promotion to captain or naval lieutenant—and the raise that goes with it.

Warning _____

The service requirements after you've earned your medical degree are pretty straightforward. But there are a couple of exceptions you should know about: If you have prior military service (many people rejoin to take advantage of this program), your previous experience won't count. By the same token, if you got your graduate degree through an ROTC program, or if you graduated from one of the service academies, the years you owe for that part of your education will need to be served on top of the years required to pay for your medical education.

The Least You Need to Know

- Not everyone qualifies for an M.D. But the military may be the best way to get one. You can have all your medical school tuition and fees paid by the government.

- The payback for a free degree is easy to make. All the military requires is one year of active duty service for every year you spent getting your medical degree.

- The program pays for your training, and it pays you a stipend, too, while you are a student.

- The military also has its own medical school at Bethesda Medical Center, near Washington, D.C. Students have all the benefits of regular military service while they are working on their degree there.

Chapter 18

Fly Me to the Moon

In This Chapter

- ◆ What it takes to be an astronaut
- ◆ Why the military is the best place to begin
- ◆ Other jobs NASA offers
- ◆ Military careers in the space program

Although the National Aeronautics and Space Administration (NASA) isn't one of the military services, many of its activities involve one branch or another. The Air Force usually helps their missions get off the ground, and sometimes the Navy picks them up when they get back.

John Glenn, the first of NASA's astronauts to go into orbit, was a retired Marine Corps pilot. Neil Armstrong, the first man to walk on the moon, flew 78 combat missions as a Navy pilot during the Korean War. Buzz Aldrin, who piloted the lunar module, was a former Air Force pilot. Michael Collins, who was the command module pilot on the Apollo 11 mission, was a West Point graduate who had chosen an Air Force career.

The Pioneers

Maybe you've put the dream behind you by now. But admit it, you probably did once wish for a career in space. It's not too late, you know.

There aren't any age restrictions in the astronaut program. Over the years, the average age of those selected has been 35. But NASA has accepted candidates as old as 46 and as young as 26.

Back in 1959, NASA went to the military to find the right candidates for the manned space program. What they were looking for, they said, were men (yes, men!) with experience flying jet aircraft and engineering training. They also insisted that none of these people could be more than 5 feet, 11 inches tall. That was so they could fit inside the space capsule they had in mind.

The military came up with 500 matches. After tough physical and psychological testing, NASA hired seven of them. Three were from the Air Force, three from the Navy, and one from the Marine Corps.

The military connection faded into the background in 1964, when the space agency turned to the scientific community for its astronaut candidates. The qualifications were changed to educational background rather than flight experience.

The new breed became known as "scientist astronauts," and in the first round of hiring, NASA picked 6 out of 400 who applied for the job.

In Their Footsteps

You may think of John Glenn as a U.S. senator. But his 25 years in the Senate may be the least part of his legacy to America. After he graduated from college with a Bachelor's degree in engineering (he has since been awarded nine honorary doctorates), he went into the Navy's Air Cadet program and earned a Marine Corps commission in time to fly 59 combat missions during World War II.

A few years later, after flying F-86 Sabrejets for the Air Force in Korea, he became a Navy test pilot. During his military career, Glenn logged some 9,000 hours of flying time, 3,000 of them in jet aircrafts. He also flew the first transcontinental mission at supersonic speed, flying from coast to coast in a record 3 hours, 23 minutes.

He joined NASA as a Project Mercury astronaut in 1959. Three years later, he piloted *Friendship 7* on a three-orbit mission around the earth—the first for an American. The mission lasted 4 hours, 5 minutes, and 23 seconds. Glenn went back into space in 1998 with the crew of a nine-day Discovery mission, which involved, among other things, the deployment of the Hubble Space Telescope. He was 77 years old at the time.

> ### In Their Footsteps
>
> The first man in space was the Russian cosmonaut, Yuri Gagarin, who spent 1 hour, 48 minutes in space on April 12, 1961. Since then, through the end of 2001, 97 Russians have flown in space. Over the same period, 267 Americans have gone into Earth orbit. All together, 422 humans have broken the bonds of gravity. There are 11 Germans among them, and 9 Canadians. Eight who have flown in space, and 2 were from Japan.

The Shuttle Program

By the time the space shuttle program was in place in the late 1970s, it was obvious that some of the astronauts were going to have to fly those things. Although the scientist astronauts all had doctorates or equivalent experience, it was decided that flying experience was important, too.

Besides, those scientists had other things to do when they went into orbit. So a new class of astronaut was created, "pilot astronauts." The group of 35 who formed the first potential shuttle crews included 15 pilots. Overall, the group included six women and four minorities.

The picture is still changing. The future of space exploration is going to be launched from a manned space station. That means that the space agency has to cast a wider net beyond its traditional pool of military personnel, and into the civilian world to find the right men and women to take it into the future.

How to Qualify

You don't have to be in military service to become an astronaut. In fact, if you are, you're going to need to go up through the chain of command and get yourself nominated for the job.

As a civilian, though, you can send in your application any time at all. Jobs are filled on an as-needed basis, on average about every two years. When they say they'll keep your resumé on file, they really mean it. What that resumé better show is that you have at least a bachelor's degree in engineering, biological or physical science, or mathematics.

If you think you'd like to be a mission specialist, you'll also need to back up your degree with three years of experience in a related field. It will help if you've been promoted a few times. An advanced degree might make up for what you lack in experience, though.

To become a pilot astronaut, military experience will probably still be helpful. The first requirement is a minimum of 1,000 hours in command of a jet aircraft. It's possible that someone could log that many hours as a civilian airline pilot, but the most obvious way is through a military aviation career.

There are also some physical benchmarks NASA insists on for its astronaut candidates. The height requirement is still part of it. But now you can be as tall as 6 feet, 3 inches. Those little orbiting modules went out of style years ago.

Tip

If you're thinking of a future at NASA, these are a few of the programs you might become involved with:

◆ Space Infrared Telescope Facility to launch December 2001.

◆ Gravity Probe B (to help prove Einstein's Theory of General Relativity) to launch May 2002.

◆ International Rosetta Mission (to rendezvous with comet 46P/Wirtanen) to launch January 2003.

◆ Planck-Herschel Satellite (to study the origins and nature of the Universe) to launch in 2007.

Plus, of course, a host of research activities aboard the International Space Station, scheduled to be operational in 2005, after 44 separate assembly missions.

The Screening Process

Once you have passed the physical and educational hurdles, you may be invited to spend a week with panels of administrators at the Johnson Space Center in Houston, Texas. Your medical records will be fine-tuned, and your psychological profile probed. There will be an endless round of interviews, too.

Typically, there are a few hundred applicants for every job that's open. The elimination process comes during these interviews. Like the military, NASA is looking for team players. They also insist on a high level of individuality.

An impossible combination? Possibly, but those are qualities the military looks for, too, and people who are self-reliant but still eager to be part of a team aren't as rare as you might think. That's what a military career brings out in you.

Most help-wanted ads, for any job, insist that you have a "proven track record" before you'll be considered. Obviously, the best place to get the right track record, and be able to prove it, for this particular job is by starting out with a military career.

Making the Cut

Going to Houston for orientation doesn't mean you have the job. The next step, if you make it that far, is assignment to NASA's astronaut office for a year or two of training and more evaluation. Once you're past that phase, you'll get the title and a contract that requires you to stay on the team for a minimum of five years.

If you are in the military, you will be, in effect, "loaned" to NASA for your tour of duty. You will still be considered on active military duty, and your pay and benefits won't change.

Civilian astronauts, on the other hand, are civil service employees of the government. Their pay ranges from grade GS-11, which is $56,000 a year, at the beginning of 2002, to GS-13, about $87,000. (Civil Service salaries are upgraded on an annual basis.) The difference is determined by your education and previous experience.

Candidate Training

Before you make the cut, you will go through intensive training at the Johnson Space Center. Among the academic courses that are required are such things as oceanography, astronomy, physics, and meteorology.

You will also be expected to become a qualified scuba diver, and to be able to swim three lengths of a 25-meter pool in a flight suit with your shoes on.

You'll get a taste of space travel in this early phase, too. You'll experience high and low atmospheric pressures in special altitude chambers. During that phase, you are going to have to think your way out of sudden surprise emergencies.

The training also involves flying in a special aircraft that produces weightlessness for short periods. The exercise is repeated over and over again during each flight.

Candidates for pilot astronaut fly NASA's jets a minimum of 15 hours a month. Mission specialist candidates are required to log at least four hours of flying time a month.

Advanced Training

During the first phase of advanced training, you will be expected to study NASA's training manuals and to take computer-based training in Orbiter systems. Hands-on training comes after you've made it through the first stage.

> **Tip**
>
> The "Orbiter systems" is NASA's description of the technology that allows the space shuttle (usually called just the "Orbiter") to be maneuvered as it is orbiting the Earth and, of course, to bring it in for a landing back on Earth. The term also applies to unmanned space probes that orbit the planets and are controlled from Earth.

Next comes one-on-one instruction in a single-systems trainer. This is where you get familiar with the Orbiter and learn to deal with any glitches that might come up.

After that, you'll "graduate" to the shuttle mission simulator, where the experience is exactly the same as would be in space, except that you never leave the ground. It comes in two versions, one that doesn't move and another that gyrates all over the place to give you a better feel for actual flight.

This part of the training, which usually involves 300 hours of simulation, also includes links to Mission Control, just as it would be during an actual mission. It is as real as NASA can make it. By the time you are ready to blast off, the experience will be second nature to you.

Other Job Opportunities

Although they represent the glamour of NASA, there are fewer than 150 astronauts in the space program. There are also nearly 19,000 other people on the payroll.

The personnel list includes university researchers and students, but the majority of NASA's employees are federal civil service workers. The jobs they handle include the following:

- **Administrative professionals.** This includes computer programmers, public affairs specialists, accountants, human resources people, and administrators.
- **Lawyers.** This involves dealing with patents and contracts, and the all-important lobbying that keeps the agency funded.
- **Aerospace technologists.** This is far and away the biggest category because it breaks down into more than 70 different specializations for scientists and engineers.
- **Doctors.** These are not just for the care of the agency's staff, but for research in the field of space medicine.
- **Pilots.** There are pilot astronauts, but there is also a need for men and women to operate NASA's fleet of fixed-wing aircraft and helicopters.
- **Logistics.** This includes secretaries and clerks.

Tip

You can get just about any specific information you need about NASA's programs and how to get involved in them through the agency's website at www.nasajobs.nasa.gov.

Anybody can compete for any of these jobs. But as your own job hunting has probably shown, it helps to have experience that perfectly matches the opening. If a job calls for selling soap, for instance, interviewers will often look down their noses at you if all you've ever sold are washcloths.

NASA doesn't give preference to people with military backgrounds, at least not officially, but when it comes to having the right experience, a previous military career may be as right as it gets.

Bet You Didn't Know

If you've ever watched a space launch on television, you've heard a lot of chatter about "Houston." The more formal name for it is the Johnson Space Center, which happens to be located in Houston, Texas. It is where mission control is located, where all operations are planned, and where astronauts are trained. More than 3,300 people work there. But Houston isn't all there is to NASA's operation.

The launching you watched was probably from the Kennedy Space Center on Florida's "Spacecoast." More than 1,725 people work there, preparing the four space shuttle orbiters for launching and servicing them when they get back. The next generation of spacecraft is being developed at the Jet Propulsion Laboratory in Pasadena, operated for the agency by the California Institute of Technology. The more than 5,000 people who work there are classified as independent contractors.

The U.S. Space Command

As impressive as it is, NASA isn't the only branch of the government with its eye on space. The military is very much involved. That involvement is centered around the U.S. Space Command, an operation that coordinates the space-oriented activities of the Army, Navy, and Air Force from its base at Peterson Air Force Base in Colorado.

Each of those services has special responsibilities for putting satellites into orbit and operating them. The Space Command is also involved with NASA in developing new technologies that have uses for defense.

Right now, the military is deeply involved in developing reusable launchers for future NASA missions. It was also on the cutting edge of the development of the X-33, a reusable suborbital space plane that was originally intended to replace the space shuttle. Although NASA has scuttled the idea, the Air Force has put the wheels in motion to revive the project on its own.

That's just one example of how your military career can also be a space-related career. Many of NASA's facilities are located on Air Force bases, and there is often a mingling of jobs.

The Ames Research Center, which does research in such fields as computing, astrobiology, and information systems, is at Moffet Field in California. Its Flight Research Center, where advanced aeronautic technology is developed, is at Edwards Air Force Base in California.

Computers in SPACECOM

The opportunities at the U.S. Space Command also include some of the most impressive computer learning experiences in the world. A division called Joint Task Force–Computer Network Operations (known as JTF-CNO, of course) is charged with all military computer network defense and attack capabilities.

Its staff of about 50, monitors computer networks around the clock. They are on the lookout for intruders, and they are prepared to recommend what to do about them. The task force is also responsible for making sure that new computer operations within the military will be able to do what they were intended to do.

If you are now, or ever have been, or ever wanted to be, a computer hacker, the military's Space Command may have a job for you. Its personnel come from all the services except the Coast Guard.

When all is said and done, maybe it would be more fun to be a (legal) computer hacker than an astronaut. It all depends on whether you're looking for a career in outer space or in cyberspace.

The Least You Need to Know

- You don't need a military background to be an astronaut, but for many years it was the key to success.
- Training for space flight is as intense as for any military career, possibly even more so. Both physical and technical training are intense.
- You can be involved in space research without going there. Thousand of people work behind the scenes to make sure every space launch is perfect.
- There are careers within the military that involve the launching and tracking of satellites.

Chapter 19

The New Heroes

In This Chapter

- The best background for a law enforcement career
- How military experience gets you to the top of the list
- How a military career can also be a career in law enforcement

Back during the Vietnam War, it was fashionable to shun people in the military. The mood of rejection even extended to West Point cadets, who had been the pride of America for more than 150 years. It was also fashionable to turn your back on police officers, and to call them "pigs."

All of that has changed, fortunately. In a *New York Times* interview, a cadet at the U.S. Military Academy noted with pleasure that nowadays "… when people see the West Point military van go by, they yell 'Hi,' and salute. It makes you feel really proud."

Pride has come back into the lives of police officers and firefighters, too. Back where it belongs.

Some of that pride is reflected among young men and women who are filling out applications in record numbers for jobs at police and fire departments all over the country. One thing they are discovering, though, is that many of those organizations are giving special preference to people who have served in the military.

It makes perfect sense. They prefer people with related experience. Even veterans whose military MOS had nothing to do with fighting fires or fighting crime are more welcome in these jobs.

Getting the Perfect Background

The most obvious way to get the right kind of experience for police work is with the military police (MP) or the Adjutant General Corps. You can get that in any one of the services. Once you've been an MP, there isn't much you won't be able to do in any civilian police department. And do it better than most.

There are military careers for firefighters, too. The best can be found in the Navy or the Air Force. The only problem you might have when you move over to the civilian side is that the equipment you'll be working with may seem a little old-fashioned.

But if there is a career in law enforcement in your future plans, there is absolutely no better way to prepare yourself for it than by joining the Coast Guard, where just about everyone is actively engaged in law enforcement in one way or another. Many of them even wear badges that identify them as federal officers.

Bet You Didn't Know _____

When you were a preschooler, you probably made up your mind that you would be a policeman or a fireman someday. Most of us did, and not all of us got over it. If anything, it seems to have become a more popular career choice among young adults than it ever has been.

But not all of them know this secret: These are jobs you can prepare for before you ever set foot in a police academy. And when you do, you'll not only get hired faster, but you'll move up faster, too.

What's the best way to get yourself ready? There isn't any better way than with a tour of duty in the military.

Seagoing Stakeouts

The boarding team is the backbone of the Coast Guard's law enforcement operation. They are the ones who board ships looking for all kinds of violations of federal law, from drug smuggling to safety violations. The officer in charge is one of the Coasties who wears a badge.

The people who back up the boarding officer are teams made up of members of a Coast Guard cutter's crew. Even cooks can get in on the action. Sometimes, a member of the team may outrank the boarding officer, but during the operation, they are subordinates. When it is over, everybody goes back to their normal jobs on deck, on the bridge, or in the galley.

In order to qualify for one of these jobs, it is necessary to pass special tests of your judgment potential. You also have to meet the right physical requirements. And you need to qualify firing a 9mm pistol, which every member of the team carries.

Bet You Didn't Know

In 1982, a boarding team from the Coast Guard cutter *Munro* went aboard a ship off the coast of Mexico and found nearly 200 illegal Chinese immigrants headed for the United States. They called for help, and teams from two other cutters got there as fast as they could. But by the time they arrived, the smuggler who had hired the vessel had stirred up his clients, and they were on the edge of a riot. The Coasties calmed them down, but they were still a long way from an American port. On the way, the teams fought off riots, dealt with hunger strikes, and prevented a couple dozen suicides. They managed to get all the migrants to San Diego and turned them over to the Immigration Service.

In response to such incidents, which have become common, the Coast Guard added a fleet of 38-foot pursuit boats whose crews of six are all qualified for boarding team duty. It also armed them with M-14 rifles as well as the traditional pistols. Each of the so-called "go-fast" boats also carries a shotgun whose scattershot can be used to disable a ship's engine and stop it in its tracks.

Criminal Investigations

Boarding teams are required to wear uniforms, but there is also a lot of plainclothes work available through the Coast Guard's Investigative Services unit.

Like the military police in the other services, these people have a responsibility for investigating internal problems within the service. But in the Coast Guard, the mission also extends to counterintelligence investigations and criminal investigations related to maritime affairs. The work includes illegal immigration, drug smuggling, and environmental crimes. Coast Guard investigators also frequently work hand in hand with other federal enforcement agencies, for example, the Drug Enforcement Agency (DEA).

Coast Guard personnel are selected for boarding teams and for investigative services based on qualifications demonstrated during their regular tour of duty. You can't join up and get one of these jobs right away. You have to volunteer for them, and then prove that you are right for the job.

Investigators come from the ranks of warrant officers and petty officers. Boarding teams can be composed of a variety of rates.

Investigative jobs are also open to members of the Coast Guard Reserve with a rating of warrant officer or petty officer. In fact, nobody but reservists can serve as port security specialists.

Everyone who qualifies for a job as a Coast Guard Investigative Service agent must also qualify for security clearance (which limits the pool of candidates to American citizens). Once you are accepted, you will be sent for intensive courses at the Federal Law Enforcement Training Center at Glynco, Georgia. Boarding officers are sometimes given special training at the Coast Guard's own Maritime Law Enforcement School at Yorktown, Virginia.

Bet You Didn't Know

In spite of its name, the Coast Guard's Pacific Tactical Law Enforcement Team's responsibilities extend from the Pacific to the Caribbean to the Gulf of Arabia. Under the National Defense Authorization Act, the Department of Defense is responsible for preventing drug trafficking into the United States. That is one of the Coast Guard's specialties, but the Coast Guard is part of the Department of Transportation. The answer was to put Coast Guard personnel aboard Navy ships as "guest experts." They are aboard every Navy ship that is navigating through waters where drug cargoes are likely to be found.

To qualify for one of the assignments, a Coastie has to qualify under the Navy's rules to be able to fly in one of its helicopters. That calls for a tougher swimming exam than the Coast Guard usually requires. Using sophisticated drug detection equipment, it is the Coast Guard people who decide whether a ship should be boarded. And it is Coast Guard boarding crews who actually do the job.

Opportunities in the Other Services

The Coast Guard isn't the only military organization with openings for careers as criminal investigators. The Navy and Marine Corps calls theirs the Naval Criminal Investigation Service; the Army's program is called the Criminal Investigation Command; and the Air Force calls it the Office of Special Investigations.

Except for the uniforms their people usually wear—unless they're doing plainclothes work, of course—the missions of all of them are almost the same:

◆ They conduct counterintelligence activities.

◆ They investigate violent crime.

- They safeguard information systems.
- They counteract attempts at fraud.

All of these departments train their agents in every aspect of law enforcement, from the law itself to writing reports. Many are trained in electronics, forensics, polygraph operation and analysis, and even photography.

Once they have been trained and certified, most of the armed forces investigators are on 24-hour standby for special assignments that can take them anywhere in the world. Most of the time, they turn on a dime, but sometimes they can plan their trips.

For instance, whenever one of the Navy's carrier groups sets out on a cruise, teams of Navy special investigators visit their ports of call in advance. Making contact with the local police, they go to work finding and arresting street drug dealers. By the time the big ships tie up, the supply of drugs is usually dried up, and temptation is removed from the sailor's paths.

Every once in a while, they get really lucky. During a sweep of the streets in Gibraltar back in 1993, the Navy's special agents found $375,000 worth of hashish. The perpetrators had disappeared, but two days later the local police caught up with them and netted another cache of drugs. The combined haul was worth more than $937,000.

These military investigators routinely get involved with local law enforcement agencies, and they all learn from one another. One advantage the military people have is that they range beyond city and state lines, not to mention national boundaries. They go anywhere their services are needed.

Your Postmilitary Career

Since the terrorist attack on the World Trade Center, the New York City Police Department has become the poster child for police careers. Even without the disaster, television shows like *Law and Order* and *NYPD Blue* have made the Department a popular choice among job-seekers looking for law enforcement careers.

If you want to work for the NYPD, there is something you need to know: There is a big advantage to starting out in the military.

New York's Police Department requires that all candidates have at least 60 credits from a college or university. But, instead of that, they'll accept two years of active military service.

The NYC Fire Department requires 30 higher education credits, but it will waive the rule if you have served in the military for two years. Although you can be as old as 35 to become a police officer, rookie firefighters can't be older than 29. But they'll bend that rule if you have military experience. They will deduct your years of military service from your actual age, up to six years. That means you *can* become a New York City firefighter when you're as old as 35.

Bet You Didn't Know _____

Among the city's heroes of September 11, in addition to New York's Finest, as police officers are called, and New York's Bravest, the nickname of the city's firefighters, were the men and women of the Emergency Medical Service, including paramedics. These people are employees of the Fire Department, and they're first in line for promotion to firefighter. Like every other desirable job, it takes time, and it helps to know that one too many birthdays isn't going to put you out of the running, thanks to the policy of extending age eligibility for military veterans.

New York City's uniformed services, as is the case with police and fire departments just about everywhere, provide benefits that in many ways resemble the ones the military gives you.

It starts with retirement, which starts with 20 years of service. The pensions are based on an average of your compensation over the last couple of years you serve. That includes overtime pay and other cash benefits such as night differential—the extra pay you get when you pull duty after dark. You will collect half of that amount.

New York's police officers and firefighters start out at slightly less $35,000 a year, and can count on increases to $60,000 over the first five years. They start out with 20 paid vacation days in the first year, and they always get unlimited sick leave at full pay.

Is all that better than a career in the military? It's a matter of opinion. Both careers have remarkable advantages. But if you want to be a uniformed civilian employee, it's a good bet that your chances will be better if you start out in a military uniform.

The Least You Need to Know

- ◆ A career in law enforcement or as a firefighter is similar to a military career. The jobs are related, and the benefits, especially retirement, are almost as good.
- ◆ The military offers scores of similar jobs. In many instances, such as in the Coast Guard, military people have the power to arrest civilians.
- ◆ Civilian uniformed services value military experience, even if that experience didn't involve police work or firefighting. They know they are getting people who understand the discipline that the job requires.
- ◆ There is more flexibility in the military. There are more different kinds of jobs related to police work than can be found in any individual police department.

Chapter **20**

Serving as a Civilian

In This Chapter

- ◆ Civil Service in the military
- ◆ Financial advantages
- ◆ Better than most civilian jobs
- ◆ How to snag one of these jobs
- ◆ Why you should consider it

Whenever the economy takes a dive, which happens with some regularity, factory workers have traditionally found themselves out on the street, laid off.

As the economy has become more sophisticated, white collar workers have often found themselves in the same boat. There seems to be nothing that warms a Wall Street investor's heart more than the news that a company is getting rid of people because it represents an effort by management to curb costs, with the result of higher profits. Most of the time, it is called "downsizing."

But whatever it's called, the effect is the same. There are bills to pay and families to feed; replacement jobs seem to be few and far between.

When a recession hits home, there really aren't any safe havens except, possibly, the military. But there is an employer that is more recession-proof than the average company: the federal government. It is called Civil Service, and some of the best jobs in that category are with—but not in—the military.

You can serve your country without putting on a uniform.

What Is Civil Service?

Since ancient times, governments have insulated themselves from changes that come about when new people are elected to the top jobs. The people who actually do the work are known as civil servants, and their jobs are secure in spite of political change.

The idea makes sense. Without it, in America for instance, whenever we get a new president or the balance of power shifts in Congress, thousands of people might lose their jobs.

Make that hundreds of thousands. The U.S. Office of Personnel Management (itself staffed by Civil Service employees) reports that in 2000 there were 1.9 million civilians on the federal payroll.

Civil Servants in the Military

The Department of Defense is the government's biggest civilian employer, with more than 623,000 jobs. Of those, 207,000 work for the Army, 177,000 for the Navy, and 148,000 for the Air Force. The rest work directly for the department itself, largely at the Pentagon.

There are civilians working at every military installation in the United States, and the job opportunities extend to bases in other countries as well. The jobs are comparable to what you'd expect in any civilian organization, from typists to administrators. In fact, the job descriptions on Civil Service lists cover the whole range of opportunities available in the private sector. One business that the government doesn't engage in very much is selling, so the military prefers to let their recruiters handle those jobs.

On the other hand, one of the big sources of civilian jobs in the military is working with its retail contractors at post exchanges. Most of those jobs are sales-oriented, and they offer the security and protection of Civil Service laws.

Advancement

The federal Civil Service operates exactly like the private sector, although there are some minor differences. Most of the jobs available in professional categories call for a college degree. But office workers and most support jobs only require a high school diploma.

In most Civil Service jobs, they will train you, and many connected with the military offer tuition assistance. Most training takes place on the job, but sometimes it extends to colleges and universities.

Advancement is guaranteed through what is known as a "career ladder." Most workers begin at the starting grade for an occupation, and all are given promotions at regular intervals. The only qualification is satisfactory performance. Sometimes, but not always, these promotions involve moving up two steps at a time in the pay grade scale.

People without a high school diploma are usually hired as clerks at Grade 1, the lowest level, which pays about $14,000 a year. If you have your high school diploma, your entry-level salary will be higher, in the neighborhood of $17,500. Increases, which usually come every six months, will quickly get a Grade 1 employee up to $17,800; and Grade 3, the high school graduates, will earn a maximum of $22,700.

If you have some technical training or experience in another job, your starting salary will be about $19,500, and it goes up to $25,500.

The salary levels vary by job and by your qualifications, and if you have a Bachelor's degree, you'll start out at about $27,000 a year, and advance through the career ladder to $35,000. Exceptions to the rules abound. The government is anxious to make its civilian salary levels competitive with other jobs you might consider.

Tip

You might think that a Civil Service job at a military installation seems perfect for military personnel spouses. Some do take advantage of the opportunity, but for the most part, people from the outside fill the jobs. The reason is one of the disadvantages of being in the military—chances are that the family is going to be moving to another base sometime soon. It happens every couple of years, and the people who do the hiring are aware of that. They prefer to fill their jobs with people who are going to stick around for a while.

It Gets Better

Once you reach the top of your entry-level track, you will still get frequent raises. Better still, you'll have the opportunity to compete for a better job. By the time you reach this point, you'll also qualify for bonuses based on performance. They are generous, and they are more frequent than in other civilian jobs.

Like a career in the military, you can also qualify for a recruitment bonus when you sign up. It can be as much as 25 percent of your starting salary, and even more than that if you have professional experience. The Department of Defense even offers a civilian employment program that will give you up to $40,000 to help wipe out your student loan debt.

Special Educational Programs

In order to improve the effectiveness of its civilian employees, the Army's Materiel Command offers two special programs for higher education on the job.

One of them is a four-year program for skill development. It includes on-the-job training and classroom work that leads to journeyman status, often with related college credit.

The skills involved, defined by the Department of Labor for apprenticeships, include sheet metal mechanics, aircraft mechanics, and machinists. It also extends to electronics and heavy mobile equipment mechanics. Participants are paid for their regular Army-related jobs while they are going through the program, and the raises keep coming.

The other plan, known as the Fellows Program, is a five-year commitment available to most college graduates. It offers a starting salary of nearly $30,000, with a possible 25 percent signing bonus. By the end of the fourth year, your salary will have increased to between $51,00 and $55,000 a year. By the time you finish the last year of the program, your pay level can reach as high as $65,000.

During the first two years, you'll be a full-time student at a graduate school. The government will pay your tuition and your expenses for moving there, and your travel costs as well if the graduate school isn't within commuting distance of where you live. It will also cover the cost of books.

As soon as you get on the payroll, you'll get six months of military orientation at AMC's Logistics Leadership Center in Texarkana, Texas. No, this is not Basic Training. You are a civilian working for the Army, not a soldier.

The Other Services

The Air Force Materiel Command, like the Army's version, is responsible for the development and purchase of just about everything the service needs, from jet fighters to combat boots. It employs about 60,000 civilians in 13 states, and anticipates hiring 17,000 more civilians before 2005. The jobs range from receptionists to electrical engineers.

The Navy, Marine Corps, and the Coast Guard have similar divisions, similar jobs, and similar training incentives. Your choice will more than likely depend on which service has a location close to home. But these jobs can take you anywhere you want to go. Military civilian jobs are available anywhere the military is based, all over the world.

Part-Time Jobs

The Air Force, for one, offers temporary jobs to high school and college students. They can range from lifeguard duty to laborers to office workers. The opportunities are available all the time but, because of the nature of the pool of applicants, most of these jobs are filled between May and September.

It also offers the Student Career Experience Program. It makes jobs available in the field you ultimately plan to enter. The jobs give you a taste of what to expect in that field. And they usually lead to permanent jobs once you've finished the training program and come back with a degree.

Management Training

The Army also offers an intern program for its civilian employees, which will undoubtedly extend to the other services at some point in the near future. It is intended to encourage entry-level civilian employees to move up to middle management and beyond. It is a two-year program that includes training on the job coupled with classroom work.

There are 22 different career programs involving more than 150 different job classifications. They range from personnel administration to library sciences and from housing management to law enforcement. If you participate in the intern program, you'll be hired at a Civil Service level of GS-5 or GS-7 ($22,000–$27,000) as a full-time civilian employee.

During the first two years, you will live on an Army post, where you'll get a specialized classroom education while you are working at the job you signed on for. After that, you'll be promoted to GS-9 or GS-11 ($33,000–$40,000). Not a bad increase after just two years on the job.

The only drawback—and it may not seem so bad to you—is that before you start the program, you'll have to sign a mobility agreement. It means that the Army will have the right to send you anywhere that a relevant job is open. If the stars are in the right alignment, you could wind up on Waikiki Beach. Wherever you go, you'll still be a civilian.

Job Opportunities

Open jobs in the civilian military are posted on a variety of Internet locations. You're going to be surprised at how many there are—and the variety.

A recent posting for jobs with the Army included announcements for such vacancies as running the bowling alley at West Point and decorating a hotel being built in Europe for military personnel. They were looking for someone to run a golf club in Japan, too.

The same page also included several "recreation management" jobs for military people and their families around the world. The job descriptions vary, but they run the gamut from arts and crafts specialists to recreation center managers.

Tip

Some of the websites you'll find in Appendix C will list open opportunities for civilians, even though they are military-oriented. You can find links to others, as well as more information on civilian/military jobs, by logging on to the Department of Defense website: www.defenselink.mil. Or by going to the Civil Service site: www.usajobs.gov. By the way, if you are using a search engine to find others, you'll see many that offer to help you find "unadvertised" jobs or inside help with the entrance exams. Many of those are scams and should be avoided. If the web address doesn't end with ".gov," be wary.

In that category, the job may include running dance classes and planning social dancing events. Sports directors run fitness centers and organize intramural tournaments. Depending on the location, they also get involved in organizing ski weekends or mountain-climbing excursions. Some run marinas and organize deep-sea fishing tournaments.

If it's fun, they do it.

The Corps of Engineers

The Army engineers are more than a military organization. An amazing 97 percent of its people are civilians. They include architects, engineers, landscapers, and zookeepers. And they are represented everywhere in the world that the Army needs them. Most of the jobs are right here in America. The Corps of Engineers is involved in every federal public works project in every state, from flood control to beach erosion.

Tip

Civilian employees in the Corps of Engineers are also allowed to sign up for jobs overseas. Volunteers go abroad for three years, and then come back to the job they left behind with all of their benefits intact.

Among their most recent accomplishments was the rebuilding of the Washington Monument. They built most of the monuments and public buildings in Washington, in fact. The Corps also supervised the building of most of the big hydroelectric dams in the country. They still run some of them, too. They are America's fourth-biggest supplier of hydro power.

Army–Air Force Exchange Service

This civilian organization is one of the biggest retailers in the world. It has 8.7 million customers and more than 50,000 employees. It runs base exchanges for the Air Force, and post exchanges for the Army all over the world. Its personnel aren't Civil Service employees, but they aren't active duty military people, either. The exchanges it runs are like small shopping malls. They usually include retail stores, snack bars, fast food outlets, and often a movie theater.

AAFES is looking for college graduates with degrees in business administration or marketing. It is also on the lookout for people with degrees in hotel and restaurant management. Even if you don't have those qualifications, you can apply for an extensive management training program that involves on-the-job training and classroom work.

Why Should You Consider a Civil Service Job?

On average, Civil Service employees earn $51,565 a year. At the low end of the scale, the salary can be as low as $15,000; at the high end it goes up to nearly $103,000. Although the salary levels are based on predetermined pay charts, just as they are in the military, exceptions are frequently made for people living in areas where the cost of living is high (they get about 17 percent more than the base figure).

If you qualify for a hard-to-fill occupation, you can expect to be paid more for it, too. There are also premium pay schedules for overtime or holiday work as well as for jobs that may be considered hazardous. The pay charts are usually upgraded every year in January to account for increases in the cost of living.

Federal civilian employees are represented by unions, which bargain for new and better contracts. Membership in a union isn't mandatory, though, and only a small percentage actually join, probably on the theory that there isn't any point in buying a cow when you get free milk.

On top of the base pay and frequent bonuses, federal employees also have a choice of several different health plans and life insurance programs. The government contributes to the cost of premiums, usually a higher percentage than you'll find in the private sector.

They also participate in the Federal Retirement System that combines a pension plan with your Social Security benefits. In some locations, they are also entitled to public transit packages that take the strain out of getting to and from work.

Vacation time in a Civil Service job is 13 days a year for the first three years, then 20 days for the next 12 years, and 26 days after that. As a federal employee, you get 13 days of sick leave every year, and the time accumulates indefinitely.

If you decide to opt for a military career, Civil Service is one of your best options when you retire. In most cases, your salary in a civilian job will offset your military retirement pay. But if you take a Civil Service job, you can keep your pay and collect full military retirement, too.

Why So Many Openings?

By now you're probably asking yourself: "If these jobs are so good, why are so many of them available?" The fact is that once people get these jobs, they stick with them until they hit retirement age. But right now, civilians in the defense department are retiring at the rate of about 20,000 a year. Under a new policy, the department is trying to fill their jobs before they leave so that new employees will be able to have the benefit of their experience.

Traditionally, Civil Service has used the model of the military for recruiting new people. They hire them in entry-level jobs and "grow" them into the higher levels. That takes time, though, and the new emphasis is to look for people with experience elsewhere, and they're willing to make attractive deals to get them.

How Do You Get These Jobs?

Civil Service jobs with the military are filled through the federal Office of Personnel Management (OPM). You'll find them in the phone book listed under "U.S. Government," or you can call the federal relay number, 1-800-877-8339. You can also find OPM through its website at www.usajobs.opm.gov.

In some, but not all, cases, you will probably have to take an examination to qualify for the job you want. You'll need to check the usajobs.gov website for specific details. Finding a Civil Service job sometimes involves wading through the bureaucracy. This is the government after all. But it doesn't take very long to get used to the drill.

In spite of its penchant for leading you through a sea of mysterious abbreviations, the federal government wants you to have these jobs, and all the information you need is available though the agency you want to work for. It's free, too. But that doesn't stop some people from trying to guide you though the process for a fee. A lot of them will sell you lists of jobs that might interest you. Many will offer to sell you copies of the exams you'll take, too.

Save your money. Surf the web. Most government agencies not only list all their available jobs and tell you how to apply for them, but they have resumé services, too. You fill out a form on your first visit, let them know what you are looking for, and they will e-mail you when a job like that opens up. Not only that, but you can go back to your original resumé and revise it. Along with the job information, you'll find tips for getting your personal information into a form that can do you the most good.

Can you name a private sector employer that does that?

The Least You Need to Know

◆ Not all military jobs require an enlistment. Every U.S. military installation in the world has civilian employees.

◆ Civilian benefits may equal many active duty perks. The pay is better, too.

◆ There is more security in government jobs. They aren't subject to ups and downs in the economy, as with many other civilian jobs.

◆ You can work around the corner or on the other side of the world—it's your choice. There are Civil Service jobs everywhere the federal government has a presence, from Corps of Engineers project sites to military bases—even consulates and embassies.

◆ Civil Service is a great way to serve your country and have a good-paying job at the same time.

Cutting-Edge Technology

In This Chapter

- ◆ Your future in high tech
- ◆ Keeping ahead with the people who developed it all
- ◆ More than just traditional uses for computers
- ◆ If you like computer games, check out the ultimate
- ◆ Staying far ahead of state of the art

Have you ever noticed that the messages your computer flashes at you seem a bit aggressive, even military-like?

UNIX systems prompt you to "kill" files. DOS programs tell you to "abort" them. And when you do something wrong, your PC will tell you that you've just been the perpetrator of an "illegal" action. What law did you break? And how in the world did that mistake get classified as "fatal"?

Yet, they like to tell you that the computer hardware and software you're working with is "user friendly."

If your machine talks tough, it's because its ancestors were developed for the military, where toughness is considered an asset.

Where It All Started

Although home computers, laptops, handhelds, and other such marvels are relatively recent developments that keep business thriving and global villages in touch with one another, most of them were originally created for military applications. And the military has a lot more up its sleeve. You have the opportunity to be part of making it happen.

Most histories of computerization go back to the ancients and their methods of counting beads on an abacus. Over the centuries, dozens of devices were developed for counting and keeping track of things. But the first electronic digital computer worthy of the name didn't come along until 1945. It was called ENIAC, the Electronic Numerical Integrator and Calculator, and it was used at the U.S. Army's Aberdeen Proving Ground in Maryland.

Bet You Didn't Know

In the early days of computer development, it was the people who operated these machines, and not the machines themselves, that were called "computers." The word wasn't used to describe an electronic digital machine until the late 1950s. Today, any device that has a memory and a central processing unit is considered a computer. It must be able to carry out different sets of instructions based on its own calculations and store those instructions. It's all so new and yet so much a part of our culture today, it makes you wonder what people did for a living—and for fun—in your grandfather's day.

Tip

"Servo-mechanisms" that were key to the computerized aiming devices on World War II antiaircraft guns are hydraulic systems (or motors) that are activated and controlled by low-energy electronic impulses transmitted to them. They were integral parts of early computers that used rotating disks turned by what was called a "servomotor." They are still in use today in such devices as garage door openers.

The ENIAC machine had been developed to solve one of the military's biggest headaches during World War II. Aircraft had become much more maneuverable since the First World War, but antiaircraft guns were still singing from the same old songbook.

Gunners fired round after round of flak into the air, and more often than not planes were able to dodge out of the way. The only reason any shells ever brought a plane down was that there were too many of them to avoid. It wasn't because the gunners had any way of knowing where a plane would go between the time it appeared in their sights and the shells got there. It was an incredibly expensive way to fight a war.

The problem was solved, sort of, with "servo-mechanisms" that used input from analog computers to compute a plane's position. The work of putting together the trajectory tables that made them work, also done at Aberdeen, required the efforts of hundreds of people working with desk calculators and a primitive electromechanical analog computer. It was called the "differential analyzer" and used motor-driven rotating disks and a complex series of gears and pipes to solve complicated equations.

It was a slow process, and subject to all sorts of human error. Something better was needed, and that turned out to be ENIAC.

Building a Dinosaur

The digital solution to the Army's problem cost half a million dollars. But it seemed worth every penny. The best analog computer of the day was only about 50 times faster than a human with a desk calculator, but ENIAC was able to do most of its calculations at the speed of light.

Its reliability had yet to be tested, but its designers were pretty sure it could run for about 12 hours without crashing.

> **Tip**
>
> Although ENIAC seemed to be the last word in computers, Remington Rand, whose business was making electric razors, added another word to the nation's vocabulary in 1951—UNIVAC. It was smaller, at only 352 square feet, and it only needed 5,400 tubes. Yet it was six times faster than its predecessor.
>
> The first model was used for number-crunching by the Census Bureau, but CBS Television used one to predict the outcome of the 1952 presidential election. The machine used early returns to accurately predict that Dwight D. Eisenhower had won, but the human pundits wrongly predicted otherwise. It was the first time that a lot of Americans had ever even heard of computers. But they knew they hadn't heard the last of them.

There were plenty of opportunities for that to happen. The machine, which filled a very large room, had no less than 18,000 vacuum tubes, at least several of which burned out every day. The failure rate was reduced when the engineers decided to leave it turned on all the time. That cut the failure rate down to something like one tube every other day. But still, a technician had to locate the offending tube and replace it. That could sometimes take hours.

ENIAC used enough electrical power to light a small town, about 140 kilowatts a day. And because of the heat all those tubes generated, it needed an air-conditioning system so that it wouldn't set itself on fire. Even without its cooling system, ENIAC was much too big to fit in your living room, maybe even your whole house. If anyone had predicted that some day people would have computers on top of their desks, or in their laps, they would have been laughed out of town.

Still, it represented progress. The only problem was that the war was over. There were no planes to shoot at, and no need for computing charts to track them. The Army had produced a dinosaur.

But then, as now, the Army always has problems that need creative answers. The first digital computer was put to work making complicated mathematical models for the world's first hydrogen bomb.

Tip

Before there were transistors, all radios, TV sets, and computers needed vacuum tubes to make them work. They are glass tubes with the air removed from them, like a light bulb, with electronic filaments that control the rate of flow of electricity through the device. The more powerful the radio or computer, the more tubes were required to make it function. Like a light bulb, the flow of electricity through it generates a great deal of heat, and the hotter it gets, the shorter its life.

Onward and Upward

During the postwar years, other, better computers were developed for the military. But they were all bulky and filled with finicky vacuum tubes. There was no hope at all that they could ever be used for weapons systems.

Then in 1948, the Bell Telephone Laboratories in New York developed a thing called the transistor. It is a wafer-thin device that regulates the flow of electricity between two terminals by varying the current between one of them and a third that provides the electrical input. It was the same job vacuum tubes performed, but not only was the transistor much smaller, it didn't require any heat to make it work. It was obviously *the* way to make computers smaller. But it wasn't until 1954 that Bell Labs built the first transistor computer, which was used by the Air Force. The machine was too big to fit on anyone's desktop, but small enough to stow on a large airplane.

The next customer for a transistorized device was the Navy Tactical Data System. Its version, designed to be used aboard ships for controlling radar and weapons systems, was about 4 feet high and 6 feet long, about the size of your bathtub. It had a word size of 30 bits. That amount of memory is puny compared to today's computers. A bit, also called a binary digit, is the smallest measure of the amount of information a computer can handle. It takes 8 of them to make one "byte," a unit of data equal to one letter. A million bytes is a "megabyte." No self-respecting computer owner would even think of having less memory than that.

It was also considered one of the most reliable of all computers built up until that time. The average time between crashes was a then-incredible 2,500 hours.

Bet You Didn't Know _____

Looking back on it, it seems to go without saying that computers would never have evolved into something practical without the transistor. Yet, in the early 1950s, many engineers were convinced that the way of the future was magnetic amplifiers, which did everything a vacuum tube could do without heat or unwieldy size.

In fact, it was these magnetic tape cores that made UNIVAC work, and it was considered the prototype for all future computers. When the Air Force ordered a guidance computer system for its Titan missiles, Sperry Rand, the contractor, built two versions, one that used transistors, the other magnetic cores. After testing them, the Air Force decided that transistors were the way to go, and it's been the route for computers ever since.

What It Can Mean to You

All of the military's early computers were custom-developed by companies that have since become giants in commercial computing. In today's world, the military is turning to those same companies for "off-the-shelf" hardware and software. After all, it was the military that paid for the original research and development.

That works to your advantage when you apply for an MOS that involves computers. You'll be using equipment and programs you may have seen before and will surely see in the future.

But that doesn't mean that military computer work is "same old, same old." Like a teenager with a new car, military people go right to work souping up the basic model. They've been experimenting with their computers since day one. And they're not likely to stop any time soon.

Computers on the Battlefield

Not too far in the future, everyone, from infantry troops to the top brass, is going to be sharing the same information, thanks to already-developed systems and mobile equipment. Information used to be passed to the field by radio, and the guys on the ground had to use what they heard to plot positions on their maps. Not anymore. Now the information, including the map, is beamed to a handheld computer.

Those same minicomputers allow soldiers in combat to keep informed in real time of other units operating nearby, as well as the availability of air support. It opens up all sorts of computer-related military jobs that didn't exist even a couple of years ago. But some people see problems down the line. And solving them is one of the challenges you might consider getting involved with. Your help will be more than welcome.

Tip

If you've ever thought of yourself as a computer hacker, a career in the military is a good way to find out how good you might be at it. It takes one to know one.

The first problem that needs solving is how to prevent the information from falling into an enemy's hands. Just as important, what happens when every squad leader has the same information as the generals? Will they still continue to follow orders to the letter? And, most important of all, probably, is how to keep the system from crashing and immune to hackers.

The answers are important. But finding them calls for fresh new ideas. And it is quite possible that some man or woman going through Basic Training today might come up with the answer tomorrow.

Electronic Warfare

Battlefield losses are dramatically reduced by the use of "smart" bombs, missiles, and artillery. But because these electronically guided weapons are often flying all over the place, there is a greater danger of forces being hit by their own ordnance.

The threat of friendly fire has led to a new kind of field unit called "Identify Friend or Foe." These units are armed with technology programmed with allied and enemy hardware. Troops in the field carry devices about the size of a pack of cigarettes that send out transponder codes with the message that the unit is friendly.

Aircraft often carry electronic countermeasure devices in pods on their wings. They are designed to evade incoming missiles. Because not every missile threat is the same, the devices often need to be reprogrammed before each mission. They also include jamming technology that needs to be altered as threats change.

Even skeptics admit that in the not-too-distant future, soldiers won't need those 60-pound backpacks anymore. The future of fighting a war is in microchips. Here are some examples:

- ◆ Electric power typically comes from noisy diesel generators that cancel out any idea of stealth. Now, in many situations, the power is coming from solar panels.

- Vehicles and aircraft are already being deployed without human operators.

- Even dog tags are being replaced with smart cards that contain medical information vital to medics in the field.

Quite simply, if there is any new technology out there, it is first seen in the military. The future doesn't get any closer.

Picture Yourself in a World of Computers

Even if you go for a military specialty outside the high-tech field, you're going to find a computer in your future anyway. The U.S. Department of Defense is the biggest user of computers in the world. It maintains more than 10,000 different networks. According to a 1999 survey by *Army Times* magazine:

- 92 percent of active-duty military personnel use computers on the job or in training.

- 43 percent use computer workstations.

- 73 percent use desktop computers.

- 51 percent use LAN systems.

- 17 percent use mainframe computers.

- 13 percent use minicomputers.

More than 40 percent of all military personnel are involved in information management. Every aspect of computer skills are involved: computer operators, programmers, systems analysts, LAN specialists, and MIS managers. And you can be sure that when new job categories are developed, the military will make them available. The fact is, they will probably be the ones who will create the categories.

Research and Development

The computer was the military's gift to the world. But its research programs have come up with a lot of other things that are changing people's lives.

Many car manufacturers have begun offering optional extras that wouldn't exist without military research and development. Some of them use thermal imaging to help you see at night when a car coming the other way doesn't turn down its high-beam headlights. Some use infrared lasers to spot hazards on the road that you might not be able to see without them.

The military developed flat-panel displays for tanks and aircraft so that it isn't necessary to glance downward to check gauges. These screens are now available in luxury cars. They are at work on multimedia improvements that someday might allow you to have a conversation with your car's engine.

If you're looking for an SUV or a small truck, some are available with suspension systems that adjust themselves to the driving surface. They were developed and tested for military vehicles.

Your new car will tell you when you need to put air in the tires. It might be equipped with a radar device that warns you against collisions. And if your car has a computerized navigation system tied to a satellite, where do you think that technology came from? And the list goes on.

These days, the military is all about technology. Most of the research and development is made possible by computers, and most of the resulting innovations use them, too. The excitement is on the ground floor. And that is where a military career can put you.

In Their Footsteps

Computers have completely changed the creative process. They allow you to ask questions that were once regarded as unanswerable. And they deliver answers faster, which makes the process that much more rewarding. But sometimes the computer systems themselves call for old-fashioned inventive thinking.

When they were expanding a missile warning system at Peterson Air Force Base in Colorado, the team was faced with the problem of getting wires through a 40-foot conduit that was already filled with them. The solution came from Lt. Col. Randy Blaisdell, or rather from the family pet, a ferret named Misty. He tied a piece of yarn around her belly, and tied one of the wires to it. Then he showed her the opening in the conduit. Her natural instinct for exploring took over. It took several trips through the pipe to get all the wires in place so that the base's computers could be networked. But the mission was accomplished in less than an hour. Installing a new conduit would have taken days.

Virtual Reality

If you are a Navy maintenance worker, you have one of the most important jobs on the ship. There aren't any service stations out on the high seas, and when something goes wrong, it has to be fixed on the double.

Training for these jobs involves using virtual reality. It's a giant step above the old-fashioned hands-on experience. The Navy has developed a computer program that allows students to experience a ship's engine room through a virtual reality headset and a computer mouse. A simulated human figure on the video screen "walks" you through the room, and answers any question you might have, from keeping the engines oiled to fire control procedures.

The same technology is also used to train troops for battlefield conditions. It's the ultimate video game. Of course, you probably already knew that those war games you play down at the video arcade grew out of programs that were developed as military training devices. But have you ever played one with the screen built into a headset?

Cyberwarfare

Another connection between your own desktop computer and the military is that you need a coded password to access most information. Even some websites that are trying to sell you something won't let you have the buying information you need until you've typed in your password.

It helps to remember that the Internet was created by the military. Codes and passwords are mother's milk to the average military person. That is because information is at the heart of everything they do. And they are always looking over their shoulder to make sure nobody else has access to it.

In today's international arena, the old definitions of war between nations and terrorism have changed. These days, they are more accurately called "cyberwarfare" and "cyberterrorism." Nations use computer networks to plan attacks; terrorists use them to organize worldwide cooperation among themselves.

It is because those threats exist that it is important to watch out for gaps in the Internet that allow unauthorized persons to access information they shouldn't have, and for the military to use parts of it that only it can access. The military's networks fall into two categories: NIPRNET (Nonclassified Internet Protocol Router Network), which carries non-secret information, and SIPRNET (Secret Internet Protocol Router Network), used for moving sensitive data.

Cyberwarfare also extends into the civilian world. Back in 1999, people began worrying that when the calendar rolled around to 2000, computers around the world might think it was 1900. They would forget all kinds of things, from how much money you had in the bank to how electrical energy would get to where it was supposed to go. The computer experts were predicting all kinds of dire effects (and finding plenty of jobs reprogramming computer systems.)

Airplanes would fall from the sky, they said, and the food supply would get lost in transit. Telephone systems would crash, and an emergency call to 911 would draw a blank at the other end. Fortunately, none of the things associated with the so-called Y2K problem actually happened. But all of it was completely possible. And it could still happen if a terrorist organization were to figure out how to invade the country's computer networks. It is the job of the military to make sure that doesn't happen. And if it does, to get things up and running again as fast as they can.

All of these new technological problems require computer-savvy people to solve them. But if you still think of yourself as computer illiterate, don't worry, the military will get you up to speed. And if you haven't caught the bug yet, you're going to be surprised at how infectious it is.

Bet You Didn't Know

The U.S. Space Command has taken on the assignment of protecting the military's computers from hacker attacks. It's a big job. They experience as many as 20,000 such attacks every year.

The space command is also experimenting with a little hacking on its own to be able to penetrate and disrupt an enemy's systems.

Computer hacking is against the law, of course. You can go to jail if you get caught at it in the civilian world. But if you think it would be fun, the space command would like to hear from you. They need people who think that way.

Where Will You Go from Here?

Fascinating as it is, virtual reality isn't really real. But in the military, there's plenty of real stuff to go around when it comes to training for a career in computer science.

There are lots of different ways to become a certified player in high tech. It's a rare college that doesn't offer relevant courses. There are hundreds of distance learning programs that will prepare you, too. And if you live in a large city, you'll find that storefront computer schools are about as common as barber shops.

But none of them can possibly give you much more than a snapshot of the state of the art at the time they hand you a diploma. Not only is the field changing at lightning speed, but the hardware and software is changing even faster.

Doctors find it crucial to keep reeducating themselves, even if they've been practicing medicine for years. It's the same in the computer field. And the best way to do that is through a military job, where everything you touch is as new and up-to-date as tomorrow. And speaking of tomorrow, what sort of jobs can you expect to find after your military career is over and you're in the top tier of computer-savvy candidates?

Right now, even a computer expert might not be able to tell you what you should be looking for. You might call yourself a programmer, but some employers might pay you a lot more if you're hired as a systems analyst.

And do you know the differences among tech support, product support, and system engineers? There aren't any. It depends on who you work for.

In general, the basic job descriptions in the computer field boil down to the following:

- Consulting
- Data processing
- Engineering
- Management
- Programming
- Sales and marketing
- Systems analysts

And what's behind the names? A consultant can be anything from a freelance programmer to tech support person. Data processing, which is the fastest-growing segment of the industry, is also sometimes called information systems, and includes a whole range of service jobs. Engineering, the most specialized, also includes lab technicians. Managers, well, manage.

Programmers write the codes that make up a computer program, test them, and then get the bugs out. This is where most professionals cut their teeth. Sales and marketing are those people you meet when you go to a computer store. Think you can do a better job?

Systems analysts are basically troubleshooters. But they aren't as concerned about what made a computer crash as they are with the people who use the machines. They cut through the technical jargon, and show customers how to use new hardware or software. Naturally, those people need to know just about everything. It's true of most other jobs in the field, too.

You can learn all those things in a classroom, to be sure. But you're not going to find a way to get to be as well rounded in a high-tech world as you will through your career in the military.

The Least You Need to Know

- The military has far more high-tech careers available than any segment of the private sector.
- Computers were first developed for military use, and it is still where new technology breakthroughs are being made.
- Today's military encourages inventiveness, and it is looking for people who can help refine computer systems.
- You don't need to be computer literate to start. You will have the benefit of the best hands-on training in the world of computers.

22

D... e Motor Pool

In

... echanics

... ities

... new outlook

... important job

... anics and celestial mechanics, fluid mechanics and
... l mechanics and particle mechanics. But if you were
... game and the word "mechanics" came up, your
... shoot back: "grease monkeys."

... respect. Except in the military. And among civilian
... t for them to retire from their military careers.

... pins of every one of the services. They keep airplanes
... g full speed ahead. They keep tanks rolling and trucks
... iers rely on mechanics to make sure they'll get where

DUE TO PRODUCT DESIGN OR MATERIALS, WE WERE UNABLE TO ATTACH ALL VALUE ADDED COMPONENTS REQUESTED. COMPONENTS REQUESTED UNATTACHED THEY HAVE BEEN PROVIDED UNATTACHED

Jobs with a Future

Have you ever cooled your heels at an airport sitting out a long flight delay? Sometimes you can blame the weather. Sometimes it's security checks that are holding things up. But if you're the kind of person who likes to bet on things, put your money on mechanical problems.

The airlines have big maintenance operations at just about every major airport in the country. They have all the tools and all the parts they need to turn their aircraft around, no matter what the problem might be. What they don't have are enough trained mechanics.

The aviation industry has about 137,000 mechanics on its combined payroll. The Federal Aviation Administration says it needs another 12,000. And it says it needs them yesterday.

It's one of America's dirty little secrets. If the airlines were to admit that they are desperately short of maintenance people, a lot of passengers would think twice before they got aboard one of their planes. So they just pretend that there isn't any problem, and quietly scout military bases for trained mechanics.

A Growing Need

Like pilots, the majority of airline mechanics learned their trade in the military. The airlines consider them prime prospects because they have had the best training along with hands-on experience that's worth its weight in gold.

Although they are muddling their way through a personnel shortage right now, airline executives who will talk about the problem admit that things are going to get worse for them before they get better.

If you have airframe or power plant experience as a military mechanic, your future couldn't possibly be more secure.

Consider this: The 747 passenger jet is more than 20 years old. Many of the originals are still flying beyond the lifespan promised by Boeing. Careful maintenance is what is keeping them in the air and keeping them safe. But consider this as well: Thousands of members of airline maintenance crews are getting close to retirement age. That means that on top of the dire need to expand their maintenance operations, the airlines are going to be running in place for a long time to come.

They're going to be looking for you.

Just in the last 10 years, the Navy has lost 52 percent of its aircraft mechanics to private industry. The Air Force, which has three quarters of all the mechanics in the American military, is also having problems getting them to reenlist. The grass really is greener on the other side of that fence.

At today's scale, an aircraft mechanic can make $50,000 a year after five years on the job. Put in five more years and your pay will jump as high as $80,000. And that's at today's rates. The numbers are going to go up; you can bet on it.

What Kind of Jobs Are They?

Most aircraft mechanics specialize in preventive maintenance. They check out engines and landing gear, of course. But they also make sure pressurized sections are up to snuff, and that the air-conditioning is working. They take everything mechanical or electronic under their wing.

There are also required inspections based on the number of hours a plane has flown. This often involves removing an engine and taking it apart to measure parts for wear. The mechanics use x-ray and magnetic devices to look for cracks or stress points. They replace worn-out parts, too. And when they finish, they do test runs to make sure the job was done right.

Mechanics also troubleshoot problems a pilot may have noticed. For that part of the job, they have to be able to turn on a dime because the plane has to get moving again. There are passengers waiting over there behind the gate wondering what's going on.

Typical aircraft maintenance crews include power plant mechanics, who work on engines and sometimes on propellers, and airframe mechanics, who work on any part of a plane or a helicopter except engines, propellers, and instruments. The majority, though, are classified as A&P mechanics, a combination of airframe and power plant specialists. They work on all parts of a plane except instruments. Avionics mechanics are the only ones qualified to maintain and repair navigation and communications equipment, such as radar systems and flight computers.

Get the Best Experience

You can learn these jobs at any number of independent schools. Or you can learn them through the military. Not only does that save you tuition fees, but all aircraft mechanics need to be certified by the FAA, and its qualifications include not only training, but prior experience.

To be licensed as an A&P mechanic, for instance, you will need at least 30 months of experience working on airframes and engines—after you've spent time in the classroom learning how.

Civilians do it all the time, but for the most part, they end up wishing that they had gone to the military for their schooling and experience in the first place.

Where do you suppose the teachers at those aeronautical schools got their qualifications? There's no need for you to get second-hand training.

Keeping the Wheels Turning

Not every mechanic serving the military works with aircraft. Not by a long shot. There isn't a single military mission that doesn't count on mechanics to make sure it comes off as planned.

Automotive and heavy equipment mechanics are the people who keep jeeps and humvees, cars, trucks, and tanks rolling. They also get to work on combat vehicles like missile launchers, and heavy construction equipment.

Basically, their jobs involve solving problems in engines, electrical systems, steering, brakes, and suspension systems. It's not a lot different than what you'd expect from the people who take care of your car, your pickup, or your SUV.

As an automotive or heavy equipment mechanic, you will also tune engines, repair body damage, and follow routine maintenance schedules for all sorts of vehicles. Since the list will include bulldozers and power shovels, you can also expect to be called on to deal with hydraulics, not exactly a skill you can pick up working down at the corner gas station.

"Mechanic" MOS Training

A lot of the mechanics who take care of automobiles and other personal vehicles probably learned how down at the corner gas station. It was an experience of trial and error. In fact, you might have come up on the error side of the equation a time or two.

But there is no margin for error in maintaining military vehicles. That's why if you choose an MOS that includes the word "mechanic," you are going to spend a lot of time in school. For some of those jobs, the classroom part of your training can last as long as 29 weeks. Even the shortest course lasts two months. Then comes the on-the-job training. You'll work alongside people who know what makes things work and actually seem to enjoy sharing their experience with you.

All the services use mechanics, and all of them offer advanced courses in most specialties. By the time your tour is over, there won't be an engine you won't know like the back of your hand.

And you won't wind up at that corner gas station when you retire from the military. Of course, you'll know a lot more than anyone else down there, and it's guaranteed that you'll be the busiest mechanic in town. But there are other, better jobs available to someone with the kind of experience you'll have. Your choices range from construction companies to farm-equipment companies to local-highway agencies. Car dealers and trucking companies will be eager to talk to you, too.

Wherever you wind up, you will know what you are doing. And it will show.

Not for Men Only

Since the introduction of the Armed Services Vocational Aptitude Battery, hundreds of women have discovered, sometimes to their surprise, that they have the right aptitudes to become mechanics.

Servicing engines and vehicles has always been considered a man's job. But then, in the early days of automobiles, it was a foregone conclusion that only men were capable of driving them. That myth was put to rest so long ago that not many people remember it even existed. But still, some people are surprised to find women working under the hoods of all kinds of vehicles at military installations.

Women are still barred from jobs that might take them into combat, but those are only a small percentage of the opportunities available for mechanics. And women are welcomed into all the rest.

As often happens in military specialties, you are seen just as a person with the skills that are needed to do a job. Nobody notices what color you are, and nobody cares if you happen to be a woman. There aren't any stereotypes in uniform.

The public sector is another matter, of course. But female mechanics are beginning to show up in the civilian world, too. One such person, quoted in a magazine published by the Florida Public Transit Office, began her career as a mechanic in the Army. When her tour ended, she took a job with a school district near Orlando, servicing its fleet of buses. She went to work on the maintenance staff of the state transit network after that, handling preventive maintenance and repairing such things as brakes and fuel injectors. "I love to do more complicated repairs," she says.

> **Warning**
>
> One reason why women are barred from some MOSs in the maintenance field is that in the Army and Marine Corps, many mechanics are also trained as riflemen and can be called upon to use their weapons in combat.

One of her female co-workers worked for several years at the transit service in Rochester, New York. In spite of her training, she started work there in the office, before her employers realized that they were wasting her experience. She did towing and road service at first, but then she discovered a new skill as an expert on wheelchair lifts.

Both women say they wouldn't trade their lives as mechanics for any other career. As one of them put it, "I love 'wrenching.' Every time I've gone away from it, I've missed it."

And have they had any problems working in an all-male environment? It doesn't seem so. "There were plenty of whistles and catcalls at first," one of them says. But not for long. She says she finds the men she works with "polite and respectful." And not a bit surprised that a woman can do their job as well as they can.

Admittedly, automotive maintenance is one of the last bastions of old-fashioned ideas like that. But the old notions are fading fast. And women in military careers are helping to sweep them away.

The Challenge

There are few military occupational specialties that are more important to the big picture right now than the ones involving the skills of mechanics.

Many of the weapons systems that are being used today are decades old and are expected to stay efficient for decades longer. That means that mechanics are expected to keep them up and running.

Just as an example, the Air Force has committed itself to keeping the B-52 bomber flying for at least 40 more years. The plane has already been part of its arsenal for almost 50 years.

That's just part of the challenge.

The military has about 150 different types of aircraft, and there are no plans to junk any of them. The total number of planes that have to be kept flying is well over 18,000. There are some 500 ships that need to be maintained. There are more than half-a-million missiles, all with targeting systems and other avionics that need to be kept up to snuff. There are 250,000 vehicles to maintain, and there are millions of machines, from electrical generators to missile launchers to elevators, cranes, and radar arrays, with everything you can think of in between. If it moves, it needs maintenance. And to do that, you need mechanics who know what they're doing.

Not Exactly Like Civilian Counterparts

Being a mechanic in the military isn't as glamorous as, say, working at a Mercedes dealership. You might find yourself repairing a steam launcher on the flight deck of a carrier in the middle of a blustery nor'easter. You might wind up repairing armored personnel carriers in a mountain pass in Afghanistan, or airplanes in the heat of the Saudi desert.

But when all is said and done, mechanics in the military have a big advantage over their civilian counterparts. In the civilian world, if they are noticed at all, it is as unskilled labor.

That's a bum rap, but the label is there anyway. In the military, on the other hand, mechanics get the recognition they deserve. No one questions the fact that their jobs are critical. They also understand that every mechanic has a bag of tricks that goes far beyond simply fixing things. Sometimes they need to be welders; sometimes, machinists. They need to understand heating and ventilating as much as how to replace a carburetor. They need to know a little bit about a lot of things because you never know where the next problem is going to come form. And it's nice to know that when one does, you've been trained to handle it.

Unskilled labor? It may well be the most skill-oriented labor there is.

> **Tip**
>
> The U.S. Army Tank-automotive and Armaments Command (TACOM) is charged with the responsibility of developing new products and helping all the armed forces modernize their readiness. It has operations across the country and around the world.

The Future Is Here

One of the best things about a military career is that it keeps you a jump ahead of developments in the civilian world. It's especially true in the automotive field.

The Army has already developed what it is calling a "SmarTruck." Before its concept team went to work, according to some insiders, they were ordered to watch at least four James Bond movies. It must be true because this machine has features that Bond would love.

It is basically a Ford F350 heavy-duty pickup truck, and if someone were to drive one down your street, you might not even notice it. It's what it can do that makes the difference, not what it looks like.

If you tried to steal it, the door handles would knock you down with a jolt of electricity. Then before you could get up, it would fire pepper spray at you. On the road, it can spray oil out from under its rear bumper to give a hard time to anybody with ideas of following you. If the oil slick doesn't stop them, the SmarTruck will dump sharp tacks into their path for a plague of flat tires.

The rear roof also swings back to expose a turret equipped with a laser weapon that is operated by a joystick up front. The vehicle includes some features you might see on your own car one of these days. Among them are four-wheel steering that allows you to park in the tightest spots, not to mention taking the strain out of making U-turns. In fact, General Motors has already announced plans make it a feature in their pickup trucks.

Some features you may never need for the family bus are blinding lights, front and rear, and a pepper spray gun on the roof that shots a six-foot pattern on all four sides.

But you might be interested in the cameras that give you a full 360-degree view around the outside on flat-panel video screens inside. Its cell phone, doors, windows, and radios are all voice-activated.

The SmarTruck also carries a black box, the same kind of voice and data recorder used on airliners. It allows mechanics to diagnose and fix problems from miles away.

And that's what they're telling us. You can be sure that SmarTruck is a whole lot smarter than anyone is willing to admit. But it's what it stands for that's important. It's the first step in an amazing future for military transportation. And for the mechanics who keep the wheels turning.

Driving Into the Future

The military likes to give fancy names to its projects, but one of the most important it has come up with since the end of the Cold War is called, simply, the revolution in military affairs. They'd rather have you think of it as RMA.

Although the think tanks have been turning its basics over in their minds for more than a decade, the Army has been working for action, and General Eric Shinseki, the chief of staff has ordered the creation of a new kind of fighting force in place by 2010. He is asking for a new kind of Army where "strategic forces must be strategically deployable, with a smaller logistical footprint, and light forces must be more lethal, survivable, and tactically mobile."

What does that have to do with mechanics? It's right there in the word "mobile."

As the chief of staff was announcing his intentions, he was also unveiling phase one: the future combat system. It is a new breed of vehicles that will someday soon replace everything the Army now has for driving into combat. As it stands now, it will be wheeled—not tracked—vehicles that weigh less than 20 tons.

Reinventing the Wheel

This is a concept that has stood military strategists on their ears. It has been an article of faith since the First World War that tanks and armored personnel carriers and other combat vehicles had to be propelled on metal caterpillar-like tracks. But the prototype of the new future combat system rides on eight wheels.

No, it isn't change for the sake of change. Field tests have proven that wheeled vehicles are faster, use less fuel, require less maintenance, need less logistical support, and are more flexible in varied terrain. On top of that, they are easier to get aboard an airplane, and because they are about half the weight of existing vehicles, more of them can be moved aboard the same transport.

The Army has also unveiled a new combat helicopter, the RAH-66 Comanche, an attack and air-combat machine perfect for moving fast and hitting hard.

And that's just the beginning. Will the other services follow the Army's lead? They're not saying. But interservice rivalry being what it is, it's likely that they will. And for mechanics, the trend toward more, if not smaller, mechanization is going to present new worlds to conquer. One thing is for sure, the next decade is going to be anything but boring.

The Least You Need to Know

- Forget what you might have thought about mechanics. In the military, it isn't just a job, it's a profession.

- The job market is bright for seasoned mechanics today, and airlines and other employers are looking to the military for the best-trained people to fill those jobs.

- Schooling and training is the best there is in every military career involving mechanical skills. There is no better way to master those skills.

- Technology is booming in the military. New weapons systems and better vehicles are under development, and this is the best time to get in on the ground floor.

Military as a Second Language

One of the first things you'll notice when you begin a career in the military is that they don't always speak your language. They'll be patient with you while you learn the jargon and dope out the acronyms. But in the meantime, this short list will give you a push from the shore.

A "Alfa"

ACINT   Naval acoustic intelligence.

ACM   Air combat maneuvers (dogfights).

AD   Active duty.

AGL   Above ground level. Aircraft altimeters read height above sea level. Radar altimeters make it possible to get this more realistic number.

air boss   The head of an aircraft carrier's air department.

AK-47   The standard rifle of the Warsaw Pact nations.

alert 5   A manned aircraft ready to get into action within five minutes.

aluminum cloud   An F-14 fighter.

angels   Aircraft altitude measured in thousands of feet (15,000 feet = Angels 15).

AO   Area of operations.

AOM   All officer's meeting.

arclight   A bombing mission by B-52s.

ARTY   Artillery units.

as you were   Get back to what you were doing.

ASVAB   Armed Services Vocational Aptitude Battery.

ASW   Antisubmarine warfare.

AWOL   Absent without leave.

B   "Bravo"

back to the taxpayer   Disposing of wrecked aircraft or vehicles.

bag   A flight suit, or an antiexposure suit.

BAH   Basic allowance for housing.

bandit   Hostile aircraft.

BAR   Browning automatic rifle. A .30-caliber gas-operated weapon fed by a clip holding 450 shots a minute. At 15 pounds, it is usually fired from a bipod, but it can also be fired from the shoulder or hip.

BAS   Basic allowance for subsistence.

bat decoder   A sheet carried on flight operations for interpreting communications codes.

battalion   A unit of three or more rifle companies.

battery   The basic artillery unit, consisting of three to six cannon.

beachhead   A footing on shore after a Marine or infantry amphibious landing.

big mother   An H-3 Navy helicopter assigned to sea rescue.

billet   Assignment or job; the place where you live.

bingo field   An airstrip on land where carrier pilots can divert.

bird   Any aircraft, but usually a helicopter.

blackshoes   A naval aviator's term for nonflying personnel. The guys who fly wear brown shoes; all others wear black.

blouse   A jacket.

bogey   Unidentified, possibly hostile, aircraft.

boondocks   Isolated back country (boonies).

boondoggle   A great, easy assignment, usually at someone else's expense.

boonierat   A combat infantryman.

BOQ   Bachelor officers' quarters.

bought the farm   Died. The term refers to government policy of reimbursing farmers for crops destroyed in plane crashes, more often than not an inflated number more equal to value of the whole farm.

bouncing Betty   An antipersonnel mine with two charges, one to propel the other upward where it explodes at waist level.

brass   Officers.

bravo zulu   High praise.

brig   A place of detention in the Navy or Marine Corps (called a stockade in the Army).

brown side-out   Desert camouflage fatigues pattern.

bunker   A protective shelter.

BUPERS   Bureau of Naval personnel.

C   "Charlie"

C rations   Combat rations, usually including a can of some basic meal, a can of fruit, a packet of dessert, powdered cocoa, and some cigarettes and chewing gum. Most often called "Com-Rats."

CAG   The chief pilot in a carrier's air group.

cannon-cockers   Artillery troops.

cat shot   A catapult-assisted takeoff from a carrier deck.

CC   Company commander.

cherubs   Altitude under 1,000 feet measured in hundreds of feet (200 feet = Cherubs Two).

chopper   A helicopter anywhere except in the Navy, where it is a "helo."

chow   Food served in a mess hall.

CINCEUR   Commander in chief, Europe.

CINCLANTFLT   Commander in chief, Atlantic Fleet.

CINCNAVEUR   Commander in chief, Naval Forces, Europe.

CINCPACFLT   Commander in chief, Pacific Fleet.

Cinderella liberty   A short period of time off that ends at midnight.

civvies   Clothing that isn't military issue.

claymore   A directional mine.

CMC   Commandant of the Marine Corps.

cobra   A helicopter used as a gun platform.

COLA   Cost of living allowance.

cold nose   An aircraft flying with radar turned off, usually during air-to-air refueling.

company   A unit made up of two or more platoons and a headquarters staff.

compound   A fortified military installation.

cones   Students. Short for coneheads.

CONUS   Continental United States.

cover   Hat.

crispy critters   Burn victims.

crud   Any rash or illness picked up in jungle climates.

cruise   A tour of duty.

D   "Delta"

daisy cutter   A shell fitted with fuses for detonation several feet above ground, which clears thick brush and jungle.

delta Sierra   A dumb and stupid action.

Devil Dogs   Marine Corps.

DO   Duty officer.

DOD   Department of Defense.

dog tag   A soldier's identification tag, worn around the neck.

double time   At a run.

double ugly   An F-4 Phantom jet.

dust-off   Medical evacuation by helicopter.

E   "Echo"

ECM   Electronic countermeasures for jamming enemy communications and radar.

Eighth & Eye   Marine Corps headquarters in Washington.

electric jet   Planes like the F-15 that have fly-by-wire controls.

F   "Foxtrot"

fangs out   A pilot looking for a fight.

fatigues   Standard combat uniform.

field day   Cleaning up the barracks.

field strip   Take apart; for example, it is required that you tear cigarette butts into shreds to avoid littering in the field.

firebase   A remote artillery position.

first shirt   A first sergeant, the highest enlisted grade in a company.

fishbed   NATO code for Russian-built fighters.

flack jacket   A vest filled with fiberglass for protection against shrapnel.

fly-by-wire   Electronic computer-controlled aircraft.

four deuce   A 4.2-inch mortar.

four-by   A light truck.

G "Golf"

G-loading   Centrifugal forces that affect high-performance aircraft. One-G is equal to normal gravity, 4-Gs exerts pressure four times the weight of gravity.

gear   Equipment.

GI   The all-purpose identification of military personnel. The letters stand for "Government Issue."

GI can   Garbage can.

gizmo   A sophisticated piece of technical gear.

goldbrick   Avoiding assigned work.

grease   To kill.

Green Berets   Army Special Services.

Green Machine   Marine Corps.

green side-out   Woodland-pattern camouflage in fatigues.

grinder   Parade ground.

grunt   Originally used to describe Marines in Vietnam, it now covers infantrymen of all kinds serving anywhere.

guidon   A pennant bearing a unit's designation.

gun bunnies   A field artillery crew, also called "lanyard pullers" and "ammo-humpers."

gung ho   A tiger at your job. From Chinese words meaning "motivated."

H "Hotel"

hamburger helper   A bombardier/navigator or radar intercept officer.

heat tabs   Flammable tablets used to heat C rations, if you're lucky enough to find one.

heater   A Sidewinder heat-seeking missile.

helo   The Navy's term for a helicopter. Others call them "choppers."

high-and-tight   The standard Marine haircut.

hooah   Pronounced "who-ah," nobody seems to know exactly what this word means, except that it doesn't mean "no." Get used to hearing it everywhere, all the time.

house mouse   The drill sergeant's assistant.

hump   A hike under full pack; any tough job.

huss   A favor or a break, as in "gimme a huss."

I "India"

intel   Intelligence information.

J "Juliet"

JAG   Judge Advocate General.

jarhead   A Marine.

JO   Junior officer.

jock   A fighter pilot. Pilots often call themselves "drivers."

K "Kilo"

kick the tires and light the fires   Shortening the routine of checking out aircraft so that they can get airborne faster.

klick   A kilometer.

L "Lima"

ladder   Stairways, to Marines and sailors who more often than not climb ladders and not stairs aboard ships.

leatherneck   A Marine.

leave   More than 24 hours of time off.

liberty   Less than 24 hours of time off.

lock and load   Arm and get your weapon ready for action.

M "Mike"

M-16   The standard military rifle.

Medivac   Medical evacuation of wounded.

Mom   The ship you are assigned to in the Navy.

mortar   A short cannon that fires shells at high angles.

MOS   Military Occupational Specialty.

MP   Military police.

mud-mover   A low-level air attack.

mustang   An enlisted man promoted to Marine officer.

N "November"

NATOPS   Naval Air Training and Operating Standardization. It is an organization responsible for safe operation of all naval aircraft.

NCO   Noncommissioned officer.

number one   The best. In spite of what the movies tell you, number 10 is the worst.

O   "Oscar"

OCS   Officers candidate school.

on the mouse   Using flight-deck radios whose headsets look like Mickey Mouse ears.

over the hill   Absent without leave.

P   "Papa"

paddles   Landing signal officers on carrier flight decks.

painted   Scanned by radar.

passageway   A hallway, to sailors and Marines, at least aboard ships.

perimeter   The outer limits of a military operation. Anything beyond is enemy territory.

phantom   An F-4 fighter jet.

platoon   An element of a company composed of three squads.

pogue   A goldbricker or an office worker.

point man   The guy who walks first in formation and scouts the area.

police   Clean up an area.

PX   Post exchange. Sometimes called commissaries, these stores are often as well stocked as the biggest department stores, and their prices are lower than any discount store.

Q   "Quebec"

quarters   Living space.

R   "Romeo"

R2D2   The backseat crewman in an F-14 or F-4 aircraft.

RA   Regular Army. The letters are part of every enlistee's serial number.

rappel   Climb down a cliff face or from a helicopter on a rope.

rate   A naval or Coast Guard job specialty.

reckless   A recoilless rifle, a small artillery piece.

Regiment   A unit consisting of three battalions.

roll 'em   The time the nightly movie starts.

romp 'n' stomp   Marching and drilling.

roof   An aircraft carrier flight deck.

ROTC   Reserve Officers Training Corps, available in high schools and colleges for training of future officers.

RTO   Radio telephone operator.

S "Sierra"

SAR   Search and rescue.

SEAL   The Navy's special forces (Sea-Air-Land).

SECDEF   Secretary of Defense.

semper fi   The exclamation point after every Marine's exclamation. From the Corps' slogan: *Semper Fidelis*, "Always Faithful."

shrapnel   Pieces of metal that are sent flying from an explosion.

Sierra Hotel   High praise.

six-by-six   A truck with three axles.

skivvies   Underwear, to a sailor or a Marine.

slick   A troop transport helicopter.

SOP   Standard operating procedure.

sortie   A single mission involving one aircraft.

SP   Shore patrol, the police of the Navy and Coast Guard.

speedjeans   Nylon trousers that cover the legs and abdomen. In high-gravity situations, they fill with compressed air to prevent pooling of blood and reduce the risk of blackouts.

squad   A small team of 5 to 15.

squad bay   Marine barracks.

stand-down   Returning to the base camp for refitting.

T "Tango"

TACAMO   Take charge and move out.

tail   The last soldier in a formation covering its rear.

Texaco   An air-to-air refueling plane.

the position   Getting set to do push-ups.

tickets   The jobs you need to earn promotions.

tracers   Bullets that contain pellets that produce smoke or light along their trajectory so that the shooter can trace their flight.

U "Uniform"

up to speed   Understanding what is going on.

utilities   Olive drab Marine field uniform.

V "Victor"

volley   The firing of each individual cannon in a battery.

VSTOL   Very Short Takeoff and Landing. An aircraft like the Harrier can use its vectoring jets to take off vertically.

W "Whiskey"

wash out   Failing to make the grade at flight school.

Whiskey Charlie   A way of saying "who cares."

Willy Peter   White phosphorous.

wingman   The second pilot in a two-plane formation.

workup   Putting a ship through tests and exercises before starting a cruise.

X "X-Ray"

XO   Executive officer.

Y "Yankee"

Y   Part of an aircraft's designation identifying it as a prototype.

YTD   Year to date, as it appears on your pay statements.

Z "Zulu"

zero week   The first week before starting a school.

zero-dark-30   The term means a half-hour after midnight, but it is used to describe any mission between sunset and sunrise.

Check Your Watch

Along with having to learn strange new words and phrases, when you show up for military service, you may also have to learn how to tell time all over again.

Like the scientific community, and most of the rest of the world, the American military is on a 24-hour clock. The day begins at 00:00 and ends at 23:59.

That means if you get hauled out of bed at what you think is 5:00 AM, it's 0:500 to the guy who's shouting in your ear. And you'll be expected to line up at least by 0:530. At the end of your day, dinner may be served at 6:00 PM, but from now on, you'll have to think of it as 18:00.

You'll get used to it. Just remember that the numbers keep going up from noon, beginning with 13 at 1:00 PM in the afternoon. You can count on your fingers until you get used to it. But be careful, you might wind up counting push-ups if the drill sergeant thinks that's kid stuff.

Team Canada

The United States and Canada have been close partners in modern conflicts. Troops from both countries routinely serve side-by-side in United Nations and NATO peacekeeping operations.

The opportunities and the benefits of military service are not a lot different in both countries. Many of the things described in the previous pages are equally valid for the Canadian military. But what the military in the two countries have most in common is that they offer young people career and educational opportunities that are without equal in civilian life.

This section is intended to explore what being part of Team Canada can be like.

Fighting Around the World

During the Vietnam War, an estimated 40,000 draft-age American citizens crossed the border into Canada to avoid being drafted into the military.

Less remembered is that after World War II broke out in Europe, more than 15,000 crossed that same border and joined the Royal Canadian Air Force (RCAF). At the time, it looked like their own country was going to stay out of the war. These guys chose not to sit back while the Nazis overran all of Europe.

Long before the United States declared war on Germany, U.S. men wearing RCAF uniforms were flying Hurricanes and Spitfires and fighting the Battle of Britain. In September 1942, they were transferred into the U.S. Army Air Force. Many of them already had three years of combat experience in the air by then.

By the end of the Second World War, more than a million Canadians had joined up, and they fought in every part of the world. In the years since,

Canadian forces have served on more United Nations peacekeeping missions than any other country.

In fact, at the beginning of 2001, they were serving in 18 different overseas operations at the same time. That included more than 1,600 Canadian troops in the North Atlantic Treaty Organization stabilization force in Bosnia.

The "Secret Soldiers"

The Royal Canadian Mounted Police was charged with counterterrorism and emergency response until 1993. The job was turned over to the Army's Joint Task Force II (JTF2) and then the Task Force vanished from the public's radar screen.

Everybody who cared about military matters in Canada knew they were out there. But while nobody denied their existence, nobody would talk about their operations.

Their safety was at stake, of course. You don't fight terrorists by waving flags at them. But the secret of the "secret soldiers" turned out to be that JTF2 is a close cousin to the American Green Berets and other special service outfits.

They have been with Canadian forces, providing intelligence and commando-like support, in every operation from Rwanda to Afghanistan. The bulk of the force is still very much involved in their first mission of homeland security across Canada. But they are taking an important message to the rest of the world: Don't mess with Canada.

The Canadian Military

There are about 60,000 men and women on active military duty in Canada. Another 30,000 serve in the reserve force. They not only handle peacekeeping missions around the world, but they are at the forefront of disaster relief and security at home.

Their official duties are ...

- Protecting their country from military threats.
- Protecting Canadians during environmental and other disasters.
- Helping local governments in civil emergencies.
- Protecting Canada's fisheries and intercepting illegal drugs.
- Responding to terrorist threats.
- Providing search-and-rescue survival services.
- Participating in United Nations and NATO operations.
- Supporting humanitarian relief efforts.
- Participating in arms-control activities.

Canadian forces also work hand in hand with the United States to protect the borders of North America and the Arctic.

They are based in every province and territory except Prince Edward Island. The force includes the Canadian Army, Navy, and Air Force. There is no separate Marine Corps, although the Joint Task Force comes close to filling that bill. There is no Coast Guard, either, but every branch of the service handles jobs the Coast Guard takes on south of the U.S.-Canadian border.

The Canadian military often works together as a single team in times of emergency. There is no such thing as interservice rivalry.

Canadian Military Pay

A recruit (E-1) in the American military earns $12,500 a year before other benefits are factored in. The basic salary for the lowest rank in the Canadian Army is $23,600. That's in lower-valued Canadian dollars, but the gap is still dramatic.

At the level of lieutenant colonel (O-5), the starting salary in the American Army is $40,428. In Canada, the minimum lieutenant colonel's pay is $84,192 (Canadian).

Base salaries above that level are negotiated, not mandated, so it isn't easy to say what an admiral or a general can make in the Canadian armed forces. But it's a good bet that the top brass in Canada are right up there with the CEOs of multinational corporations.

Recruitment Bonuses

Like their counterparts in the American military, the Canadian forces offer special incentives to fill vacancies in occupations that need to be brought up to strength.

The bonuses are given to new recruits, to veterans who reenlist, and to reserve force members who sign up for active duty again after two years. The allowances, in Canadian currency, are...

- ♦ $10,000 with a college diploma or certificate.
- ♦ $20,000 with direct civilian trade experience.
- ♦ $20,000 with related military experience.

The money is paid in two installments, half at the end of Basic Training, and half a year later. It is based on a three-year enlistment.

Among the 19 specialties that qualify for a recruitment bonus are dental clinical assistants, military police, plumbing and heating technicians, and vehicle technicians. The list also includes such esoteric things as naval acoustic electronic technicians, weapons technicians, and aerospace telecommunications.

Personnel who qualify for these cash incentives are also promoted to the rank of acting corporal as soon as they have finished their basic recruit training. That brings their basic salary up from less than $25,000 to almost $42,000.

The Best Enlistment Bonus in the Military

The Canadian forces estimate that it will need to recruit some 600 new engineering officers before 2006.

In order to help make that possible, they are offering a bonus of $40,000 to qualified candidates for any one of six different engineering specialties. Yes, $40,000.

The qualifications fall into four different categories:

- ◆ Direct-entry candidates with a relevant engineering or science degree
- ◆ Reserve force members with relevant degrees who transfer to regular force engineering officer occupations
- ◆ Noncommissioned members with relevant degrees who earn commissions and assignment to engineering occupations
- ◆ Former members with relevant degrees who reenlist

In order to qualify for the $40,000, officers have to sign up for four years. The bonus is paid in two installments. The first $25,000 is paid when all the qualifications, including officer training, have been met. The balance, $15,000, is paid on the second anniversary of the first installment. The fields that qualify include electrical and mechanical engineering, maritime engineering, and airfield engineering.

If you're a student at MIT working on an engineering physics degree, you have until 2006 to qualify for the $40,000 bonus. But watch out for that first step: In order to join the Canadian Forces, you need to be a Canadian citizen.

On the other hand, the law has a loophole. It specifies that "the Chief of Defense Staff … may authorize the enrollment of a citizen of another country if he is satisfied that a special need exists and that the national interest would not be prejudiced thereby."

The need exists, to be sure. Go for it!

Surfing Your Way to a Military Career

There are literally hundreds of thousands of websites that can help you decide which military career suits you best. The ones that follow are just for starters.

You'll find that many of these websites also offer links to other sites that will add to the information they provide themselves. Keep in mind that some websites sometimes disappear without warning. Others aren't kept as up-to-date as they should be.

General Sites

Some websites offer links and information about all of the services. Among them are:

- ◆ Armed Forces Network—www.armedforces.net
- ◆ Department of Defense—www.defenselink.mil
- ◆ General Links—www.usmilitary.about.com
- ◆ Military.Com News and Information Network—www.military.com
- ◆ Military Net, Schools and Academies—www.military_net.com

ASVAB

Before you can even think about a military career, you will have to take the Armed Services Vocational Aptitude Battery. You'll find scores of books, and even videos, to help you prepare for it. These websites may be helpful as well:

- ◆ www.todaysmilitary.com/explore_asvab.shtml
- ◆ www.asvab.org
- ◆ www.learntest.com/military
- ◆ www.sealchallenge.navy.mil/careers/asvab.html
- ◆ www.usarec.army.mil/hq/warrant/asvab.htm
- ◆ www.webdesk.com/test-prep/military
- ◆ www.armyjobs.net/militaryplacementtests.html
- ◆ www.cnet.navy.mil/cetars/help/glossary/asvab_test_series.htm

Army Sites

The Army's primary recruiting website is the place to begin. It describes available careers, current benefits, and more. It even has a chat room where you can ask specific questions. Log on to www.goarmy.com.

These sites will also offer valuable information:

- Aberdeen Test Center (Automotive and Direct Fire)—www.atc.army.mil
- Armament, Automotive, and Tanks—www.acala1.ria.army.mil
- Army–Europe—www.hqusareur.army.mil
- Army–Pacific—www.usarpac.army.mil
- Army Air Defense Artillery School—www.airdefense.bliss.army.mil
- Army Armor School—www.knox.army.mil/school
- Army Aviation—www.usarmyaviation.com
- Army Aviation and Missile Command—www.redstone.army.mil
- Army Aviation Museum—www.armyavnmuseum.org
- Army Cadet Command Center—www.rotc.monroe.army.mil
- Army Chemical School—www.wood.army.mil/usacmis
- Army Chief of Public Affairs—www.dtic.mil/armylink
- Army Civilian Personnel—www.cpol.army.mil
- Army Communications/Electronics Command—www.monmouth.army.mil/cecom
- Army Continuing Education—www.armyeducation.army.mil
- Army Corps of Engineers—www.usac.army.mil
- Army Engineer Research and Development Center—www.erdc.usace.army.mil
- Army Field Artillery Center—www.sill.army.mil
- Army Field Band—www.mdw.army.mil/fband
- Army Flight School—www.armyflightschool.org
- Army Helicopters—www.acala1.ria.army.mil
- Army Intelligence Center—www.usaic.hua.army.mil
- Army Jobs—www.armyjobs.net
- Army Marksmanship Unit—www.usarc.army.mil/hq/amu
- Army MARS (Military Affiliate Radio System)—www.asc.army.mil/mars
- Army Materiel Command—www.amc.army.mil
- Army National Guard—www.arng.army.mil
- Army National Training Center—www.irwin.army.mil
- Army News And Information—www.army.mil
- Army Nurse Corps—www.perscom.army.mil/ophsdan
- Army Officers Candidate Schools—www.armyocs.com
- Army Personnel Command—www.perscom.army.mil
- Army Physical Fitness School—www.benning.army.mil/usapfs
- Army Rangers Association—www.ranger.org
- Army Recruiting Command—www.usarec.army.mil
- Army Reserve—www.army.mil/usar
- Army Reserve Recruiting—www.goarmyreserve.com
- Army Sergeants Major Academy—www.usasma.bliss.army.mil
- *Army Times* Magazine—www.armytimes.com

- Army Transportation Museum—www.eustis.army.mil
- Army Transportation School—www.transchool.eustis.army.mil
- Army Warrant Officer Center—www.army.mil/wocc
- Army Warrant Officers Association— www.penfield.org/usawoa
- Army Women's Museum—www.awm.lee.army.mil
- Association for the U.S. Army—www.ausa.org
- Canine Corps—www.gmfound.com/war_dogs
- Combined Army Support Command—www.cascom.army.mil
- Fifth Army—ww.5tharmy.army.mil
- First Army—www.first.army.mil
- Military District of Washington—www.midw.army.mil
- Military Police History—www.azstarnet.com/roveto/mphist
- National Guard Bureau—www.ngb.dtic.mil
- Reserve Recruiting—www.goarmyreserve.com
- ROTC and Junior ROTC—www.usarotc.com
- Second Armored Division Association—www.2ndarmoredhellonwheels.com
- *Soldiers Magazine*—www.dtic.mil/soldiers
- Special Forces—www.specialforces.net
- U.S. Army–Alaska—www.usarak.army.mil
- U.S. Forces in Korea—www.korea.army.mil
- U.S. Military Academy—www.usma.edu
- V Corps (Germany)—www.hq.c5.army.mil
- Walter Reed Army Medical Center—www.wramc.army.mil

Navy Sites

The Navy's primary recruiting site will give you details on ratings, bonuses, educational opportunities, and lots more. Log on to www.navyjobs.com.

You should check out some of these sites as well:

- *All Hands* Magazine—www.mediacen.navy.mil/pubs/allhands
- Arctic Submarine Laboratory—www.csp.navy.mil/as
- Atlantic Fleet—www.atlanticfleet.navy.mil
- Blue Angels—www.blueangels.navy.mil
- *Chips* Information Technology Magazine—www.chips.navy.mil
- Coastal Amphibious Warfare—www.ncsc.navy.mil
- Department of the Navy—www.hq.navy.mil
- Enlisted Careers and College Guide—www.navyadvancement.com
- Fleet Numerical Meteorology and Oceanography Center—www.fnoc.navay.mil
- Helicopter Attack Squadron—www.seawolf.org
- Military Jobs—www.navyjourney.com
- National Museum of Naval Aviation—www.naval-air.org
- Naval Academy—www.nadn.navy.mil
- Naval Air Station/Whidbey Island—www.naswi.navy.mil
- Naval Air Warfare Center—www.nawcad.navy.mil
- Naval Air Warfare Center Training Systems Division—www.ntsc.navy.mil

- Naval Construction Force—www.seabee.navy.mil
- Naval Education and Training—www.cnet.navy.mil
- Naval Facilities Engineering Command—www.navfac.navy.mil
- Naval Food Service—www.seabeecook.com
- Naval Historical Center—www.history.navy.mil
- Naval Oceanography—www.onr.navy.mil
- Naval Postgraduate School—www.nap.navy.mil
- Naval Research Laboratory—www.nrl.navy.mil
- Naval Reserve—www.navy-reserve-jobs.com
- Naval Reserve Jobs—www.cnrrc.com
- Naval School of Health Sciences—www.nshs.med.navy.mil
- Naval Space Command—www.ncwspace.navy.mil
- Naval Special Warfare—www.sealchallenge.navy.mil
- Naval Station–Everett—www.everett.navy.mil
- Naval Station–Guantanamo Bay—www.nsgtmo.navy.mil
- Naval Surface Warfare Center—www.dt.navy.mil
- Naval Test Pilot School—www.usntps.navy.mil
- Naval Undersea Warfare Center—www.nuwc.navy.mil
- Naval War College—www.nwc.navy.mil
- Navy Advancement Web—www.navyadvancement.com
- Navy Band—www.navyband.navy.mil
- Navy Chemical and Biological Defense—www.cbd.navy.mil
- Navy College Program—www.navycollege.navy.mil
- Navy Fact File—www.chinfo.navy.mil/navpalib/factfile
- Navy Jobs—www.navyjobs.com
- Navy League—www.navyleague.org
- Navy Mine Warfare Command—www.cnsl.spear.navy.mil/cmwc
- Navy Morale, Welfare, and Recreation—www.mwr.navy.mil
- Navy Official Site—www.navy.mil
- Navy on the Internet—www.refdesk.com/navy
- Navy Patrol Squadrons—www.upnavy.com
- Navy Personnel—www.bupers.navy.mil
- Navy Recruiting Command—www.cnrc.navy.mil
- Navy SEALs—www.navyseals.com
- Navy Ships—www.fas.org/man/dod-101/sys/ship
- Navy Supply Corps School—www.nscs.navy.mil
- Navy Support/Diego Garcia—www.dg.navy.mil
- *Navy Times* Magazine—www.navytimes.com
- Office of Naval Research—www.onr.navy.mil
- Osprey Program—www.navair.navy.mil
- Pacific Fleet—www.cpf.navy.mil
- Pacific Fleet—www.pacom.mil
- Pacific Fleet Air Force—www.airpac.navy.mil
- Sea Cadets—www.seacadets.org
- Sea Systems Command—www.navsea.navy.mil
- Seventh Fleet—www.c7f.navy.mil

- Shipboard Combat Systems—www.fas.org/man/dod/sys/ship/weaps
- Sixth Fleet—www.c6f.navy.mil
- Third Fleet—www.comthirdflt.navy.mil

Air Force Sites

The Air Force's main recruiting site has most of the detailed information you want. It also has a webcam at Lackland Air Force Base that will give you a live look at some of the things you may have been wondering about. Log on to www.airforce.com.

Some other sites that might be worth surfing include the following:

- Air Force Academy—www.usafa.af.mil
- Air Force Association—www.afa.org
- Air Force Band—www.bolling.af.mil/band
- Air Force Basic Training—www.usairforce.bm.com
- Air Force Civilian Jobs—www.afpc.rando/ph.af.mil/resweb
- Air Force Information—www.cio.hq.af.mil
- Air Force Intelligence, Surveillance, and Reconnaissance—www.cia.gov/ic/afi
- Air Force Library Resources—www.petersons.com/airforce
- *Air Force* Magazine—www.afa.org/magazine
- Air Force Museum—www.wpafb.mil/museum
- Air Force Office of Scientific Research—www.afosr.sciencewise.com
- Air Force Officer Accession and Training—www.afoats.af.mil
- Air Force One—www.boeing.com/defense-space/military/af
- Air Force Research Laboratory—www.afr.af.mil
- Air Force Reserve—www.afrc.af.mil
- Air Force ROTC—www.afrotc.com
- Air Force Security Forces—www.afsf.lackland.af.mil
- Air Force Space Command—www.spacecom.af.mil
- Air Force Special Operations—www.afsoc.af.mil
- Air Force Technology News—www.airforce-technology.com
- *Air Force Times* Magazine—www.airforcetimes.com
- Air Force Weapons School—www.nellis.af.mil
- Air Intelligence Agency—www.aia.af.mil
- Air National Guard—www.ang.af.mil
- Air Rescue—www.geocities.com/pentagon/8505
- Air Warfare Center—www.acq.osd.mil
- Civil Air Patrol—www.capnhq.gov
- Dryden Flight Research Center—www.dfrc.nasa.gov
- Eglin Air Force Base—www.eglin.af.mil
- Eighth Air Force Museum—www.8afmuseum.net
- First Air Force—www.1staf.tyndall.af.mil
- Hickam Air Force Base—www.hickam.af.mil
- Maxwell Air Force Base—www.au.af.mil
- NASA Langley Research Center—www.larc.nasa.gov
- National Aeronautics and Space Administration—www.nasa.gov

- National Guard Bureau—www.ngb.dtic.mil
- Office of Special Investigations—www.dtic.mil/afos
- Pararescue Teams—www.pararescue.com
- Randolph Air Force Base—www.randolph.af.mil
- Reserve Careers—www.afreserve.com
- School of Aerospace Medicine—www.sam.brooks.af.mil
- Space Wing—www.spacecom.af.mil
- Special Operations Command—www.socom.mil
- Strategic Command—www.stratcom.af.mil
- Thunderbirds—www.airforce.com/thunderbirds
- Vandenberg Air Force Base—www.vandenbergafb.af.mil
- Weather Reconnaissance—www.hurricanehunters.com
- Wright-Patterson Air Force Base—www.wpafb.af.mil

Marine Corps Sites

The Marine Corps recruiting site will fill you in on things you want to know, from available jobs to a look at what you might expect from your first weeks as a Marine. Log on to www.usmc.mil.

For more specific information, check out these sites:

- Basic Training—www.parrisisland.com
- College Programs—www.navycollege.navy.mil
- Corps Chronology—www.hila.com/reference/marines-chron.html
- Defense Environmental Resources—www.dtic.mil
- Education Opportunities—www.militaryedu.com/military-education-programs
- *Leatherneck* Magazine—www.mca,marines.org/leatherneck
- Marine Aviation—www.topedge.com/panels/aircraft
- Marine Band—www.marineband.usmc.mil
- Marine Barracks, Washington—www.mbw.usmc.mil
- Marine Corps Air Station Miramar—www.miramar.usmc.mil
- Marine Corps Air Station–Yuma—www.yuma.usmc.mil
- Marine Corps Base–Camp Lejeune—www.lejeune.usmc.mil
- Marine Corps Base–Camp Pendleton—www.cpp.usmc.mil
- Marine Corps Base–Hawaii—www.mcbh.usmc.mil
- Marine Corps Base–Quantico—www.quantico.usmc.mil
- Marine Corps Combat Service Support Schools—www.lejeune.usmc.mil/mccsss
- Marine Corps Daily Workout—www.getfitnow.com/marinecorps2htm
- Marine Corps Forces South—www.marforsouth.usmc.mil
- Marine Corps Information—www.mps.navy.mil/~library/marines
- Marine Corps League—www.mcleague.org
- Marine Corps MOS Lists—www.usmilitary.about.com/library/milinfo/b/marinejobs.htm
- Marine Corps News—www.marinecorps.com/news
- Marine Corps Raiders—www.usmarineraiders.com
- Marine Corps Reading Program—www.marinecorps.com/reading list

- Marine Corps Scholarship Foundation—www.marine-scholars.org
- *Marine Corps Times* Magazine—www.marinetimes.com
- Marine Corps Warfighting Laboratory—www.mcwl.quantico.usmc.mil
- Marine Corps Web Links—www.thefew.com
- Marine Database—www.thefew.com
- Marine Expeditionary Force—www.globalsecurity.org/military/usmc
- Marine Forces Atlantic—www.marforlant.usmc.mil
- Marine Forces Reserve—www.marforres.usmc.mil
- Marine History—www.grunts.net/usmc
- Marine Links and Information—www.inreach.com/marine
- Marine Pacific Command—www.mfp.usmc.mil
- Marine Scouts and Snipers—www.marinescoutsniper.com
- Marine Security Guards—www.usembassy.de/mission/e1_3_12
- Marine Stories—www.oo-rah.com
- Marine University—www.quantico.usmc.mil
- Marines Online—www.usmchq.com
- Naval Institute—www.usni.org
- Recruit Training—www.mcrdpi.usmc.mil
- Reference Directory—www.globalspecops.com/military/usmc
- School of Aviation Safety—www.nps.navy.mil/~avsafety
- Training and Educational Command—www.mcu.usmc.mil
- Women Marines—www.womenmarines.org

Coast Guard

The Coast Guard's main recruiting website not only describes the ratings that are offered, but it includes a list of comparable civilian jobs with each one. Log on to www.gocoastguard.com.

You may want to surf these sites as well:

- Coast Guard Academy—www.cga.edu
- Coast Guard Auxiliary—www.cgaux.org
- Coast Guard Auxiliary E-Zine—www.teamcoastguard.org
- Coast Guard Background—www.globalsecurity.org/military/agency/dot/uscg.html
- Coast Guard Careers—www.bluejacket.com/index_coastguard.html
- Coast Guard Chief Petty Officers—www.uscgpoa.org
- Coast Guard Facts—www.np.navy.mil/library/cguard.htm
- Coast Guard Foundation—www.cgfdn.org
- Coast Guard Guide—www.uscgbook.com
- Coast Guard History—www.refdesk.com/coast.html
- Coast Guard Home Page—www.uscg.mil
- Coast Guard Information—www.dot.gov/affairs/cgind.html
- Coast Guard Links—www.coopfish.siv.edu/uscg-links.htm
- Coast Guard Links and Chats—www.coastguard.org
- Coast Guard Lore—www.jacksjoint.com/seatales
- Coast Guard Navigation Center—www.navcen.uscg.mil
- Coast Guard Research—www.grotonk12.ct.us

- Coast Guard Reserves—www.uscg.mil/hq/reserve
- Coast Guard Schools—www.call.army.mil/homepage/sch_uscg.htm
- Coast Guard Training—www.fieldtrip.com/nj/98986969.htm
- Coast Guard Units—www.afic.army.mil/parade_units/thecoastguard.htm
- Coast Guard Vessels—www.hazegray.org/worldnav/usa/guard.htm
- Cutters and Homeports—www.wunclub.com/files/uscg.html
- Department of Transportation—www.dot.gov
- Drug Interdiction—www.grunts.net/uscg/drug.html
- Great Lakes Careers—www.schoolship.org/careers/coast_guard.html
- Helicopters—www.adam2fly.com/coast.html
- Housing—www.livable.org/awards/coast.html
- Ice Patrol—www.drifters.doe.gov/usos/ice_patrol.html
- International Ice Patrol—www.uscg.mil/lantarea/iip
- Interpreters—www.cgwebs.net/interpreter
- Links—www.ribb.com/cg.html
- Merchant Marine Exams—www.hawspipe.net
- National Response Center—www.nrc.uscg.mil
- Office of Boating Safety—www.uscgboating.org
- Officer Opportunities—www.minorityaccess.org/programs/cgnt.htm
- Polar Star Icebreaker—www.polarstar.org
- Recruiting Information—www.cgangel.net
- Research and Development—www.rdc.uscg.mil
- Search and Rescue—www.grunts.net/uscg/sar.html
- Student Precommissioning—www.gocoastguard.com/cspi.html
- U.S. Coast Guard–San Diego—www.sandiegocoastguard.com
- *Vision* Magazine—www.dtic.mil

Give Them a Call

If you don't have access to a computer, or would prefer to be able to talk to someone about your options, these toll-free numbers are a good place to start:

- Air Force—1-800-423-8723
- Air National Guard—1-800-864-4264
- AmeriCorps—1-800-942-2677
- Army—1-800-872-2769
- Army National Guard—1-800-464-8273
- Coast Guard—1-800-438-8724
- Marine Corps—1-800-272-7391
- Navy—1-800-872-6289
- Peace Corps—1-800-424-8580

Index

A

A&P mechanics, 293
A-10 Thunderbolt II, 204
AAFES (Army-Air Force Exchange Service), 275
academic skills, learning, 112
academies (military)
  academic requirements, 87
  admissions, 86-87
  Air Force, 92-93
  Basic Training, 93-94
  business success, 84
  Coast Guard, 94-95
  graduation, 88
  Merchant Marine, 96
  Naval, 84, 86-87
  personal requirements, 88
  service fees, 95
  tuition, 87
  West Point, 89-91
  women's admittance, 104-105
Accelerated Initial Accession program, 64
active duty (medical school graduates), 251-252
Adjunct General's Corps, 156, 264
administrative professionals (NASA), 260
Administrative Services (Army), 152
admissions
  Coast Guard Academy, 94
  military academies, 86-87
advantages
  college degrees, 77
  doctors, 253
  military mechanics, 296-297
aerospace technologists (NASA), 260
African Americans, opportunities, 109-119

age (enlistment), 16
Ahoy!, 185
Air Corps (Army), 189-190, 198
Air Defense Artillery division (Army), 154
Air Force
  academy, 92-94
  Air National Guard, 63
  aircrafts
    A-10/0A-10 Thunderbolt II, 204
    B-1B Lancers, 200
    B-2 Spirit, 200
    B-52s, 201-202
    Bombers, 200
    C-130 Hercules, 206
    E-3s, 205
    F-111s, 203-204
    F-117A Nighthawk, 203
    F-15 Eagles, 204
    F-16s, 204
    fighters, 203-204
    KC-135 Stratotankers, 205
    noncombat, 205-206
  airspeed, 203
  Army-Air Force Exchange Service, 275
  AWACS, 205
  Basic Training, 45
  careers, 195-197
  Civil Service, 272
  commissioned officers, 198
  Community College, 76
  creation, 192
  Developing Aerospace Leaders program, 196
  enlisted ranks, 199
  enlistment cutoff age, 16
  first transistor computer, 282
  flights, 193
  groups, 193

  Hap Arnold Wings, 199
  history, 190-191
  honors, 144
  insignia, 198
  major commands, 194
  Materiel Command, 272
  missiles, 194
  numbered air forces, 194
  Office of Special Investigations, 266-267
  officers, 196
  pararescue teams, 198
  part-time civilian jobs, 273
  pay scale website, 198
  personnel department, 197-198
  Personnel Readiness Center, 197
  pilots, 206
  ranks, 198, 200
  refueling planes, 205-206
  ROTC, 66-67
  scholarships, 66
  space exploration, 261
  space program, 195
  special forces, 198
  squadrons, 193
  Student Career Experience Program, 273
  technology, 195
  units, 193-194
  warrant officers, 200
  Warrior Week, 56
  wings, 193, 199
Air Force Academy, 92-94
  graduating, 94
  The Beast, 93
Air National Guard, 62-63
air wings, 179
Airborne, 154
Airborne Warning and Control System (AWACS). *See* AWACS

aircraft
  Air Force, 200-206
  Boeing B-17, 193
  C-130 Hercules, 206
  Coast Guard, 237
  combat helicopter, 299
  E-3s, 205
  electronic countermeasure
    devices, 284
  first military, 189-190
  KC-135 Stratotankers, 205
  Landing Pad Helicopters,
    224
  mechanics, 293
  refueling, 205
  Signal Corps No. 1, 189
  women, 102
airlines (commercial)
  mechanics, 292
  pilots, 5
airspeed, 203
Alaska Coast Guard, 234
Aldrin, Buzz, 255
allowances (BAS), 10
amenities (Navy), 177
Ames Research Center, 261
amphibious assault ships, 224
Amphibious Ready Groups
  (ARGs). See ARGs
amphibious transport docks
  (LPDs), 223
Argo Merchant spill, 235
ARGs (Amphibious Ready
  Groups), 222
Arithmetic (ASVAB), 34, 38
Armed Forces Qualifying
  Test score, 31
Armed Services Vocational
  Aptitude Battery test. See
  ASVAB
Armor Center, 154
Armor division (Army), 154
Armstrong, Neil, 255
Army
  Adjunct General's Corps,
    156
  Administrative Services,
    152
  Air Corps, 189-190, 198
  Air Defense Artillery
    division, 154

Airborne, 154
Armor Center, 154
Armor division, 154
army corps, 159
Army-Air Force Exchange
  Service, 275
Aviation division, 154
barracks, 165-166
Basic Training, 44, 55
battalions, 159
batteries, 158
brigades, 159
career degrees, 73, 75
Chaplain Corps, 157
Chemical Corps, 155
Civil Service, 272
Civil War, 150
civilian clothes, 163
civilian intern program,
  273
Combat Arms, 154-155
combat helicopters, 299
Combat Operations, 152
Combat Service Support,
  156-158
Combat Support, 155-156
commissioned officers, 159
companies, 158
conscription, 150
Corps of Engineers, 155,
  274
Criminal Investigation
  Command, 266-267
day-to-day life, 163
Dental Corps, 157
divisions, 159
draft, 151
Electronic Communi-
  cations, 152
Electronic Maintenance
  careers, 152
Engineering/Construction,
  152
enlisted, 160
field armies, 159
Field Artillery, 155
Finance Corps, 157
Green Beret, 155
headquarters, 159
health care careers, 152
history, 150

honors, 144
housing, 164-165
HPSP, 250
infantry, 155
Intelligence, 152
job security, 166
Judge Advocate General
  Corps, 157
Materiel Command, 272
Media, Public, and Civil
  Affairs, 152
Medical Corps, 157
Medical Specialist Corps,
  156
Military Intelligence Corps,
  155
MOSs, 151-153
MPs, 156
National Guard. See
  National Guard
Nurse Corps, 156
Ordnance Corps, 157
payscale website, 159
personal cars, 164
platoons, 158
Quartermaster Corps, 157
Rangers, 155
ranks, 162
regimentation, 163
ROTC, 67-68
salutes, 159
scholarships, 67
sergeants, 161-162
Signal Corps, 155
SmarTrucks, 297-298
special forces, 155
squadrons, 159
squads, 158
starting, 150
time off, 163
today vs. old, 151
Transportation Corps, 157
Transportation/Supply
  Services, 152
uniforms, 163
Union Army, 150
Veterinary Corps, 158
Victory Forge, 56
warrant officers, 160-161
West Point, 89-91
Army brats, 165

Army Corps, 159
Army Repayment program, 78-79
Army-Air Force Exchange Service (AAFES), 275
Army Women's Corps, 99
Artillery
  Air Defense, 154
  Field, 155
astronauts
  advanced training, 259-260
  candidate training, 259
  civilians, 259
  equipment testing, 5
  height requirements, 258
  military, 256, 259
  mission specialists, 257
  pilots, 257
  qualifications, 257-258
  scientist, 256
  screening process, 258
  training/evaluation, 259-260
ASVAB (Armed Services Vocational Aptitude Battery), 11
  auto/shop information, 37
  best time, taking, 32
  coding speed, 36-37
  cost, 32
  electronics information, 39
  enlistment purposes, 31
  format, 30
  importance, 40
  math reasoning, 34
  mathematics knowledge, 38
  mechanical comprehension, 38
  numerical operations, 36
  paragraph comprehension, 35
  science (general), 33
  scores, 29-31
  studying for, 39
  taking over, 32
  testing pressure, 32
  time, 30
  word knowledge, 34-35

AT-4 antitank rockets, 216
ATMs (Navy ships), 177
automatic grenade launcher, 215
automobiles
  ASVAB questions, 37
  mechanics, 294
  military developments, 297-298
  SmarTrucks, 297-298
Auxiliaries (Coast Guard), 242-243
auxiliary ships, 178
Aviation division (Army), 154
AWACS (Airborne Warning and Control System), 205

B

B-1B Lancers, 200
B-2 Spirit, 200
B-52s, 201-202
band (Marine), 217-218
barracks (Army), 165-166
BAS (Basic Allowance for Subsistence), 10
base pay, 6-7
Basic Allowance for Subsistence (BAS), 10
Basic Training, 44
  Air Force, 45
  Air Force Academy, 92-94
  Army, 44
  Coast Guard, 44
  drill instructors, 57-58
  eating habits, 49
  exercise preparations, 49
  exercising before, 48
  first day, 50-51
  graduating, 55-57
  graduation requirements, 45
  haircuts, 47-48
  length, 44-45
  locations, 44-45
  Marine Corps, 44
  military academies, 93-94
  Navy, 44

  needs, 46
  packing for, 46-47
  physical fitness test, 49
  running, 48
  sleeping habits, 49
  tips to follow, 50
  week-by-week, 53-56
  weight training, 49
  what to bring, 47
  women vs. men, 45
battalions (Army), 159
batteries (Army), 158
Bell Telephone Laboratories, 282-283
beneficiaries (life insurance), 133
benefits, 9
  bonuses, 122
  cash, 122
  Civil Service, 275
  education, 10-12, 77
  family, 101
  fire departments, 268
  food, 9-10
  health care, 129-130
  home loans, 134
  housing, 10
  HPSP, 250
  life insurance, 133
  medical, 10
  Montgomery GI Bill, 134-136
  National Guard, 61
  pensions, 9, 130-133
  police departments, 268
  retiree, 128-129
  retirement, 9, 124, 131-132
  Servicemember Group Life Insurance, 133
  Special Separation, 127
  Top-Up, 136
  travel, 122
  vacation, 9
  veterans, 9, 125-126, 136-137
  Voluntary Separation Incentive, 127

bits, 282
boarding teams (Coast Guard), 264-265
boats (Coast Guard), 237, 243. *See also* ships
Boeing B-17s, 193
bombers, 200
Bonhomme Richard, 168
bonuses
    Civil Service, 271
    enlistment, 8, 24-25, 122
boot camp. *See* Basic Training
bootleggers (Coast Guard), 231
Borginis, Sarah, 98
bows (ships), 185
Boyington, Maj. Gregory USMC, 212
branches. *See also* names of specific branches
    base pay, 7
    Medals of Honor, 144
    pay scales, 143
    selecting, 143
Brewer, Lucy, 98
brigades (Army), 159
Buddy Deal, 19
bytes, 282

C

C-130 Hercules, 206
Calvary (Armor division), 154
career degrees (Army), 73-75
career ladders, 271
careers
    Air Force, 195-197
    Civil Service, 276
    civilian military, 143
    computer science, 283, 288-289
    critical, 24-25
    DOD, 142
    fire department, 267
    minorities, building, 114
    NASA, 260-261
    Navy, 4, 182-183
    part-time, 273
    police, 267
    women, 6, 102-103

carriers
    air wings, 179
    groups, 178
    Kitty Hawk, 173
cars (personal), 164
Carter, Edward A., 115
cash benefits, 122
CCAF (Community College of the Air Force), 76
chaplain assistants, 152
Chaplain Corps (Army), 157
checks, 7
chefs, 9
Chemical Corps (Army), 155
Citadel Corps of Cadets, 90
citizenship
    enlisting, 16
    minorities, 117
Civil Affairs (Army), 152
Civil Service, 269-270
    advancement, 270-271
    Air Force, 272
    Army, 272-273
    Army-Air Force Exchange Service, 275
    benefits, 275
    bonuses, 271
    career ladders, 271
    Coast Guard, 272
    Corps of Engineers, 274
    Department of Defense, 270
    educational programs, 272
    employers, 270
    insurance, 275
    job applications, 276
    job openings, finding, 273-274
    management training, 273
    Marine Corps, 272
    Navy, 272
    openings, 276
    part-time jobs, 273
    raises, 271
    retail contractors, 270
    retirement, 275
    salaries, 271, 275
    union, 275
    vacation, 275
    website, 274

Civil War
    Army, 150
    Coast Guard, 233
    Marine Corps, 210
civilians
    astronauts, 259
    Civil Service. *See* Civil Service
    clothes, 163
    counterparts, 5
    DOD jobs, 142
    downsizing, 269
    job experience, 23
    job scenario example, 123-124
    mechanics, 296-297
    military jobs, 143
    pensions vs. military, 131
    related jobs after service, 23
    salary comparison, 7
    women mechanics, 295
Coast Guard
    Academy, 94-95, 104
    aircraft, 237
    Alaska, patrolling, 234
    Auxiliary, 242-243
    Basic Training, 44
    boarding teams, 264-265
    boats, 237
    bootleggers, 231
    Civil Service, 272
    Civil War, 233
    Coasties, 229
    coastline patrols, 229
    commissioned officers, 239
    dive schools, 241
    drug busts, 232
    enlisted ranks, 240
    exploration, 238
    full-time status, 233-234
    Gulf of Mexico, patrolling, 235
    gun shipments, stopping, 232
    high-endurance cutters, 236
    history, 230
    Investigative Services unit, 265-266
    Korean War, 234

law enforcement preparation, 264

Lighthouse Service, 230-231

lives, 242

marine science, 241

Mexican War, 233

national security, 229

National Strike Force, 235-236

natural resource protection, 229

oil spills, 235

opportunities, 239

Pacific Tactical Law Enforcement Team, 266

pay scale website, 239

pleasure boat problems, 243

polar class icebreakers, 236

qualifications, 239

ranks, 239-240

ratings, 240-241

Reserves, 63

Revenue Cutter Service, 231

sea security, 229

ship mobility, 229

Spanish-American War, 233

terrorist attacks, 227-228

tools, 237-238

uniforms, 243

Vietnam War, 234

War of 1812, 233

war time, 233

warrant officers, 240

water safety, 229

women, 99, 239

WWI, 233-234

WWII, 234

Coasties, 229

coats (pea), 185

College First Option, 23

college

admissions, 75

Community College of the Air Force, 76

credits, 8, 11, 75

degrees, 77

distance learning, 79-80

earning credits while serving, 75

funds, 113

kickers, 77

loans, 12

military school credits, 73, 112

minorities, 112

Montgomery GI Bill, 10

Navy Associate Degree Completion Program, 76

Servicemember Opportunity Colleges, 12

signing up after, 23

SOCs, 73

student loans, 78-79

Texas A & M Cadet Corps, 91

tuition assistance, 11

Collins, Michael, 255

combat, women, 103

Combat Arms (Army), 154-155

combat helicopters, 299

Combat Operations (Army), 152

Combat Service Support (Army), 156-158

Combat Support (Army), 155-156

combat swimmer reconnaissance units, 187

combat training (Marine Corps), 214

combat vehicles, 298

command sergeant majors (Army), 161

commissioned officers

Air Force, 198

Army, 159

Coast Guard, 239

Marine Corps, 219-220

Navy, 180

pay, 7

training, 251

Community College of the Air Force (CCAF), 76

companies (Army), 158

computer science careers, 288-289

computerized aiming devices, 280

computers

battlefield, 284

bits, 282

bytes, 282

creative process, 286

cyberwarfare, 287-288

first electronic digital, 280-282

first transistor, 282

hackers, 288

history, 280-281

megabytes, 283

military careers, 283, 288-289

military presence, 285

Navy Tactical Data System, 282

research and development, 285-286

Space Command, 262

transistors, 283

UNIVAC, 281

virtual reality training, 286-287

Congressional Medal of Honor, 144

conscription, 150-151

construction (Army), 152

contracts

enlistment papers, 162

medical school, 251

cooks, 9

corporals (Army), 162

Corps of Cadets, 88

Corps of Engineers, 155, 274

countermeasure devices, 284

countermeasure ships, 174

courses (ROTC), 68-69

cows, 90

credits

college, 8, 11

earning while serving, 75

military schools, 73

crimes, enlisting, 16

Criminal Investigation Command, 266-267

criminal investigators
Air Force, 266-267
Army, 266-267
Coast Guard, 265-266
Marine Corps, 266-267
Navy, 266-267
critical careers, 24-25
Crucible, 56
cruisers, 178
cyberterrorism, 287-288

D

D&C (Drill and Ceremony), 52
DACOWITS (Defense Advisory Committee on Women in the Service), 100-101
day-to-day life (Army), 163
Defense Advisory Committee on Women in the Service (DACOWITS). *See* DACOWITS
delayed entry, 23
Dental Corps (Army), 157
Department of Defense. *See* DOD
destroyers, 178
Developing Aerospace Leaders program, 196
development (research), 285-286
Devil Dogs, 211
dirty-shirt wardrooms, 176
disabled veterans, 125-126
discharges, 101, 127
discounts (military), 123
discrimination, 110-111
distance learning, 79-80
dive schools (Coast Guard), 241
doctors
active duty, 252
advantages, 253
assignments, 252
enlistment papers, 250
HPSP, 249-250
in-service, 253

learning while serving, 251
medical degrees, 247-249
medical school, leaving, 250
military medical school, 253
NASA, 260
physical training, 251
residencies, 251-252
second active duty tour, 251
USUHS interns/residents, 254
DOD (Department of Defense), 142
civilian careers, 142-143, 270
pay scale table website, 7
website, 274
dog tags, 285
downsizing, 269
draft, 150-151, 233
drawdown, 151
dress blues (Marine Corps), 218
Drill and Ceremony (D&C). *See* D & C
drill instructors, 57-58
drug busts, 232
duty (National Guard time), 61

E

E-3 rank, 7, 205
e-mail, 177
Eagle, 95, 237-238
education
academic skills, 112
Air Force Community College, 76
Air Force scholarships, 66
Army career degrees, 73, 75
Army scholarships, 67
benefits, 10
Civil Service programs, 272

college admissions, 75
credits, 8, 11, 75
degree advantages, 77
distance learning, 79-80
Fellows Program, 272
funds, 113
GED, 16
high school diploma, 16
high school equivalence diploma, 80
kickers, 77
learn while serving, 75
mechanics, 294-295
military school credits, 73
minorities, 112
Montgomery GI Bill, 10, 72, 134-136
Navy Associate Degree Completion Program, 76
Navy scholarships, 66
reservist benefits, 77
Servicemember Opportunity Colleges, 12
Servicemen's Readjustment Act of 1944, 11
SOCs, 73
student loans, 12, 78-79
Top-Up, 136
tuition assistance, 11
Edwards Air Force Base, 13
eight bells, 185
Eighth Fleet, 171
Electronic Communications (Army), 152
Electronic Maintenance careers (Army), 152
Electronic Numerical Integrator and Calculator (ENIAC), 280-282
electronic warfare, 284-285
Emergency Medical Service, 268
employers, Civil Service, 270
Engineering (Army), 152
English, learning, 117
ENIAC (Electronic Numerical Integrator and Calculator), 280-282

enlisting
   age, 16
   Air Force ranks, 199
   Armed Forces Qualifying
      Test score, 31
   Army, 160
   ASVAB scores, 31
   bonuses, 24-25, 122
   citizenship, 16
   Coast Guard ranks, 240
   College First Option, 23
   convicted crimes, 16
   delayed entry, 23
   final interview, 26-27
   height restrictions, 16
   high school diploma, 10,
      16, 116
   limitations, 16-17
   Marine Corps, 220
   marital status, 16
   MEPS, 25-27
   Navy, 181
   papers, 162
   recruiters, 18-20
   requirements, 16-17
   ten commandments, 17-18
   weight restrictions, 16
enlistment papers, 162
entry (delayed), 23
equipment
   astronauts, 5
   women, changes for,
      105-106
Escadrille Américane, 190
Esprit de Corps, 221
exam. *See* tests
exercises (graduation), 56-57
exploration (Coast Guard),
   238
Exxon Valdes spill, 235

F

F-111s, 203-204
F-117A Nighthawk, 203
F-15 Eagles, 204
F-16s, 204
family benefits, 101
fathoms, 185

federal government. *See* Civil
   Service
Fellows Program, 272
field armies (Army), 159
Field Artillery (Army), 155
Fifth Fleet, 170
fighter aircraft, 203-204
final interview (enlistment),
   26-27
Finance Corps (Army), 157
fire departments, 267-268
firefighters, 263
first day (Basic Training),
   50-51
First Fleet, 171
first military plane, 189-190
first sergeants (Army), 161
firsties, 90
Fiscal 2000 Defense
   Authorization Bill, 130
Fleet Activities Sasebo, 173
fleets, 170-174
Flying Fortress, 193
food
   Army books, 165
   cooks, 9
   free, 9-10
   Marine Corps, 225
   midnight rations, 176
   Navy, 176
forecasting weather, 5
format (ASVAB), 30
Foulois, Lt. Benjamin, 189
Fourth Fleet, 171
French Air Force, 190
friendly fire, 284
frigate, 178
frogmen, 187
funds (college), 113

G

Gagarin, Yugi, 257
games (war), 55
Gator Navy, 222-224
GED (General Educational
   Diploma), 16
   creation of, 16
   development, 116

enlisting, 10
enrollment, 116
ghost fleets, 171-172
GI Bill. *See* Montgomery
   GI Bill
Glenn, John, 255-256
graduating
   Air Force Academy, 94
   Basic Training, 45, 55-57
   military academies, 88
Gravity Probe B, 258
Green Beret, 155
ground combat (women), 103
groups
   Air Force, 193
   Navy carriers, 178
Gulf of Mexico, Coast Guard,
   235
Gulf War, Marine Corps, 212
guns
   issuing, 53
   shipments, 232

H

hackers, 288
haircuts (Basic Training),
   47-48
handheld computers, 284
Hap Arnold Wings, 199
headquarters (Army), 159
health care
   Army careers, 152
   veterans, 129-130
Health Professions
   Scholarship Program,
   248-249
heavy equipment mechanics,
   294
height
   astronauts requirements,
      258
   enlisting restrictions, 16
helicopters, 299
high school diploma
   enlisting, 10, 16
   requirement, 116
high school equivalence
   diploma, 80

high seas, 185
High-3 pension plan, 130
high-endurance cutters, 236
hikes, 216
Hispanics
    military representation,
        111
    opportunities, 116
home loans, 134
honors
    Air Force, 144
    Army, 144
    Marine Corps, 145
    Medals of Honor, 144
    Navy, 145
    Purple Hearts, 144
housing
    Army, 164-165
    free, 10
    Navy, 174
    substandard, 174
HPSP benefits, 250
humps, 216

I

infantry
    Army, 155
    Marine Corps, 214
    training, 215-216
instant response (Marines),
    222
instructors (drill), 57-58
insurance
    Civil Service, 275
    life, 133
Intelligence (Army), 152
intern programs, 273
International Rosetta
    Mission, 258
Internet
    Civil Service job openings,
        273
    Navy access, 177
internships, USUHS
    Program, 254
interviewing recruiters, 18
inventions, technology, 12

Investigative Services unit
    (Coast Guard), 265-266
issuing
    checks, 7
    rifles, 53
Iwo Jima Marine Corps
    invasion, 224
Izak, Edouard, 172

J

Jet Propulsion Laboratory,
    261
job descriptions
    MOSs, 153-154
    Navy, 183-184
job security (Army), 166
jobs. See careers
Johnson Space Center, 261
joining. See enlisting
Joint Chiefs of Staff, 141
Joint Task Force-Computer
    Network Operations
    (JTF-CNO), 262
Jones, Captain John Paul, 168
JTF-CNO (Joint Task Force-
    Computer Network
    Operations), 262
Judge Advocate General
    Corps (Army), 157

K-L

KC-135 Stratotankers, 205
Kelly, Lt. George, 190
Kennedy Space Center, 261
kickers, 77
Kitty Hawk, 173
Korean War
    Coast Guard, 234
    Marine Corps, 212

Lafayette Escadrille, 190
Landing Pad Dock (LPDs),
    223
Landing Pad Helicopters
    (LPHs), 224

Landing Ship, Dock (LSD),
    223
landings (Marine Corps), 223
languages
    barriers, 117
    Navy, 184-186
law enforcement
    Adjutant General Corps
        backgrounds, 264
    Coast Guard, 264-266
    Emergency Medical
        Service, 268
    fire departments, 267-268
    military investigators,
        266-267
    military police background,
        264
    New York Police
        Department, 267
    New York Fire
        Department, 267
    police departments,
        267-268
lawyers (NASA), 260
learning (distance), 79-80
Leathernecks, 211
leave, 9
length (Basic Training), 44-45
Life Accelerator, 182
life insurance, 133
Lighthouse Service, 230-231
limitations
    enlisting, 16-17
    women, 103
living arrangements
    Marine Corps, 225
    Navy, 175
living conditions
    Navy, 174
    West Point, 90
loans
    college, 12
    home, 134
    student, 78-79
locations
    Army barracks, 166
    Basic Training, 44-45
log books, 185

logistics personnel (NASA), 260
low-income veterans, 126
LPDs (Landing Pad Dock), 223
LPHs (Landing Pad Helicopters), 224
LSD (Marine Corps Landings), 223
Luke, Frank, 192

M

M16A2 rifles, 215
M2.50 machine gun, 215
M2249 machine gun, 215
M240 machine gun, 215
M9 pistol, 215
mach, 203
machine guns, 215
major commands (Air Force), 194
management training (Civil Service), 273
Marine Corps
　advancement, 220-222
　automatic grenade launcher, 215
　Band, 217-218
　Basic Training, 44
　Civil Service, 272
　Civil War, 210
　combat training, 214
　commissioned officers, 219-220
　creation, 209
　Crucible, 56
　Devil Dogs nickname, 211
　dress blues, 218
　emblem, 219
　enlisted ranks, 220
　Esprit de Corps, 221
　first battle landings, 211
　first recruiting station, 209
　food, 225
　Gator Navy, 222-224
　Gulf War, 212
　high standards, 213

history, 212
honors, 145
humps, 216
infantry, 214-216
instant response, 222
Iwo Jima invasion, 224
Korean War, 212
Landing Ship, Docks, 223
landings, 223
Leathernecks nickname, 211
living arrangements, 225
Marine Forces Reserves, 63-64
master sergeant, 8
Mexican War, 210
MOSs, 214
motto, 219
Naval Criminal Investigation Service, 266-267
pay scale website, 219
physical training, 216
ranks, 219
retention rate, 213
size, 213
SOI East, 214
SOI West, 214
tasks, 212
toughness, 213-214
training officers, 221
uniforms, 211
War of 1812, 210
war on terrorism, 212
weapons, 215-216
Women Marines, 99, 216-217
WWI, 211
WWII, 211
Marine Forces Reserves, 63-64
marine science, 241
marital status (enlistment), 16
marksmanship, 53
Mary Baldwin College, 93
master sergeants
　Army, 161
　Marine Corps, 8

Materiel Command, 272
math (ASVAB) questions, 34, 38
McMurty, Captain George, 158
mechanical comprehension (ASVAB), 38
mechanics
　A&P, 293
　aircraft, 293
　airlines, 292
　automotive, 294, 297-298
　challenges, 296
　future vehicles, 298
　heavy equipment, 294
　leaving, 292
　military advantage, 296-297
　new combat vehicles, 298
　training, 293-295
　women, 295-296
medals
　Medals of Honor, 144
　Purple Hearts, 144
Medals of Honor, 144
Media Affairs (Army), 152
medical benefits, 10
Medical Corps (Army), 157
medical degrees, 247-249
medical schools
　active duty, 252
　assignments, 252
　contracts, 251
　enlistment papers, 250
　HPSP benefits, 250
　learning while serving, 251
　leaving preparations, 250
　military, attending, 253
　physical training, 251
　residencies, 251-252
　second active duty tour, 251
　USUHS interns/residents, 254
Medical Specialist Corps (Army), 156
megabytes, 283
MEPS (Military Entrance Processing Station), 25-27

Merchant Marine Academy, 96, 104
Meuse-Argonne campaign, 158
Mexican War
    Coast Guard, 233
    Marine Corps, 210
midnight rations, 176
midrats, 176
military pride, 263
military academies
    academic requirements, 87
    admissions, 86-87
    Air Force, 92-94
    Basic Training, 93-94
    business success, 84
    Coast Guard, 94-95, 104
    graduation, 88
    Merchant Marine, 96, 104
    personal requirements, 88
    service fees, 95
    tuition, 87
    Virginia Military, 93
    West Point, 89-91
    women admittance, 104-105
military discounts, 123
Military Entrance Processing Station (MEPS), 25-27
Military Intelligence Corps (Army), 155
military medical schools, 253-254
military occupational specialty. See MOS
Military Police (MPs), 156, 264
military school credits, 73
minorities
    academic skills, learning, 112
    African Americans, 115
    career building, 114
    citizenship, 117
    civilian jobs, 112
    college, 112
    college funds, 113
    high school diploma requirement, 116

Hispanics, 116
    language barriers, 117
    representation, 111, 118
    ROTC, 113-114
    women, 117-118
mission specialists, 257
missiles, 194
Mk19s, 215
money
    Air Force pay scale website, 198
    Army payscale website, 159
    ASVAB cost, 32
    base pay, 6-7
    checks, 7
    civilian comparison, 7
    Civil Service pay scale, 271, 275
    Coast Guard pay scale, 239
    college, 8
    commissioned officers, 7
    E-3 rank, 7
    enlistment bonuses, 24-25, 122
    Marine pay scale, 219
    master sergeant (Marine Corps), 8
    Navy payscale website, 180
    pay scale table website, 7
    raises, 7
    recent graduates, 8
    signing bonus, 8
Montgomery GI Bill, 10, 72
    new college students, 72
    original law, 72
    signing up for, 134-136
MOS (Military Occupational Specialty), 21-22
    Army, 74, 151-152
    job descriptions, 153-154
    Marine Corps, 214
    no openings, 22
    Partnership for Youth Success, 23
    previous skills, 147-148
    qualifying for, 146-147
    selecting, 146
    subspecialties, 152-153

MPs (Military Police), 156, 264
Mullen, Robert, 209

N

NASA (National Aeronautics and Space Administration), 255. See also United States Space Command
    Administrative professionals, 260
    aerospace technologists, 260
    astronauts, 256-260
    careers, 260-261
    doctors, 260
    first man in space, 257
    Gravity Probe B, 258
    International Rosetta Mission, 258
    Jet Propulsion Laboratory, 261
    Johnson Space Center, 261
    Kennedy Space Center, 261
    lawyers, 260
    logistics personnel, 260
    Orbiter systems, 259
    pilots, 260
    projects, 258
    Space Infrared Telescope Facility, 258
    space shuttle program, 257
    website, 260
National Guard, 60
    benefits, 61
    educational benefits, 77
    full time employers, 60
    kickers, 77
    time on duty, 61
    training, 61
national security, 229
National Strike Force (NSF), 235-236
NATO, women & weapons, 105
natural resources, protecting, 229

Naval Criminal Investigation
Service, 266-267
Naval Forces Central
Command (NAVCENT), 170
Naval Surface Reserve Force,
64
NAVCENT (Naval Forces
Central Command), 170
Navy
Academy, 84, 86-87
Accelerated Initial Accession
program, 64
air wings, 179
Associate Degree
Completion Program, 76
ATMs, 177
auxiliary ships, 178
Basic Training, 44
birthplace, 169
careers, 182-183
carrier groups, 178
Civil Service, 272
commissioned officers, 180
commuting time, 175
cruisers, 178
destroyers, 178
dirty-shirt wardrooms, 176
e-mail, 177
enlisted rates, 181
Fleet Activities Sasebo, 173
fleets, 170-171
food, 176
frigate, 178
frogmen, 187
Gator Navy, 222-224
growth, 169
history, 168-169
honors, 145
housing, 174
Internet access, 177
job descriptions, 4, 183-184
language, 184-186
Life Accelerator, 182
living conditions, 174-175
Naval Criminal Investiga-
tion Service, 266-267
Naval Surface Reserve
Force, 64

officers, 176, 181
on-board amenities, 177
payscale website, 180
rates, 180-181
RDCs, 57
recruiting website, 182
ROTC, 65-66
scholarships, 66
Seabees, 186
SEALs, 186-188
ship recreation areas, 177
starting, 169
strength, 169-170
submarines, 178
Tactical Data System com-
puter, 282
television systems, 176-177
virtual reality training,
286-287
warrant officers, 181
Women Accepted for
Volunteer Emergency
Service, 99
world travel, 177
Netter, Lt. Col. Teri, 6
New York Fire Department,
267
New York Police
Department, 267
Nichols, Samuel, 209
NIPRNET (Nonclassified
Internet Protocol Router
Network), 287
Non-Prior Service Accession
Course. See NPSAC, 64
Nonclassified Internet
Protocol Router Network
(NIPRNET), 287
noncombat aircraft, 205-206
NPSAC (Non-Prior Service
Accession Course), 64
NSF (National Strike Force),
235-236
numbered air forces, 194
numerical operations
(ASVAB), 36
Nurse Corps, 98-99, 156

O

O'Hare, Lieutenant Edward
H., 174
occupational specialty. See
MOS, 21
Office of Personnel
Management, 276
Office of Special
Investigations, 266-267
officers
Air Force, 196, 198
commissioned. See com-
missioned officers
Navy, 176, 181
training, 221
warrant. See warrant
officers
oil spills, 235
on-board amenities (Navy),
177
openings (Civil Service), 276
Operation Desert Storm, 201
opportunities
Hispanic, 116
women, 6
Ordnance Corps (Army), 157
Orbiter systems, 259

P

Pacific Fleet, 172-174
Pacific Tactical Law
Enforcement Team, 266
paragraph comprehension
(ASVAB), 35
pararescue teams (Air Force),
198
part-time Civil Service jobs,
273
Partnership for Youth
Success, 23
pay
Air Force payscale website,
198
Army website, 159
base, 6-7
branches, 143

Civil Service, 271, 275
civilian comparison, 7
civilian military employees, 143
Coast Guard pay scale, 239
commissioned officers, 7
E-3 rank, 7
enlistment bonuses, 25
Marines pay scale, 219
master sergeant (Marine Corps), 8
Navy website, 180
raises, 7
recent graduates, 8
scale table website, 7
signing bonus, 8
pea coats, 185
Pearl Harbor draft, 150
pensions, 9
benefits, 130-131
civilian vs. military, 131
VA, 132-133
veterans, 126
Pentagon, 142
personnel department (Air Force), 197-198
Personnel Readiness Center (Randolph Air Fore Base), 197
PFT (Physical Fitness Test), 49
physical examination, 25
physical training
Marine Corps, 216
medical schools, 251
pilots
Air Force, 206
astronauts, 257
learning to fly, 5
NASA, 260
salaries, 5
pirates, 168
pistols, 215
planes. *See* aircraft
platoons (Army), 158
pleasure boats, 243
plebes, 89
polar class icebreakers, 236-237
Polar Sea, 236

Polar Star, 236
police departments
benefits, 268
careers, 267
New York, 267
pride, 263
Powell, Colin, 114
pregnancy discharges, 101
privateers, 168
projects
NASA, 258
rocket propulsion system, 13
promotions, 23
protection
computer hackers, 288
natural resources, 229
Public Affairs (Army), 152
Puller, Lewis B., 221
Purple Hearts, 144

Q-R

qualifications
astronauts, 257-258
Coast Guard admittance, 239
enlistment bonuses, 24
Health Professions Scholarship Program, 249
MOS, 146-147
naval officers, 181
Quartermaster Corps (Army), 157

RAH-66 Comanche, 299
raises, 7, 271
Rangers (Army), 155
ranks
Air Force, 198, 200
Army, 159-162
Coast Guard, 239-240
E-3, 7
Marine Corps, 219
rates, compared, 180
rates (Navy), 180-181
ratings (Coast Guard), 240-241
RDCs (Recruit Division Commanders), 57

recreation areas (Navy ships), 177
Recruit Division Commanders. *See* RDCs, 57
recruiters, 18
advice, 20
ASVAB scores, hiding, 31
devil's advocate present, 19
interviewing, 18
looking around, 18
Marine Corps first station, 209
Navy website, 182
questions for, 20-21
REDUX, 132
refueling planes, 205
regimentation (Army), 163
regular military compensation (RMC), 130
religion, chaplain assistants, 152
requirements
Army Basic Training graduation, 55
astronauts, height, 258
Basic Training graduation, 45
enlisting, 16-17
high school diploma, 116
Marine Corps, 213
Medals of Honor, 144
medical school residency, 251
MEPS, 27
military academies, 87-88
retirement, 131
research and development, 285-286
Reserve Officer Training Corps. *See* ROTC
reservists, 60
Air National Guard, 62-63
Coast Guard, 63
educational benefits, 77
home loans, 134
kickers, 77
Marine Forces, 63-64
National Guard, 60-61
Naval Surface Reserve Force, 64

residencies (medical school), 251-252
respect, earning, 54
retail contractors, 270
retirement, 9, 124
  benefits, 128-129
  Civil Service, 275
  pensions, 130-133
  REDUX, 132
  years of service requirement, 131
Revenue Cutter Service, 231
Revolution in Military Affairs (RMA), 298
Rickenbacker, Eddie, 190
rifles
  issuing, 53
  M16A2, 215
RMA (Revolution in Military Affairs), 298
RMC (Regular Military Compensation), 130
rocket propulsion system project, 13
rockets
  AT-4, 216
  V-2, 194
ROTC (Reserve Officer Training Corps), 65
  Air Force, 66-67
  Army, 67-68
  Corps of Cadets, 88
  courses, 68-69
  history, 65
  Mary Baldwin College, 93
  minorities, 113-114
  naval, 65-66
  service obligations, 68
  women enrollment, 101
Russian cosmonaut, Yuri Gagarin, 257

S

safety (water), 229
sailors (uniforms), 244
salaries
  airline pilots, 5
  base, 6-7
  branches, 143
  checks, 7
  Civil Service, 271, 275
  civilian comparison, 7
  civilian military employees, 143
  commissioned officers, 7
  E-3 rank, 7
  master sergeant (Marine Corps), 8
  raises, 7
  recent graduates, 8
  signing bonus, 8
  table of website, 7
saluting (Army), 159
Sampson, Deborah, 98
scholarships
  Air Force, 66
  Army, 67
  health-care professionals, 253
  Navy, 66
science (ASVAB), 33
scores
  Armed Forces Qualifying Test, 31
  ASVAB, 29-31
screening process (astronauts), 258
scuttlebutt, 185
sea security, 229
Sea, Air, Land (SEALs), 186-188
Seabees (Navy), 186
SEALs (Sea, Air, Land), 186-188
Second Fleet, 170
Secret Internet Protocol Router Network (NIPR-NET), 287
Secretary of State Colin Powell, 114
security
  job, 166
  national, 229
  sea, 229
selecting
  branches, 143
  Coast Guard ratings, 240-241
MOS, 146
Navy careers, 182
Semper Fidelis, 219
Semper Paratus (SPARS), 99
Serapis, 168
sergeant first class (Army), 161
sergeants, 161-162
service obligations (ROTC), 68
Servicemember Opportunity Colleges (SOCs), 12, 73
Servicemember Group Life Insurance, 133
Servicemen's Readjustment Act of 1944, 11
servo-mechanisms, 280
Seventh Fleet, 170
Sewaren spill, 235
ships. *See also* boats
  auxiliary (Navy), 178
  Bonhomme Richard, 168
  bows, 185
  countermeasure, 174
  cruisers, 178
  destroyers, 178
  draft, 233
  Eagle, 237-238
  frigate, 178
  high-endurance cutters, 236
  Kitty Hawk, 173
  mobility, 229
  polar class icebreakers, 236-237
  Polar Sea, 236
  Polar Star, 236
  recreation areas, 177
  Sasebo, 174
  starboard, 185
  stern, 185
  submarines, 178
  trophy, 237-238
  USS *Blue Ridge*, 170
  USS *Coronado*, 170
  USS *Eisenhower*, 177
  USS *Essex*, 174
  USS *Fort McHenry*, 174
  USS *Germantown*, 174
  USS *Guardian*, 174

USS *Juneau*, 174
USS *LaSalle*, 170
USS *Mount Whitney*, 170
USS *Patriot*, 174
USS *San Antonio*, 224
Signal Corps (Army), 155
Signal Corps No. 1, 189
signing bonus, 8
signing up. *See* enlisting
SIPRNET (Secret Internet Protocol Router Network), 287
sites (web)
  Air Force pay scale, 198
  Army payscale, 159
  Coast Guard pay scale, 239
  Civil Service, 274
  Department of Defense, 274
  Marine Corps pay scale, 219
  NASA, 260
  Navy payscale, 180
  Navy recruiting, 182
  Office of Personnel Management, 276
  payscale, 7
  VA, 130
Sixth Fleet, 170
SmarTrucks, 297-298
SOCs (Servicemember Opportunity Colleges), 12, 73
SOI East, 214
SOI West, 214
solar panels, 284
sore muscles, 49
Space Infrared Telescope Facility, 258
space program (Air Force), 195
space shuttle program, 257
Spanish-American War, 233
Spar and Storis, 238
SPARS (*Semper Paratus*), 99
special forces
  Air Force, 198
  Army, 155
  Navy SEALs, 186-188
  WWII, 156
  WWII Air Corps, 198
Special Separation Benefit, 127

squadrons
  Air Force, 193
  Army, 159
squads (Army), 158
staff sergeants (Army), 161
starboard, 185
starting
  Army, 150
  draft, 150
  Marine Infantry Training, 216
  Navy, 169
Stefanyshyn-Piper, Naval Lt. Commander Heidemarie, 66
stern, 185
Storis and Spar, 238
Student Career Experience Program, 273
student hierarchy (West Point), 90
student loans, 78-79
studying, ASVAB, 39
submarines, 178
subspecialties (MOS), 152-153
substandard housing (Navy), 174
summer training (Coast Guard Academy), 95
Supply Services (Army), 152

T

technicians (Air Guard), 62
technology
  Air Force, 195
  battlefield computers, 284
  computer careers, 283
  computers, 285-287
  cyberwarfare, 287-288
  dog tag replacements, 285
  electronic warfare, 284-285
  ENIAC, 280-282
  first electronic digital computer, 280-282
  history, 280-281
  inventions, 12
  military careers, 288-289

Navy Tactical Data System computer, 282
servo-mechanisms, 280
solar panels, 284
transistor, 282-283
transistor computers, 282
UNIVAC, 281
television systems (Navy), 176-177
ten commandments of enlisting, 17-18
Tenth Fleet, 171
tests
  ASVAB. *See* ASVAB
  college credits, 75
  physical exam, 25
Texas A & M Cadet Corps, 91
The Beast, 92-94
Third Fleet, 170
Thunderbolt, 204
time
  ASVAB, 30-32
  commuting, 175
  National Guard duty, 61
time off
  Army, 163
  Civil Service, 275
  West Point, 89
tools (Coast Guard), 236
  aircraft, 237
  boats, 237
  high-endurance cutters, 236
  polar class icebreakers, 236-237
  trophy ship, 237-238
Top-Up, 136
training
  aircraft, women, 102
  astronauts, 259-260
  Basic. *See* Basic Training
  Coast Guard Academy, 95
  combat, 214
  commissioned officer, 251
  cooks, 9
  infantry, 215
  management, 273
  marksmanship, 53
  mechanics, 293-295
  Navy SEALs, 187

officers, 221
physical
    Marine Corps, 216
    medical schools, 251
virtual reality, 286-287
West Point, 91
women, 104
transistors, 282-283
Transportation Corps (Army), 157
Transportation Services (Army) 152
travel, 122, 177
trophy ship (Coast Guard), 237-238
tuition
    assistance, 11
    military academies, 87
Twelfth Fleet, 171

U

Uniformed Services University of Health Sciences (USUHS). *See* USUHS
uniforms
    Army, 163
    Coast Guard, 243
    differing, 180
    Marine Corps, 211, 218
    pea coats, 185
    sailors, 244
    women, 106
Union Army, 150
unions (Civil Service), 275
United States Space Command, 261-262. *See also* NASA
    computer hacker protection, 288
    Joint Task Force-Computer Network Operations, 262
UNIVAC, 281
USS *Blue Ridge*, 170
USS *Coronado*, 170
USS *Eisenhower*, 177

USS *Essex*, 174
USS *Fort McHenry*, 174
USS *Germantown*, 174
USS *Guardian*, 174
USS *Juneau*, 174
USS *LaSalle*, 170
USS *Mount Whitney*, 170
USS *Patriot*, 174
USS *San Antonio*, 224
USUHS (Uniformed Services University of Health Sciences), 253-254

V

V-1 missile, 194
V-2 rocket, 194
VA pensions, 132-133
VA website, 130
vacations, 9
    Army, 163
    Civil Service, 275
Vargas, Jay (Marine Captain), 145
Veteran's Group Life Insurance, 133
veterans
    benefits, 9, 125-126, 136-137
    disabled, 125-126
    discharge status, 127
    health care benefits, 129-130
    home loans, 134
    life insurance, 133
    low-income, 126
    pensions, 126, 130-133
    retiree, 128-129, 130-131
    Servicemen's Readjustment Act of 1944, 11
Veterinary Corps (Army), 158
Victory Forge, 56
Vietnam War, 234
Virginia Military Academy, 93
virtual reality training (Navy), 286-287
Voluntary Separation Incentive, 127

W-X-Y-Z

WAAC (Women's Army Auxiliary Corps), 99
WAC (Women's Army Corps), 99
Walt Disney World, military discounts, 123
war games (Basic Training), 55
War of 1812
    Coast Guard, 233
    Marine Corps, 210
wardrooms, 176
warfare (electronic), 284-285
warrant officers
    Air Force, 200
    Army, 160-161
    Coast Guard, 240
    Navy, 181
Warrior Week, 56
Washington, George, 150
WASPs (Women Air Force Service Pilots), 99
water safety (Coast Guard), 229
WAVES (Women Accepted for Volunteer Emergency Service), 99
weapons
    electronic, 284-285
    Marine Corps, 215-216
    women, carrying, 105
weather forecasting, 5
websites
    Air Force pay scale, 198
    Army payscale, 159
    Civil Service, 274
    Department of Defense, 274
    Marine Corps pay scale, 219
    NASA, 260
    Navy payscale, 180
    Navy recruiting, 182
    Office of Personnel Management, 276
    payscale, 7
    VA, 130

weeks (Basic Training), 54-56
weight restrictions, 16
West Point, 89-91
    academic training, 91
    cows, 90
    firsties, 90
    living conditions, 90
    military training, 90-91
    plebes, 89
    student hierarchy, 90
    time off, 89
    yearlings, 90
Westpac, 172
Whittlesey, Major Charles, 158
wings (Air Force), 193, 199
wives (military), 106-107
women
    aircraft training, 102
    auxiliaries, 99-100
    Basic Training, 45
    Coast Guard, 99, 239
    difference between sexes, decreasing, 104
    equipment changes, 105-106
    family benefits, 101
    ground combat, 103
    jobs, 102-103
    limitations, 103
    Marine Corps, 216-217
    Marine dress blues, 218
    Mary Baldwin College, 93
    mechanics, 295-296
    military academy admittance, 104-105
    military admittance, 101
    military history, 98
    military wives, 106-107
    minorities, 117-118
    Nurse Corps, 99
    nurses, 98
    opportunities, 6
    pregnancy discharges, 101
    ROTC program enrollment, 101
    training, 104
    uniforms, 106
    volunteers, number of, 101

weapons, carrying, 105
Women Air Force Service Pilots, 99
Women Marines, 99
Women's Armed Services Integration Act, 100
Women's Army Auxiliary Corps, 99
World War II, 99
Women Accepted for Volunteer Emergency Service (WAVES). *See* WAVES
Women Air Force Service Pilots (WASPs). *See* WASPs
Women's Armed Services Integration Act, 100
Women's Army Auxiliary Corps (WAAC). *See* WAAC
Women's Army Corps (WAC). *See* WAC
word knowledge (ASVAB), 34-35
WWI
    Coast Guard, 233-234
    German artillery observers, shooting, 192
    Marine Corps, 211
    Meuse-Argonne campaign, 158
WWII
    Air Corps special forces, 198
    Coast Guard, 234
    Marine Corps, 211
    special forces, 156

yearlings, 90

U.S. $16.95
CAN $25.99

ISBN 0-02-864381-X

0 21898 64381 0

Find out if you've got what it takes to serve!

You're no idiot, of course. You know that the armed forces of the United States are responsible for the security and protection of our nation. However, each branch performs specific duties—offering more than 2,000 career specialties for those willing to serve. Which one is best for you?

You don't have to listen to the sales pitch of every recruiter! *The Complete Idiot's Guide® to Careers in the U.S. Military* will show you exactly what to expect should you enlist—and what is expected of you! In this *Complete Idiot's Guide®*, you get ...

- How to enlist—both as a recruit and with an advanced rank.

- A description of the Armed Services Vocational Aptitude Battery Test (ASVAB) including sample questions, study preparation, and how it is scored.

- Basic Training routines and how to get in shape for the daily physical exertion the military demands.

- Military college fund information for all the armed forces—as well as the GI Bill and the Montgomery GI Bill.

See the world and serve your country!

- **Get in on the cutting edge of technology.**

- **Decipher military jargon.**

- **Learn the history and importance of military traditions.**

- **Find out what it's like to live a day in the life of a soldier.**

- **Discover the perks of military service: free health care, early retirement, discount shopping, and more vacation time.**

- **Review the qualifications needed to get into a service academy such as West Point or Annapolis.**

- **Explore possible career paths in medicine, the space program, law enforcement, and civil service.**

BILL HARRIS spent 18 years at *The New York Times* in a variety of editorial and public relations positions, and has held similar positions with King Features Syndicate and Western Publishing. His articles have appeared in *The Wall Street Journal*, *International Herald Tribune*, and *U.S. Air Magazine*. He is also the author of more than a dozen books including *America's Medal of Honor*, *Civil War Battlefields*, and *The History of America*.

ISBN 0-02-864381-X

5 1 6 9 5

9 780028 643816

ALPHA